MANAGEMENT PRINCIPLES FOR PHYSICAL THERAPISTS

MANAGEMENT PRINCIPLES FOR PHYSICAL THERAPISTS

LARRY J. NOSSE, P.T., M.A.
Associate Professor
Program in Physical Therapy
Marquette University
Milwaukee, Wisconsin

DEBORAH G. FRIBERG, P.T., M.B.A.
Vice President of Rehabilitation Services
Sacred Heart Rehabilitation Hospital
Milwaukee, Wisconsin

Williams & Wilkins
BALTIMORE • PHILADELPHIA • HONG KONG
LONDON • MUNICH • SYDNEY • TOKYO

A WAVERLY COMPANY

Editor: John P. Butler
Managing Editor: Linda Napora
Copy Editor: Janet M. Krejci
Designer: Norman W. Och
Illustration Planner: Raymond Lowman
Production Coordinator: Anne Stewart Seitz

Printed in the United States of America

Library of Congress Cataloging in Publication Data

Nosse, Larry J.
　　Management principles for physical therapists / Larry J. Nosse,
　Deborah G. Friberg.
　　　　p.　　cm.
　　Includes index.
　　ISBN 0-683-06576-9
　　1. Physical therapy—Practice.　2. Small business—Management.
　I. Friberg, Deborah G.　II. Title.
　　[DNLM: 1. Physical therapy—organization & administration.　WB
　460 N897m]
　　RM713.N67　　1992
　　615.8′2′068–dc20
　　DNLM/DLC
　　for Library of Congress　　　　　　　　　　　　　　　　　　91-10344
　　　　　　　　　　　　　　　　　　　　　　　　　　　　　　　CIP

94　95
3　　4　　5　　6　　7　　8　　9　10

PREFACE

Management Principles for Physical Therapists was developed through the joint efforts of an academic physical therapist and a practicing physical therapist manager. For several years the authors have team-taught a management course to entry level physical therapy students who had no prior course work in business or management content areas. Much of the material in this book has been presented in the classroom and revised based on student feedback. Some of the material has also been presented to practicing physical therapists in inservice training sessions and continuing education seminars. Suggestions offered by practitioners have also had an impact on the content of this book. We undertook this project because were unable to find a single text book that met the projected needs of our students, was at their level of understanding, and was directed specifically to physical therapists' interests.

Important issues for physical therapists today include payment for services, preparation of management personnel, physical therapy practice act changes, manpower needs, and practice opportunities.

Seven specific areas that have direct fiscal implications for physical therapists are:

1. Governmental reimbursement methods;
2. Growth of managed care organizations;
3. Increased attention to utilization patterns;
4. Increased demand for accountability;
5. Increased competition among providers of services for clients and staff;
6. Diversification of health care delivery systems;
7. Greater attention to the business aspects of health care.

In the early 1970s there were occasional educational offerings centered on these topics. Today, there are many educational opportunities to help the physical therapist deal with changes in the health care environment. Some of the reasons for physical therapists' interest in management may be related to the following:

1. Organizational structures that allow physical therapists to advance within the managerial hierarchy;
2. Formal on-the-job training programs for managers and supervisors;
3. Greater accessibility to graduate programs in business administration and health care management;

4. An increasing percentage of physical therapist managers and faculty with advanced training in business and management;
5. Availability of high quality continuing education programs in the area of management specifically for physical therapists;
6. Establishment and growth of the APTA Sections on Administration and Private Practice;
7. Recognition of management competencies as an essential component of entry level physical therapy education;
8. New criteria for educational programs which include management competencies.

Two other important changes which affect physical therapists have occurred. Since 1979, more than 20 states have altered their physical therapy practice acts to allow clients to have some degree of direct access to physical therapists. This new practice opportunity may have stimulated among therapists the expression of an entrepreneurial spirit that was not as evident in earlier decades. Growing numbers of physical therapists are becoming employers of physical therapists or are self-employed. Under either circumstance the need for business and management information becomes at least as important as the need for current treatment-related information.

Employers have diversified their services and increased their need for therapists. Private practice, home health care groups, sports therapy clinics, managed care organizations, and others offer practice opportunities that were not prevalent a decade ago. These changes have resulted in competition between employers hiring physical therapists. Marketing directed to all levels of physical therapists encourages frequent job changes. To counteract this, employers provide development programs and a career ladder in an effort to retain staff. The recruitment and retention of staff is one of the major concerns of physical therapist managers today.

In response to these changes in the health care environment we have included a broad discussion on the health care environment as it is now and how it is anticipated to change during the 1990s.

We have presented the salient aspects of management needed for effective functioning in the health care environment. Management principles are presented in a discipline-specific manner directed to physical therapists. An understanding of the information in this book will provide a solid preparatory background for anyone who will have managerial responsibilities without prior educational preparation in this area and will also serve well those who have recently assumed a managerial role. In addition, this book will be useful to physical therapist managers seeking a review resource.

This book enables the reader to practice the application of management principles. There are case studies at the end of most chapters so that the reader may apply the principles emphasized in the chapter. More complex cases are presented at the end of the book; these call for integration of many management concepts to solve management problems. These integrated cases are appropriate for use in small groups where individuals work as a team to reinforce the development of practical skills in applying managerial principles.

Management principles for dealing with human resources, operations, and fiscal matters make up the core of this book. Complementary information is provided in chapters on documentation and reimbursement, law, facilities planning, and values and ethics. The inclusion of this last topic was done to strike a balance between the desire to succeed as a manager or an organization and the need to hold the welfare of others in high esteem.

We are indebted to our students and colleagues for the honest criticisms and helpful suggestions they have given us as we worked to organize what we believe to be an appropriate body of management-related knowledge for entry level students and therapists with management interests. We sincerely welcome readers' comments to guide us in our future efforts.

CONTENTS

4 Personnel Management: Practical Applications 59

5 Fiscal Management 95

6 Reimbursement and Documentation 127

7 Operations Management 141

8 Facilities Planning 167

9 Health Care Marketing 177

10 Law and Legal Concepts 193

11 Values and Ethics 215

12 American Health Care Environment: Beyond 1990 231

American Health Care Environment

OVERVIEW

Since the legislation and implementation of Titles XVIII (Medicare) and XIX (Medicaid) in 1965 the American health care system has undergone a series of significant changes. Most of the changes can be related to the cost of health care, who pays for care, and efforts to control health care costs. Some of the significant changes in the health care system which have resulted from financial concerns include:

1. *A revision of health care philosophy articulated by the federal government;*
2. *New method of payment for Medicare services;*
3. *Shifting of health care costs among payers;*
4. *Increased competition for clients who can pay for services;*
5. *Increased competition for staff to provide services;*
6. *Demands for accountability with regard to the need for services and the effectiveness of the services;*
7. *New modes of delivering health care services.*

The practice of physical therapy has also been influenced by these and other forces. Technological advances, the enactment of legislation in some states to allow clients to have direct access to physical therapists, and increased workplace opportunities have also impacted on physical therapy practice. To be able to function in the health care system physical therapists need to understand the

1

historical and evolutionary features of the American health care system which have have brought about changes that impact on them. Toward that end, this chapter will present a pertinent perspective of the past and current American health care system with attention given to implications for physical therapy practice.

Introduction

If there is one word which describes the American health care environment during the last decade, that word is change. Professionals joining the health care industry during the 1990s will find little resemblance to the work environment their predecessors found a mere 10 years earlier. The single greatest impetus for change was the rapid and uncontrolled escalation of health care costs (1). Between 1980 and 1985, national expenditures for physician and hospital services increased from 148.4 to 250 billion dollars. Expenditures for physician and hospital services were projected to increase to 383 billion dollars by 1990. This represents an estimated 158% increase over a 10-year period. In 1980, the government and private health insurance, supported largely by the business community, paid for 84% of these services at a cost of 125.1 billion dollars. They were projected to pay 320.32 billion dollars (84%) for physician and hospital services by 1990 (2).

Economic changes during the 1980s worked in favor of the health care industry evolution. During the 1980s, America continued its shift from an industrial to a service-based economy. The strength and ability of American labor unions to hold onto workers' health care benefits diminished. As a result, workers were less insulated from rising health care costs. Increasing numbers of workers received no health care benefits at all. To meet the needs of the underinsured and uninsured, health care providers were forced to shift costs to remaining corporate payers. Businesses were faced with triple-digit increases in the cost of providing their employees with health insurance. Meanwhile, the rate of increase in health care expenditures threaten the government's ability to meet other financial demands and to control the ever growing federal budget deficit (1).

During this same period, there was a shift in the American social philosophy about the delivery of health care. Traditionally, Americans had viewed health care as a basic human right. The accepted model of health care was authoritarian, with the consumer purchasing whatever the health care provider recommended. The consumption of health care found its basis in the philosophy "if a little is good, more must be better" (3). Responding to the increasing federal budget deficit and growing tax burden, the American people began to struggle with their desire for equal access for all to the best possible health care and the tax burden which was the price of that access. The traditional beliefs about health care were increasingly questioned. "Do all people have a right to access all available health care services? Who should make choices about the health care services received—the provider or the consumer? Should we ration health care services? If so, how should health care be rationed?" (3).

The push for change has come from a variety of sources outside the health care industry. The government and business community were at the forefront of the efforts. Their involvement was driven by the need to control the escalating cost of health care services. Their efforts were based on the belief that, "Increased consumer choice, more efficient health care providers and lower costs" were going to be the answer (1).

The forces of change brought threats, challenges, and opportunities for health care professionals and organizations. The magnitude of these forces and the resulting health care industry responses have left today's health care providers in a state of transition and, often, turmoil.

The forces for change evoked a largely reactive response from the health care industry. Decreasing reimbursement for health care services, a declining demand for services, and severe manpower shortages resulted in increased competition for paying customers and staff. The search for less costly health care delivery methods opened the door to alternative types of health care providers. To respond, health care professionals and organizations needed to change their structures, their facilities, and the way they approached the business of health care.

To perform effectively as part of the health care industry, physical therapists must understand their work environment. To understand today's health care environment we must first understand what it was and why it changed. Toward that end, this chapter will provide a historical review of the development of the American health care delivery system. The forces for past and future change will be identified. Against that backdrop, the current health care delivery environment will be discussed. Special emphasis will be placed on the implications for physical therapy practice.

American Health Care Delivery System

The American health care industry encompasses the products and services offered by a multitude of individuals and organizations. Any individual or organization that makes available services or products which contribute to health maintenance or health improvement is a provider of health care. Who are these health care providers? The list is a long one. For ease of discussion, a distinction between direct and indirect providers will be made. A direct provider would be one that deals directly with the person receiving the health care services. A hospital, health department, physician, orthotist, pharmacist, and physical therapist are all direct care providers. An indirect provider would make available products and services that allow the direct care providers to meet the needs of the clients they serve. A drug company, medical equipment manufacturer, medical researcher, and medical waste disposal company are all indirect providers. Together, direct and indirect providers make up our national health care industry.

In the broadest sense, references to health care providers include individuals and organizations providing direct and indirect services. For the purposes of this text, the term "provider" will be used to refer to direct providers only. The terms "health care industry" will be used to refer collectively to all direct and indirect providers of health care products and services. The terms "health care delivery system" will be used to refer to all direct providers of health care products and services.

Historical Perspective: Prior to the 1980s
TRADITIONAL HEALTH CARE DELIVERY SYSTEM

Until the early 1980s, the American health care delivery system consisted of a network of physicians, hospitals, a limited number of other private practitioners, such as physical therapists and chiropractors, and government-sponsored public health providers. Depending on the availability of specialized equipment and expertise, these traditional providers were further categorized as primary, secondary, and tertiary providers. These categories refer to the relationship between the provider of health care services and those served.

Primary Care

A primary care provider is the initial point of contact between the health care delivery system and the client. It is the entry point into the health care system. Traditionally, the primary care physician, trained in general practice, pediatrics, or internal medicine, was that entry point. Primary care services were most frequently delivered on an outpatient basis outside of the hospital setting.

Secondary Care

Secondary care providers represent the next level of care. Secondary care providers make available equipment, skill, or expertise not provided at the primary care level. Medical specialty, diagnostic laboratory, and radiology services, therapies, and surgical and medical monitoring are all secondary level services. Hospitals, medical specialists, and therapists are examples of secondary care providers. Traditionally, secondary care services were most often delivered in the hospital setting. They were often more expensive than primary care services.

Tertiary Care

Tertiary care providers offer the next level of sophistication in the provision of specialized health care services. A university medical center which acts as a regional diagnostic and treatment center for community hospitals and physicians is an example of a tertiary care provider. Tertiary care was hospital based.

SOCIAL PHILOSOPHY AND PUBLIC POLICY

During the 1960s and 1970s, popular social philosophy recognized that all citizens were entitled to the highest quality and equal access to health care services. This entitlement philosophy of health care was reflected in the public policy adopted during that period. Reflective of the times, the 1960s and 1970s saw the passage of several pieces of health care legislation. This legislation was for the most part intended to meet the health care needs of the poor, the elderly, and the disabled. With the establishment of the government-sponsored Medicare and Medicaid health

Table 1.1.
Percent of Expenditure for Health Services and Supplies by Payer Type (6)

Payer Type	Percentage of Expenditure by Year	
	1965	1980
Federal government	10.9	17.0
State and local government	11.5	11.9
Business	17.4	30.0
Household and philanthropy	60.2	41.1

care payment systems, the federal and state governments became a driving force behind the growth of health care industry and the escalation of health care expenditures (4).

Medicare

The signing of Title XVIII of the Social Security Act in 1965 is considered to be the "most significant piece of health care legislation ever passed by the U.S. Congress" (5). Perhaps surprisingly, support for the adoption of Medicare did not come from the health care industry. It came instead from organized labor. Medicare, through an extension of the Social Security Act, was intended to improve the availability of health care services to the elderly. The Medicare bill had an administrative provision that was to have a significant impact on the health care delivery system. Health care providers were to be reimbursed according to their costs. They were not restricted to a fee schedule.

Medicaid

Medicaid, mandated by Title XIX of the Social Security Act, is a state-administered program intended to provide access to health care services for the poor, the elderly, and the disabled who do not receive coverage under Medicare. Also signed into law in 1965, Medicaid established minimum coverage requirements and provided for a sharing of expenses between the federal and state governments. States retained the option of providing health care coverage at or above the minimum level. As a result, Medicaid coverage varies from state to state (5).

REIMBURSEMENT FOR HEALTH CARE SERVICES

There are four major sources of reimbursement for health care services. They are: 1) the federal government; 2) state and local governments; 3) business, directly and through the provision of health care insurance benefits; and 4) household (personal payment) and philanthropy (donated money or services) (6). The percentage of the total expenditures for health services and supplies borne by these four sources has been in transition since the enactment of the Medicare and Medicaid legislation in 1965. Table 1.1 outlines the percentage distribution of expenditures for health care services and supplies by type of payer for 1965 and 1980. Table 1.1 clearly shows a change in 1980 from 1965 in who paid for health care. Clients and other sources paid a lesser percentage while business and government paid a greater proportion (7).

During the 1960s and 1970s, there were few attempts to control reimbursement for health care services. At the start of the 1960s, Blue Cross/Blue Shield introduced the concept of paying for medical services at usual, customary, and reasonable levels. This system was widely adopted and by the mid 1960s had generally replaced the use of standardized fee schedules (7).

As mandated by Medicare, the government reimbursed health care providers on what was known as a cost plus basis. Under this system the health care provider could get reimbursed for the cost of the services provided plus a small amount to cover the depreciation of capital equipment. The governmental reimbursement system was similar to that used by the private insurance industry in that it was not tied to a specific fee schedule.

Under these reimbursement systems, there were no significant constraints on the utilization of health care services. The use of diagnostic and therapeutic interventions was at the sole discretion of the providers. In an environment of minimum payment restrictions, the inflation of health care costs accelerated. The cost of health care services increased dramatically for Medicare and non-Medicare clients alike. The profitability of health care providers increased (5). Under this new-found prosperity, the health care delivery system expanded. There were few restrictions on investment in facilities or technology. Consumers were encouraged to utilize all the medical services the expanded health care system offered (1). Increased use resulted in increased reimbursement which facilitated continued growth in facilities, technology, and services (7).

PHYSICAL THERAPY PRACTICE

Physical therapy practice during the 1960s and 1970s was largely limited to three settings: the hospital, private practice, and extended care institutions (8–10). Private practice followed the medical practice model and served primarily ambulatory outpatients (11). Throughout this period, as secondary level providers, private practitioners were dependent on primary referral sources, physicians, for their business. The first direct access legislation did not take effect until 1979 (12). Hospital-based practice accounted for the majority of practice opportunities. Along with some limitations on professional autonomy, employment in hospital-based practice generally offered the greatest opportunities for variety in clinical practice (11).

Evolution of the American Health Care Delivery System

The 1980s was a period of evolution for the American health care delivery system. Driven by a need to bring escalating health care costs in line government and business led major efforts to control health care expenditures. Their efforts were supported by the insurance industry and, in part, by consumers who were increasingly affected by the costs of health care services. The collective effects of these cost containment efforts were far reaching. Ultimately, they led to a shift in the power base controlling the health care delivery system and a major restructuring of the health care delivery system (3).

COST CONTAINMENT EFFORTS

Under the cost plus method of health care reimbursement the payer assumed all of the financial risk of providing health care services. If the cost of providing health care services increased, the burden of increased expenditures was placed on the payer. Yet, the payer had no mechanisms for controlling the utilization or cost of health care services. On the other hand, the health care delivery system had no incentive to control the utilization or cost of the services they were providing. They were reimbursed for their services no matter what they provided. Cost containment efforts of the 1980s were directed at both shifting and limiting the financial risk of the payers (3).

Capitated Risk

Efforts aimed at limiting the risk of payers attempted to put a ceiling on the amount that would be paid to providers for specific types of health care services. Limiting risk in this fashion is referred to as risk capitation (3). The first and most notable efforts at capitating risk came from the Medicare system. Through the Tax Equity And Fiscal Responsibilities Act of 1982 (TEFRA), Congress began efforts to control the federal government's expenditures on health care. TEFRA (Public Law 97-248) began efforts to control the amount and method of Medicare payment for inpatient hospital services. In 1983, Congress enacted the Social Security Act of 1983 (Public Law 98-21) which restructured the mechanism of reimbursement for inpatient health care services through the creation of the prospective payment system (PPS) (13).

Under PPS, all medicare inpatients are assigned, based on their primary diagnosis, to one of 467 diagnostic-related groupings (DRGs). DRGs are a set of mutually exclusive categories that are used to describe a client's medical condition and medical needs. The reimbursement rate for each DRG category is set in advance or "capped." The provider gets paid the same amount of money regardless of the costs they incur. If the provider's costs of providing services to an inpatient are less than the reimbursement cap, they make money. If the provider's costs exceed the reimbursement cap, they lose money. In this way the financial risk of providing health care services is shared by the payer and the provider. The provider has an incentive for controlling the utilization and cost of the services they provide. There are some provisions under PPS which limit potential losses on unusual cases where costs become excessive. Some inpatient providers remain exempt from the PPS system. They are psychiatric hospitals, long-term care facilities, children's hospitals, rehabilitation hospitals, and psychiatric and rehabilitation units operating under exemptions from the PPS systems. Since first implemented by the federal government, the concept

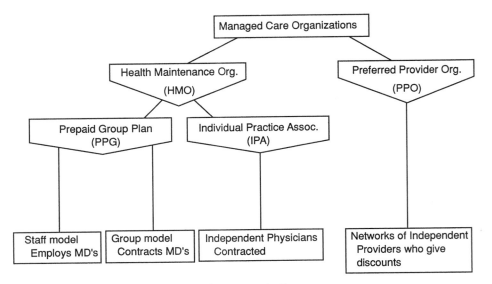

Figure 1.1. Basic features of managed care organizations.

of capitated risk sharing has been adopted by many state governments for control of Medicaid expenditures.

Businesses, particularly large organizations, have sought to limit their financial risk through the use of managed care. Managed care organizations function as a link between providers and consumers. As an intermediary, managed care organizations seek to control the utilization and/or cost of health care services. They also assume responsibility for the quality of health care services. The 1980s saw the strengthening of two types of managed care organizations. The health maintenance organization (HMO) and the preferred provider organization (PPO). The general characteristics of managed care organizations are summarized in Figure 1.1.

Two major HMO models are the Prepaid Group Plan (PGP) and the Individual Practice Association (IPA). There are two types of PGPs, the staff model and the group model. The staff model employs its own physicians who practice out of the HMO facility. Group model HMOs contract with an independent group of physicians who provide services exclusively to enrollees of the HMO at the group practice location. The IPA functions like the group practice HMO except that the physicians contract independently with the HMO. Enrollees receive services at physician practice location instead of one central location (6).

HMOs offer business an alternative to traditional indemnity (fee for service) insurance. The HMO estimates the cost of providing health care services to its enrollees and sets premiums based on their estimated costs. In return for the premium, the HMO assumes financial responsibility for the enrollees' health care services. The HMO's success is dependent on its ability to control the utilization and cost of services provided to enrollees. It achieves control of its financial risk through a variety of mechanisms. First, it controls access to health care supplies and services through the use of a gatekeeper. The gatekeeper is usually the primary physician. The gatekeeper must authorize all secondary and tertiary level services.

Second, the HMO can provide diagnostic services, pharmaceuticals, and supplies directly, eliminating extra administrative expenses. Third, the HMO can enter into provider relationships for secondary and tertiary services which use capitated or discounted fee for service payment arrangements (6).

PPOs are networks of providers which have agreed to provide services at a discounted rate and to comply with preadmission and ongoing utilization review in anticipation of a guaranteed volume of business. The PPO contracts directly with the employer. PPOs can be successful at decreasing the employers health care expenditures to the extent that PPO services are utilized by its employees. Employee cooperation is obtained through the use of incentives such as variable deductible or co-pay requirements (14).

Risk Shifting

The primary methods used by payers to shift risk and cost have been increased premiums, deductibles, and co-payments payable by the employee. These methods shift a portion of the financial risk from the insurer and employer to the consumer. Under these methods it is presumed that the consumer will be more likely to monitor and control utilization of health care services.

Another form of risk shifting has been the use of capitation by government and large business. The net effect of capitation is that it shifts financial risk from the payer to the provider. The provider who is receiving less reimbursement from large payer sources, but must still meet the health care needs of the underinsured and uninsured, continues to cost shift to the fee for service payers. These payers are usually small businesses and private pay consumers. This form of cost shifting makes it increasingly difficult for small businesses to provide employees with even basic health care coverage.

RESTRUCTURING OF THE HEALTH CARE DELIVERY SYSTEM

Cost containment efforts created incentives for inpatient care providers, hospitals, to control both the cost and utilization of inpatient services. These incentives led to several notable changes in the way health care services were delivered. These changes included:

1. A significant decrease in the average length of inpatient hospitalizations. In one study, the average length of stay for Medicare patients dropped 20.4% within the first years after the implementation of PPS (15).
2. A decreased use of routine diagnostic testing during inpatient hospitalizations.
3. An increased use of outpatient diagnostic testing and treatment.
4. An increase in the utilization of home care and skilled long-term care (15).

These changes in the patterns of health care delivery created some serious consequences for the traditional health care system, particularly hospitals. Most notable were:

1. Decreased inpatient census resulting in excess capacity.

2. Decreased profit margins due to decreases in service volume and limited reimbursement with the resultant need to reduce the overall cost of operations.
3. Financial constraints on investment in technology and new facilities.
4. Increased internal competition for now limited resources.
5. Increased external competition for consumer business.

Hospitals responded in a variety of ways to the challenges they were facing. Typical responses included:

1. Cost reductions through staff reductions, service changes, and structural reorganizations.
2. Diversification into new service areas which are exempt from the PPS such as ambulatory care, specialty care, and long-term care. From 1983 to 1987, there was a 20% increase in the number of hospitals providing home health services (16). More than 9000 inpatient rehabilitation beds were opened between 1980 and 1987 (17).
3. Organizational restructuring through vertical and horizontal integration (3). Through vertical integration health care providers link a continuum of services used by customers which allows them to capture more of the customers' health care business. A health care corporation which offers primary care, secondary care, tertiary care, home health care, and long-term care is vertically integrated. Horizontal integration is accomplished through the consolidation of like providers, such as hospitals. This allows them to strengthen their competitive advantage by capturing a greater portion of the marketplace. Organizational restructuring was accomplished through mergers, joint ventures, alliances, acquisitions, and/or the sponsorship of HMOs and PPOs (16).
4. Increased attention to traditional marketing efforts (18).

Cost containment efforts also encourage the growth and development of new entrepreneurial alternative health care providers, for example, the provision of emergency services offered by storefront urgent care centers as an alternative to hospital-based emergency care. Physicians looking for alternative sources of income also began providing services traditionally reserved for hospital settings. Office-based laboratories, radiology services, and diagnostic imaging became common. All of these alternative care settings offered hospitals increased competition for a dwindling consumer base.

Shift of Power

Under the pre-1980s health care delivery structure, the power to make health policy and practice decisions was in the hands of the health care provider. The consumer and payer were passive participants. The 1980s brought a shift in power to both the buyer and consumer of health care services (3). Where the provider had set the fees and the norms of practice, the buyer was now assuming greater control. The consumer now accepting more of the financial risk for health care services was developing new knowledge and expectations of the health care delivery system.

This shift in power created a demand for increased accountability from providers. Consumers and payers began questioning providers about both the cost and quality of the services they provide. The demand for accountability has grown in intensity and specificity throughout the 1980s. Providers have been challenged to develop methods of evaluating efficiency and effectiveness in quantifiable terms. Providers are being selected on the basis of the information they provide.

Regulation and Accreditation of Health Care Providers

Regulation of Health Care Providers

Government regulation of American health care providers occurs at the federal, state, and local level. Regulation from the federal level comes in the form of public health care policy. Public policy regulates health care providers in a variety of ways. The two most common examples of federal regulation specific to health care providers include:

1. Legislation that makes the receipt of federal funding or the right to maintain a nonprofit and thus, a nontaxable status, conditional on compliance with federal standards for health care providers.
2. Legislation that requires health care providers to comply with federal standards as a condition of participation in federally funded health care programs such as Medicare. A health care provider must be an authorized provider to bill for services rendered to beneficiaries of federal health care programs.

State and local governments also regulate the activities of health care providers. The degree and type of regulation will vary significantly between states and local governments. Some examples of state and local regulation specific to health care providers include:

1. Legislation that requires health care providers to comply with state and local standards as a condition of participation in state or locally funded health care programs such as Medicaid or county assistance programs. Nonparticipation in these programs could mean the loss of substantial business in some geographical areas.
2. Legislation that controls the licensure and/or certification of organizational and individual health care providers. The federal government relies on states to determine which providers are eligible to provide what services within their jurisdiction. This allows states the independence to define and control the quality of health care services available to its residents.
3. Legislation which allows state or local governments to control the amount of specific types or levels of health care available to its residents. In this way, the availability of services as well as the amount of resources which are committed to health care can be controlled. An example would be state control over the total number and location of skilled nursing home beds. Or, a requirement for state government review and approval of health care provider expenditures on equipment and facilities when the cost exceeds a predetermined level.
4. Legislation that controls what health care providers may charge for the services they provide. This legislation is often designed to protect the community from rising health care costs by controlling provider revenues and, indirectly, their expenditures.

Through the use of these methods, the government regulates most of the operating practices of health care providers. Government standards for health care providers set down specific guidelines for such things as organizational structure, accounting methods, service documentation, service evaluation, personnel practices, and facilities design.

Accreditation

Accreditation differs from regulation in one important way: where compliance with regulation is mandated, compliance with the standards of an accrediting organization is often, for the present, optional. The receipt of accreditation is usually sought by the individual or organizational health care provider. Accreditation is given after the provider demonstrates compliance with the performance or competence standards of the accrediting organization. The most widely recognized accrediting organization for health care organizations is the Joint Commission On Accreditation of Health Care Organizations (JCAHO). Another accrediting organization which has a special focus on rehabilitation is the Commission On The Accreditation of Rehabilitation Facilities (CARF). Various organizations representing health care professionals, such as the American Physical Therapy Association (APTA), also provide specialty accreditations or certifications for members who have met standards for the recognition of advanced expertise in a specialty area of practice.

Implications for Physical Therapy Practice

The changes in the health care delivery system are reflected in the changes in physical therapy practice patterns. Table 1.2 summarizes employment-related information from four descriptive studies conducted in the 1960s, 1970s, and 1980s. All of these reports provide data from nationwide samples.

Worthingham's data was collected in 1966 on 1961 and 1965 physical therapy graduates from all existing educational programs (8). These data reflect the physical therapy workforce one year after the introduction of Medicare and Medicaid. The large difference between the group's percentages of therapists not working was attributed to the fact that the 1965 graduates were newer graduates who had only practiced for two years. Although the exact figure was not presented, the inference was that the great majority of respondents worked in hospital settings. This conclusion was based on the job titles of the respondents, the percentages of people in the other work location categories, and the absence of additional categories.

The largest sample studied was reported on in the 1978 APTA membership profile (9). Over 13,000 APTA members participated in this survey. Clear differences are evident between this profile and Worthingham's data, particularly in the percentage not working, in private practice, and working in schools and home care categories. The actual term used in the 1978 survey was private office. This category combined those working in any type of private office, physician's office, or physical therapy office. This lack of distinction makes it difficult to identify the actual increase in the percentage of therapists reporting being in private physical therapy practice.

The 1982 APTA membership profile (9) was obtained by a sampling procedure to ensure representation of the membership rather than including the entire membership in the survey. This stratified sampling procedure produced data which were considered statistically valuable.

Table 1.2.
Physical Therapist Work-Related Data 1966–1987

Variables Target yr(s)	Worthingham (8) 1961	1965	APTA (9) 1978	APTA (9) 1982	APTA (10)[a] 1987
Respondents	520		>12,000	>3,000	<2,000
Females	75%		71%	72%	75%
Not working	32%		5%	3%	3%
Primary work setting					
Hospital	NN[b]		47%	43%	44%
Rehab center	NN	NN	9%	8%	16%[c]
Nursing home	10%	7%	8%	7%	18%
Private practice	3%[d]	NN	NN	11%	24%
Self-employed	NN	4%	10%[e]	13%	15%
K-12 school	NN	NN	6%	7%	10%
Home care	NN	NN	6%	8%	22%
Physician's office	NN	2%	—[e]	3%	4%

[a]The percentages listed are not additive because respondents indicated that they worked in more than one setting.
[b]NN, not noted.
[c]In 1987 rehabilitation center with inpatients (11%) and rehabilitation center without inpatients (5%) were separate categories. These percentages were added together in this table.
[d]Estimated from article text.
[e]In 1978 the category heading Private Office combined both private physical therapy practice and physician office data.

Compared with the 1978 APTA membership profile the changes in 1982 were: a decrease in the percentage of therapists not working, a decrease in the percentage working in hospitals and nursing homes, and increases in the percentages of those working in private practice and home care. The actual percentage increase of therapists in private practice is likely greater than the 1% listed because of the 1978 combined data discussed above.

The 1987 APTA study (10) was conducted to identify the profile of former APTA members and to make comparisons with a representative sample of active members. The primary work setting of respondents was not clearly identified. An average of 1.6 work settings per respondent was noted. The lack of differentiation in work setting is probably a good reflection of current work patterns. However, the absence of a primary work setting category makes it impossible to make comparisons with the earlier studies.

While the preceding studies (8–10) primarily describe employment patterns of APTA members it is likely that these patterns reflect the changes in the health care system that affect all physical therapists.

The general trends presented by the reports summarized in Table 1.2 are:

1. A decreasing percentage of physical therapists not working;
2. A decreasing percentage of physical therapists working primarily in hospitals;
3. Little or no change in the percentage of therapists working in nursing homes;
4. An increase in the percentage of therapists working in private practice settings;

5. A slight increase in the percentage of therapists working in school environments;
6. An increased percentage of therapists working in home care;
7. A consistent small percentage of therapists reporting that they work in a physician's office.

In the wider perspective of physical therapy in the health care system it must be recognized that the practice of physical therapy has also been affected by the push for cost containment. The effects have been varied and include expanded demand for physical therapy services, expanded practice opportunities, escalation of the physical therapy manpower shortage, less favorable work schedules, greater demands for efficiency, productivity, and accountability, and more emphasis on documentation and data collection with less time spent with clients. A move toward board-certified specialization with its expectation of expanded expertise has also influenced physical therapy practice in the 1980s (19, 20). There is debate about whether these changes in physical therapy practice have been positive or negative. Available evidence would indicate that, for the most part, the changes have had a positive impact on the prestige and the practice of physical therapy (21).

GROWING DEMAND FOR PHYSICAL THERAPY SERVICES
Opportunity

Cost containment efforts had the most immediate impact on hospital-based therapists. Prior to cost containment, inpatient physical therapy departments were a source of revenue for hospitals. After cost containment, inpatient departments became a cost which hospitals needed to control.

Initially, there was concern about the PPS leading to a decreased utilization of physical therapy services for inpatients. Those concerns proved to be unfounded. The relationship between physical therapy services and timely discharges was quickly recognized. This fact was supported by a study of Medicare referral patterns at seven acute care hospitals before and after PPS. The study found that the percentage of physical therapy Medicare referrals increased after the implementation of PPS (22).

Shorter acute care lengths of stay lead, with increasing frequency, to the discharge of patients still unable to manage independently in a community setting. This resulted in an increased demand for post hospital home care and skilled nursing facility (SNF) care (15). An increased demand for physical therapy services to be provided in both SNF and home care settings occurred as well.

The demand for physical therapy services also increased as a result of hospital diversification into rehabilitation programs. Inpatient, outpatient, and long-term care-based rehabilitation programs have experienced tremendous growth in the 1980s. Data from the American Hospital Association indicated a 65.4% increase in the number of PPS exempt inpatient rehabilitation beds between 1980 and 1987 (17). During the same period, the number of hospitals reporting organized outpatient rehabilitation programs increased by 156%. This growth, often attributed to the exclusion of rehabilitation from the PPS system, has created a tremendous demand for physical therapy services.

The growth in demand for physical therapy services has not been limited to traditional settings. Factors such as the aging population, advanced medical technology, and increased evidence of the benefits of rehabilitation have encouraged a variety of alternative providers to diversify into physical therapy (17). A recent study of trends in outpatient physical therapy utilization indicated that less than one-third of the respondents receiving physical therapy did so in a hospital setting (23). Findings showed that private practice physical therapists or physicians' offices delivered the majority of physical therapy services. Often, physical therapy private practices have been built around the provision of specialty care such as work hardening or sports physical therapy.

The growing demands for physical therapy services have led to an increased recognition of the physical therapist's value to health care organizations. With this has come a market-driven improvement in status and compensation. Because of their value, physical therapists are gaining increased control over their professional activities. They are more often afforded the opportunity to participate in organizational decision making.

Challenge

"According to the Bureau of Labor Statistics, the demand for physical therapists is expected to grow by 87% by the year 2000" (24). Physical therapists have benefited from this increased demand. Growth has meant a wider variety of practice opportunities. It has led to a demand-driven increase in available compensation. However, growth has had its down side.

First, the need for physical therapy services seven days per week, for extended hours, has impacted on some physical therapists' work schedules (25). Evening and weekend work schedules are now common.

Second, increased demand has escalated the shortage of physical therapists to critical levels. Many physical therapists work in settings where staff shortages are the rule rather than the exception.

Third, the concurrent demands for increased accountability, efficiency, and productivity have added stress to the physical therapy work environment. The physical therapist is called upon to devote an increasing percentage of time to documentation and data collection. This information is essential to demonstrate the effectiveness and efficiency of services delivered. At the same time, physical therapists are frequently asked to increase the amount of direct patient care they provide, supervise students, provide inservice training, and participate in other time-consuming activities. The demand on time can have mixed results. There can be increased frustration and job dissatisfaction at one time and exhilarating and rewarding feelings at another time.

Fourth, the shortage of physical therapists to meet the demand has made our profession vulnerable to competition from other professionals. The service voids created by the shortage of physical therapists represent opportunities for other professions to grow.

OTHER IMPLICATIONS FOR PHYSICAL THERAPY PRACTICE

The shift in power over health care decisions has also affected physical therapists. Physical therapists are increasingly accountable to consumers and payers. This has changed the way physical therapists provide and market their services. Utilization control systems have extended to physical therapy. Coming from government and managed care payment sources, these control systems can limit patient access to physical therapy services. In addition, these systems often increase the paperwork demands placed on the physical therapist. Consumer participation in goal setting and treatment planning is expected. Physical therapists can no longer make clinical decisions independent of consideration of payers' and consumers' viewpoints.

At the same time, the drive for cost containment and utilization control has supported the physical therapist's bid for direct access legislation. By 1989, consumers could access physical therapy services without a physician referral in 24 states (26). One of the arguments in favor of direct access is the cost savings which results from a decrease in unnecessary physician office visits.

The 1980s brought increased attention to the issues surrounding physician-owned physical therapy practices (POPTS). Physicians seeking alternative sources of revenue have found the provision of physical therapy services to be financially rewarding. Although acceptable to some physical therapists, others question these relationships (27). Should a referring physician gain economically from the physical therapy referral? Is there adequate control to ensure that physical therapy services are not prescribed solely for economic gain? The answers to these questions are not simple. The APTA is "... opposed to situations in which physical therapists or physical therapist assistants are employed by or under agreement with referring practitioners or organizations owned by referring practitioners and in which the referring practitioner receives compensation either directly or indirectly as a result of referring for, prescribing, or recommending physical therapy ..." (28). This issue and offshoots of it will undoubtedly continue to be discussed into the 1990s.

SUMMARY

The rate of change experienced by the health care industry during the 1980s is unprecedented. There has been, in fact, a complete evolution of the American health care delivery system. Driven by economic and social change, both the structure and the power base of the health care delivery system have changed. Consumers and payers are making decisions about health care delivery. Providers are competing against each other to survive and grow. Consumers have more service options than ever before, while their access to services is limited by the payers who assume the risk for their care. Those organizations and professionals who stay in tune with the changes will be in a position to seize opportunity. Those providers who ignore current and future changes will find continued practice a struggle as they enter the 1990s.

References

1. Tokarski C. 1980's prove uncertainty of instant cures. Mod Health Care 1990;8(Jan):51–58.
2. American Hospital Association: Council on Long Range Planning and Development. The environment of medicine. Chicago: American Medical Association, 1989: publication no. OP-223/9:15–23.
3. Kiesler CA, Morton TL. Psychology and public policy in the "health care revolution." Am Psychol 1988;43(12):993–1003.
4. American College of Hospital Administrators. Health care in the 1990's: Trends and strategies. Chicago: Arthur Anderson, 1984:15.
5. Rheinecker P. Catholic health care enters a new world. Health Prog 1990;June:31–36.
6. Levit KR, Freeland MS, Waldo DR. Health spending and ability to pay: Business, individuals and government. Health Care Financing Rev 1989;10(3):1–11.
7. Horting M. HMOs and the physical therapist: A growing relationship. Clin Manage 1987;7(6):30–35.
8. Worthingham CA. The 1961 and 1965 graduates of the physical therapy schools. Phys Ther 1969;49:476–499.
9. American Physical Therapy Association. Active member profile—1982. Alexandria, VA: APTA Department of Practice.
10. American Physical Therapy Association. 1987 former active membership profile survey—1988. Alexandria, VA: APTA Department of Practice.
11. Blood H. The administrative environment. In: Physical therapy administration and management. Baltimore: Williams & Wilkins, 1974:1–14.
12. Burch E, Jr. Direct access. In: Mathews J, ed. Practice issues in physical therapy. Thorofare, NJ: Slack, 1989:24.
13. Zollar CC, Liljestrand JS. Legislation and regulation of rehabilitation. DRG Monitor 1988;5(5–6):1–11.
14. Report of managed care focus meeting. Section For Metropolitan Hospitals, American Hospital Association. 1989;Oct:16.
15. Neu CR, Harrison SC. Posthospital care before and after the Medicare prospective payment system. Santa Monica: Rand, vi.
16. American Hospital Association. Vision, values, viability: Environmental assessment—1989/1990. Chicago: American Hospital, 1988:60–72.
17. Koska M. Rehabilitation growth: Is the heyday over? Hospitals 1989;March 5:29.
18. Wiess R. Hitting the target. Health Prog 1990;March:18–20.
19. Crutchfield C, Barnes M. Specialization—An overview. Prog Rep 1983;12(1):18.
20. Mathews J. Physical therapy specialization presents wide ranging challenges. Prog Rep 1988;17(5):6–7.
21. Kyes K. A sense of adventure. Rehab Manage 1990;June–July:101–102,104.
22. Dore D. Effect of the Medicare prospective payment system on the utilization of physical therapy. Phys Ther 1987;67(6):964–966.
23. Koska MT. Growth in outpatient PT services aids consumers. Hospitals 1989;Dec 5:78.
24. American Physical Therapy Association. Occupational outlook of physical therapy. Alexandria, VA: APTA Department of Practice, 1988.
25. Blosser G, Howells J, Mckelvy B, Pierson F. The prospective payment system: Its realties and opportunities. Clin Manage 1985;5(3):34–43.
26. Anonymous. Direct access states. Prog Rep 1989;18(10):5.
27. Anonymous. Should physician-owned physical therapy services be eliminated? Prog Rep 1982(5):10–11.
28. American Physical Therapy Association Policy Statement, 1983. Alexandria, VA: APTA Department of Practice.

CHAPTER **2**

Organizations

OVERVIEW

When more than one person is involved in doing work there is a need for an organized way to coordinate the activities associated with carrying out the work, selling the product, accounting for input and output, and many other essential actions. This chapter presents a formal introduction to principles for structuring an organization to meet organizational goals efficiently. The parts of an organization are identified as the operating core (the professional staff), management, and support staff. Various options or structural configurations depicting how these different groups can interact effectively are compared and contrasted. The purpose or mission and stated values of an organization are identified as having fundamental influences on the configuration of an organization. Other major influences, internal and external, to the organization are discussed regarding the choice of an organizational configuration. Special considerations for a physical therapist manager in designing an organizational structure are presented. This chapter contains a case study which gives the reader the opportunity to write a mission statement and test his/ her understanding of design principles.

Introduction

Whenever two or more individuals come together to achieve a goal there is an inherent need to coordinate their efforts. Coordination is needed to define common goals, make decisions about activities required to achieve goals, assign responsibility, and control activity. As the number of individuals involved or the complexity of the activity increases, the need for coordination increases. The act of organizing involves arranging activities by systematic planning and united effort into a coherent whole (1). The process of arranging the activity of an organization into a whole is called organizational design. The outcome of the process is an organizational structure for the achievement of common goals.

Mintzberg (2) refers to the process of organizing human activity as one of balancing two basic and opposing requirements. The first is the division of tasks to be performed. The second is the need to coordinate the tasks done by different individuals to achieve the common goal. Coordination of tasks can be achieved through mutual adjustment, standardization of tasks, output, and skills, or direct supervision of activities. The simplest form of coordination is mutual adjustment. It is used in the simplest and in the most complex situations. In the simplest organizations mutual adjustment is all that is needed to organize activity. In the most complex situations, standardization and direct supervision may not be possible or effective. Mutual adjustment may be the only alternative. Direct supervision involves one individual overseeing the activities of one or more individuals. The one supervising coordinates the activities of all of the others. Standardization reduces the need for supervision or ongoing communication to achieve coordination of activities (2). A single organization may use all of these mechanisms to coordinate the activities of its members.

With growth, the number and types of tasks an organization must perform become more diverse and often more complex. When this occurs, increased efficiency and effectiveness may be achieved through the subdivision of tasks to be performed. The subdivision of tasks allows the individual members of the organization to become more skilled at the performance of a few tasks. With increased skill comes increased speed and accuracy of performance. Subdivision also allows the skill level of an individual to be matched with the tasks they are required to perform. The methods chosen to divide and coordinate the work of an organization will determine how effectively and efficiently the organization will operate. Physical therapy managers will need to establish an organizational structure for the individuals under their direction. To do this effectively they must be knowledgeable about the basic parts of an organization and the structural configurations that an organization can adopt. They should be aware of the internal and external factors that could influence the design process. Also, they should recognize the effects of organizational structure on the performance of the organization and the individuals within it.

Organizational Characteristics
PARTS OF AN ORGANIZATION

There are three basic parts to every organization. First, there is the operating core. This is the part of the organization which actually does the work to produce goods and services. If the organization is small, the work of the operating core can be coordinated through mutual adjustment. Second, there is the management part of the organization. As the size and complexity of the organization increases, the reliance on management to provide direct supervision to coordinate activity will likely increase. A concurrent increase in the size and layers of the management hierarchy would be expected. Third, there is the part of the organization that supports the activity of the operating core and management. This support part of the organization would grow as the organization increases its reliance on standardization to achieve coordination of activities.

The initial addition of supervision represents the first division of labor within an organization. At this point the organization has a division between those who do the work and those who supervise the work. Managers may be subdivided into two groups. The first subdivision is executive management. These are the managers at the top of the management hierarchy. They make strategic decisions about the goals of the organization, determine the activities necessary to achieve goals, and assign responsibilities. Executive management has high decision-making authority and responsibility for overall organizational performance. The second management subdivision is often referred to as middle management. Middle management stands between and connects executive management to the operating core. Middle management directly supervises the operating core. Middle management generally has less decision-making authority and more responsibility for day to day operations.

As the organization continues to grow and subdivide the activities to be performed, it begins to rely more on support functions to achieve coordination of activities. Mintzberg (2) proposes that support staff are made up of two distinct groups of individuals. The first he calls technical support staff or analysts. Analysts direct their efforts at standardizing the tasks to be performed and helping the organization to adapt to its environment. The second group of support staff includes a variety of functions such as public relations, mailroom, and cafeteria that support the work done in the operating core but are not directly related to the performance of its work. The type and size of the support staff will vary with the size and needs of the individual organization.

Figure 2.1 presents the interacting parts of an organization according to Mintzberg's functional concepts (2). Independent Physical Therapists, Incorporated (IPT, Inc.) a small private practice, employs an owner-manager, physical therapists, physical therapist assistants, aides, and a clerk. It purchases accounting, benefits management, and legal services from outside consultants. The owner-manager is responsible for the development of policies and procedures which direct operations. One physical therapist has job duties related to staff training and development.

STRUCTURAL CONFIGURATIONS

The structural configuration of a organization defines the relationships between organizational parts and members. Through these relationships, it assigns decision-making authority and accountability for performance. An organization's structural configuration can be most easily

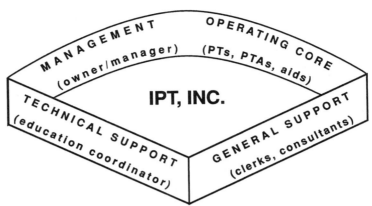

Figure 2.1. Functional organization for a small physical therapy practice. (Adapted from: Mintzberg H. The Structure of an Organization. Englewood Cliffs, NJ: Prentice-Hall, 1979:20.)

demonstrated through the use of an organizational chart. An organizational chart is a graphic representation of an organization's structure. As an organization grows, the need to divide and coordinate the activities of its members will increase. Correspondingly, the configuration of its structure will change, usually becoming more complex. The developmental stages have been described by the terms simple or craft, entrepreneurial, bureaucratic, divisionalized, and adhocracy or matrix (2).

Craft Stage

The first stage of organizational development is presented in Figure 2.2. This is the craft stage. At this stage the organization is generally small with little, if any, division of labor. The term craft should not be interpreted to imply anything about the level of skill required to perform the necessary tasks. It does imply that all members of the operating core perform all of the tasks necessary to achieve the common performance goal. All members are considered equally competent in providing service. Often, if there is a division of supervision and labor, the supervisor will also be able to and have to be involved in performing all of the tasks performed by members of the operating core. This is certainly the case in

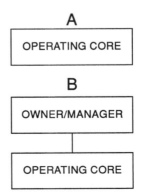

Figure 2.2. Craft stage of organizational development. **A,** without division of labor; **B,** with division of labor and supervision.

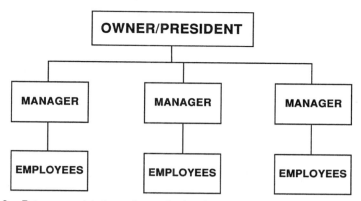

Figure 2.3. Entrepreneurial stage of organizational development.

many small physical therapy departments and practices. In a small private practice the major investor may take this responsibility. In these types of settings, the "working" manager will have both supervision and client care responsibilities. The amount of direct supervision will be minimal, with frequent reliance on mutual adjustment to achieve coordination of activities.

Entrepreneurial Stage

The second stage of organizational development is represented by the organizational chart in Figure 2.3. This is the entrepreneurial stage. At this stage, the organization can no longer rely on mutual adjustment for the coordination of activities. It has reached a point where the division of labor is necessary to achieve maximum efficiency of operation. At this stage the organization will began to add layers of supervision between the executive management level and the operating core. The advantage of this change is increased efficiency of internal operations. The disadvantage is a decreased ability to respond quickly to changes in the environment. This occurs because there are more levels of organization involved in decision making and the implementation of change. These additional layers slow down the organization's response time.

Bureaucratic Stage

The next stage of organizational development is the bureaucratic stage. Organizational structures associated with the bureaucratic stage are presented in Figure 2.4, A–C. The structure of the bureaucratic organization can be somewhat varied. The bureaucratic organization is characterized by highly specialized jobs, an extensive hierarchy of authority, much standardization, and large support structures. Figure 2.4A presents the bureaucratic organization with a support component. The support component represents the utilization of technical and/or general support functions. Figure 2.4B presents the organizational chart of a tall bureaucratic organization. The term "tall" indicates that there are many layers of management between the top executive group and the operating core. Figure 2.4C presents the organizational chart of a flat bureaucratic organization. Here, there are fewer layers of management. The current trend

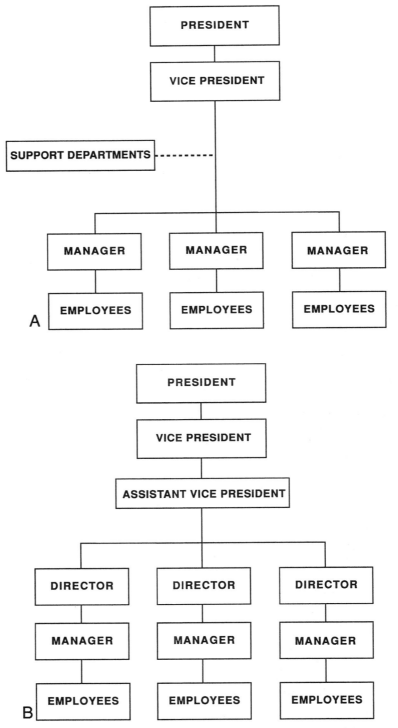

Figure 2.4. **A,** bureaucratic stage of organizational development with line (direct reporting relationships) and support (indirect reporting relationships) organizational structure. **B,** tall bureaucratic organizational structure.

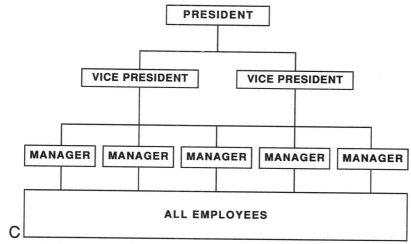

Figure 2.4. (Continued).   **C,** flat bureaucratic organizational structure.

in organizational design is toward the flat structure. This trend is driven by the need to improve an organization's ability to respond quickly to external forces.

Divisionalized Stage

The next stage of development occurs when an organization moves toward a divisional structure. Figure 2.5 presents an organizational chart for a divisionalized organization. An organization may chose to adopt a

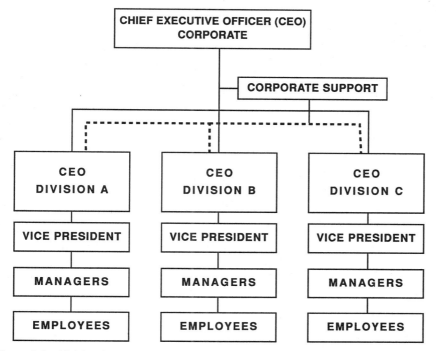

Figure 2.5.   Divisionalized stage of organizational development.

divisionalized structure based on differences in output, different geographic locations or the service needs of different markets. The health care industry has seen a shift toward the divisionalized structure due to recent trends toward vertical integration of health services. In health care, vertical integration refers to the ability of a single provider to meet the primary, secondary, tertiary, rehabilitative, and custodial care needs of all clients requesting those services from a specific geographical region (3). The vertically integrated organization would then have several divisions providing different levels or types of health care. In the design of a divisional structure the key question rests with how much decision making should be done by the corporate management (centralized decision making) and how much should be left to each division (decentralized decision making). The greater the centralization of the decision-making authority, the more time it takes to make a decision and the less responsive each division will be to external forces.

Adhocracy/Matrix Stage

The final stage of development described by Mintzberg (2) is the adhocracy. A more commonly used name for Mintzberg's adhocracy is matrix. Within the matrix there is a tendency to organize specialists both by functional departments, such as physical therapy, and by product line or program, such as orthopedics. The matrix generally relies heavily on the standardization of performance that comes from specialized formal training and mutual adjustment as its primary mechanism for coordination. Figure 2.6 presents the organizational chart for a matrix structure. The matrix organizational structure has the advantage of integrating the interests and goals of the functional departments with those of the product lines. It can also integrate the activities of a variety of professionals from different functional departments in ways impossible under a more traditional structure. The disadvantage of the matrix system includes the potential conflict between functional departments and product lines if the organization does not recognize and reward the achievement of mutual goals. The matrix may also place greater demands on its professionals. Because of the dual authority structure, the professionals within the structure may face conflict resulting from a two-boss system and the possibility of unclear expectations and priorities (4). Professional roles may need to be redefined and the concept of interdisciplinary functioning promoted (5).

STRUCTURAL CONFIGURATION AND ORGANIZATIONAL EFFECTIVENESS

The structural configuration of an organization has a direct impact on its performance. MacMillan and Jones (6) identify three areas of operation that can be strengthened or weakened by the organization's structure. The first area is the organization's ability to respond to external competition. The second area is the organization's ability to respond to market changes. The third area is the efficiency and effectiveness of internal operations.

The organization's competitive response determines the quality of its competitor intelligence. Competitor intelligence refers to the ability to

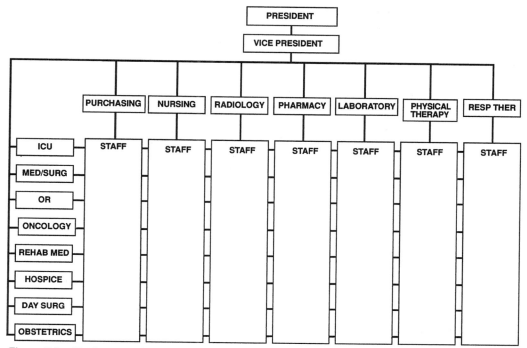

Figure 2.6. Matrix stage of organizational development.

recognize and take advantage of opportunities for product and market expansion. Quickly responding to a need by introducing competitive products and services into the marketplace is an advantage in gaining a market share.

The ability to respond to market conditions is determined by the organization's ability to focus on needs of its customers. It relates to how well the organization understands its customers and how well the organization integrates all of the service needs of each customer.

The efficiency and effectiveness of internal operations is determined by a number of factors. First, there is the expertise of its workers. Second, there is the quality of its output. Next, there is the efficiency with which it uses resources in the production of goods and services. Finally, there is the speed with which it can meet its customers' needs.

Factors That Influence Organizational Design

Management literature discusses a number of factors which are thought to influence the structure of an organization. The initial factor is the organization's fundamental principles, often referred to as its values and mission. The organization's environment, technology, competitive strategy, size and age, past history, and ownership are other factors which influence its structure. Current trends in organizational design may also influence the structure of an organization. There is much dispute over the relative importance and interrelationships of these factors as they impact the organizational design process. Of these factors, fundamental princi-

EXAMPLE 2.1
Contents of a Mission Statement

Independent Physical Therapists, Inc.

Mission Statement

Independent Physical Therapists, Inc. (IPT, Inc.) is a (1) for profit organization (2) dedicated to becoming a widely recognized provider of high quality, (3) outpatient physical therapy services to (4) persons residing in the Milwaukee metropolitan area. In addition to the (5) provision of general physical therapy services, IPT, Inc. shall provide (6) specialized treatment to adult and pediatric clients with neurological disorders. IPT, Inc. is also (7) committed to meeting the continual educational needs of physical therapists and future physical therapists; therefore, the organization will host professional meetings and maintain affiliations with accredited physical therapy programs. (8) All activities of IPT, Inc. shall reflect a recognition of the basic dignity and rights of all employees, clients, students, referral sources, and community members.

ples, the environment, technology, competitive strategy, size, and age seem to be the most critical and will be reviewed here. The importance of these factors is supported by a growing appreciation for the need to adopt a design which can respond readily to demands from the external environment, even at the risk of decreased operating efficiency (3, 4, 6).

FUNDAMENTAL PRINCIPLES

Fundamental principles are an adopted set of values by which executive management evaluates the performance of the organization and its members. According to MacMillan and Jones these values must be ". . . explicitly generated, consciously managed and clearly disseminated" (6). Recent research has identified a number of organizational characteristics which should be specified by an organization's fundamental principles. The characteristics include the scope of an organization's activities, identification of its critical functions, the style of managing people which should be used throughout the organization, the ethics with which the organization approaches business decisions, the organization's self-image, and its attitudes toward its employees, customers, competitors, and external groups (7, 8). In health care, the written statements of an organization's fundamental principles are often referred to as values and mission statements (see Chapter 11 for additional discussion of values and ethics). These statements define the organization for both members and external parties.

In Example 2.1, important characteristics of a mission statement are underlined and the significance of each point is discussed.

The numbered parts of the mission statement of IPT, Inc. identify the following characteristics of the organization:

1. It is a for profit organization; inferred is a willingness to take some risk and to meet the challenges of competition.
2. Importance is placed on earning a positive reputation nationwide for quality services. The self-perception of the organization is that it can provide very high quality service as measured on a national scale. Also inferred is a commitment to employing and retaining staff capable of achieving national recognition. Marketing will be active in disseminating information about the organization.

3–6. The critical functions of the organization, the areas in which service excellence will be demonstrated, and the geographical focus of the organization are defined.

7. A positive attitude toward education is stated. In addition to high quality services, the organization will actively support educational efforts related to its perceived expertise.

8. The desired attitude of employees toward those within and external to the organization are clearly defined. The implication is that management style will be participative. Respect for human dignity is a value all members of the organization shall demonstrate.

ENVIRONMENT

By definition, the environment of an organization is everything that is outside of its structure (1). The organization's technology (knowledge base), products, markets, competitors, geographical location, outside regulation, the economy, political climate, and even the weather are part of an organization's environment. We can view the environment's potential impact on organizational structure by considering the condition of the environment. An organization's environment can be defined by its stability, complexity, market diversity, and hostility (2).

Stability

The stability of an organization's environment has to do with both the rate of change as well as the predictability of change in environmental conditions. The more unstable or dynamic the environment, the more difficult it becomes to predict future needs and required activities. An organization in a dynamic environment should be designed in a way that allows it to respond quickly to a variety of unpredictable circumstances.

Complexity

An organization's environment can be considered complex when the organization must have in-depth knowledge about its market, products, regulations, etc. A simple environment is one in which the knowledge needed is easily understood. The design impact of a complex environment is the need to subdivide complex activities into easily understood components.

Market Diversity

Market diversity refers to the number of customers served and variety of services provided. A market can be integrated or expansive. An integrated market is one with few customers and/or few products. An expansive market is one with many customers and/or many products. The greater the market diversity, the more varied the activities of the organization. The organization's design must support the various activities while maintaining the required level of coordination.

Hostility

A hostile environment is an unpredictable environment. An unpredictable environment causes the organization to face an unpredictable demand. The hostility in the environment can arise from the organization's relationship with its labor force, competitors, the government, or other outside parties. In the presence of a hostile environment, an organization must be designed for flexibility of response.

Structures for the 1990s

In the 1990s, health care providers will generally find themselves in dynamic, highly complex, and frequently hostile environments. Market diversity varies with the competitive strategy of the specific organization. The environment of the 1990s will dictate the need for special attention to design of a structure which maximizes flexibility and coordination of complex services.

TECHNOLOGY

Technology refers to the body of knowledge required to complete the activities of an organization. A general consensus is that at least the design of the operating core should be influenced by the technology which guides its activity. Woodward (9) describes three types of technological production systems that could influence organizational design. These are unit, mass, and process production systems. Unit production describes a system of production based on a customer's special requirements, the production of prototypes, or the production of small batches. Mass production describes a system which produces large quantities of similar output. Process production refers to the continuous-flow production of liquids or gases and intermittent production of chemicals. Of these technological production systems, unit production most closely describes the technological system of most health care providers. Because the service needs of patients are diverse, the activities of the operating core of a health care provider must also be diverse and nonstandard. Woodward indicates that the work coordination in a unit production system is achieved through standardization of the skills of workers in the operating core and through mutual adjustment. A unit production organization would have a large operating core and first line manager level arranged into small work groups with a relatively small administrative structure.

COMPETITIVE STRATEGY

An organization's competitive strategy reflects its plan for defending and taking a market share from its current and future competitors. The success of the plan depends on having an organization that can carry out the chosen strategy successfully. MacMillan and Jones (6) suggest that by varying the relationships between the organization's functional departments, its outputs, and its markets an organization can improve its competitive advantage in the marketplace. For example, the traditional health care organization has been organized around functional units and their activity. This structure results in high levels of expertise and good internal efficiencies. It is also slow to recognize and respond to market changes because its focus is inward on its internal operations. Under a matrix structure, the organization is organized around the product line first and, within the product line, by functional units. This structure results in high

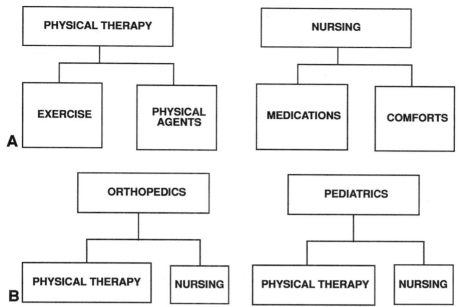

Figure 2.7. **A,** a simplified activity/activity matrix to organize services by distinct functional differences. **B,** an output/activity matrix. Here the organizational structure is based on differences in the output (orthopedics and pediatrics).

product-specific expertise and market knowledge. It is lacking in total market perspective because the focus is product specific. It may also result in inefficient staff utilization. Figure 2.7, A and B, presents examples of the matrix form of organizational charts for physical therapy and nursing functions which are part of a larger organization. Figure 2.7A represents the structure based on a division of activities, while Figure 2.7B depicts the structure by output (specialized services also called a program line structure) and activity. Each possible organizational structure has its strengths and weaknesses. The challenge is to find the most competitive structure for a particular organization in a particular marketplace (6).

SIZE AND AGE

Mintzberg (2), in summarizing current hypotheses regarding the impact of size of an organization, concluded that increased size results in greater division of labor, greater differentiation of organizational units, more levels of management hierarchy, more need for coordination, and greater formalization of behavior. Age is often related to the process of organizational development previously described under structural configurations.

Organizational Structure and Job Design

The job design process should result in a description of each job in the organization. The job description is the outcome of the job design process. The job description is a written description of the responsibilities, accountabilities, and authority for decision making for each job within the organization. To effectively guide performance, each job must be defined in the following terms:

1. Its relationships with other individuals and functions within the organization;
2. Required job tasks;
3. The skills required to perform the tasks;
4. The knowledge and/or formal training required;
5. The extent of responsibility for their own work and the work of other individuals;
6. The decision-making authority of the job.

More specific information about writing a job description will be discussed in Chapter 4. At this point, it is important to recognize the impact of organizational structure on the work design process.

The design of an organization's structure and the design of the specific jobs within it are interdependent activities. The job design process will be influenced by all of the factors that influenced the design of the organization's structure. Job design will be guided by the fundamental principles (values and mission statement(s)) of the organization. The fundamental principles will determine broadly the types of activity in which the organization will engage. It will determine the attitudes that the organization holds about the capabilities and motivations of its employees. Technology will influence the type of skills a job will require. Can skills be learned on the job or will formal training be required? How should tasks be subdivided to gain maximum efficiency? Will the organization rely on mutual adjustment or direct supervision to obtain needed coordination between jobs? The environment and competitive strategy will likewise influence the design of jobs within the structure. In a stable environment, the traditional bureaucratic organization may grow and prosper. With increasing hostility and market diversity, the need for rapid decision making may outweigh the importance of maximum internal efficiency. Decisions will need to be made more quickly. This may result in the adoption of a flat organizational structure with increased authority for decision making incorporated into jobs at all levels of the organization.

Organizational Structure for Physical Therapy Practice

The factors that influence organizational design for organizations in general apply to organizational design for physical therapy practice. This is equally true for the physical therapy practice that is part of a larger organization and the practice that is an independent organization. There are, however, some practical issues that should be taken into consideration when designing an organizational structure for physical therapy.

DESIGN ISSUES
Constraints

The first issue is the constraints on organizational and job design which come from regulations outside of the organization. There are several possible sources of outside regulation. Government regulation comes in many forms. Regulation of physical therapy practice is found at the federal and state levels in the form of reimbursement regulations. Governmental reimbursement for physical therapy services is often contingent on the training and licensure of the physical therapist, and sometimes the physical therapist assistant, providing the service. There may also be specific requirements for supervision of nonlicensed personnel involved in the delivery of physical therapy services. State licensure laws for physical therapists and physical therapist assistants place constraints on organizational design. Licensure effectively standardizes training and skill requirements as well as the limits of decision-making authority of physical therapy personnel related to patient care services. Regulation of physical therapy practice also comes from health care accreditation agencies such as the Joint Commission on Accreditation of Health Care Organizations (JCAHO) and The Commission of Accreditation of Rehabilitation Facilities (CARF).

The organizational design of a physical therapy practice may also be constrained if it is part of a larger organization. This can occur if the physical therapy practice is a department of a larger organization or is a division of a larger corporation. In either case, the larger organization may require standardization of organizational and job design between departments or divisions.

Personnel Shortage

Personnel shortages are and will continue to be a reality of physical therapy practice in the 1990s. Limits on available personnel may interfere with the physical therapy manager's ability to design the most effective organizational structure.

Advancement Opportunities and Retention

The final issue for consideration on the topic of organizational design is the impact of design on opportunities for advancement. Manpower shortages in physical therapy make staff retention a critical concern. Often staff retention is dependent on opportunities for advancement. Creating opportunities for growth and advancement along clinical and management tracks should be a priority for the physical therapy manager during the organizational design process. In addition to the traditional opportunities related to the supervision of other employees, consideration should be given to the subdivision of tasks which might offer advancement opportunities through specialization and/or responsibility for supervision of support functions, such as education and quality assurance. The creation of a career ladder can be particularly challenging for the manager of a small practice or a practice which is part of a large organization that is moving toward a flatter structure. Chapter 4 will deal with retention strategies in more depth.

ORGANIZATIONAL STRUCTURES

The organizational structures for physical therapy practice mirror the structures presented earlier during the discussion about structural

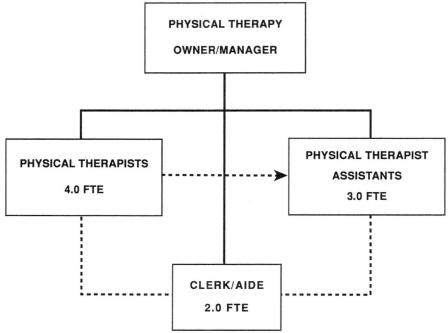

Figure 2.8. Simple organizational structure for a physical therapy practice. *Solid lines* indicate a direct reporting relationship while *broken lines* indicate indirect reporting relationships.

configurations and the development of organizations. The impacts of structure on internal operating efficiency, effectiveness, and the ability to respond to market needs and competition remain the same. Figures 2.8–2.10 present the organizational charts for physical therapy practice at three different levels of development. Figure 2.8 presents a structure for a practice at the simple or craft stage of development. Note the division of labor made necessary by regulation of physical therapy practice.

Figure 2.9 presents a structure for a practice at the entrepreneurial stage of development. At this stage there is an increased reliance on supervision which is not related to outside regulation. Support functions are minimal and related to nontechnical support functions.

Figure 2.10 presents a structure for practice that is at the matrix stage.

Note the dual reporting relationships for staff functions. The functional managers are responsible for meeting the service needs of the programs in coordination with the program managers. Functional managers are responsible for staff recruitment, training and development, and quality assurance. The program manager is responsible for coordinating the services of multiple functional areas to meet the needs of the program customers. This matrix structure would best meet the needs of a practice which is part of a larger organization.

SUMMARY

There are many factors for the physical therapy manager to consider when involved in the organizational design process.

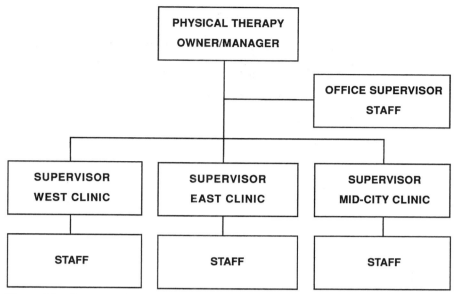

Figure 2.9. Entrepreneurial organizational structure for physical therapy practice.

The values, mission, size, and age of the practice will influence the constraints that come from being part of a larger organization and from government regulation of physical therapy practice. Organizational structure may influence the manager's ability to compensate for chronic staff shortages. To begin the design process the manager must identify constraints to be accommodated and the opportunities for improved efficiency and effectiveness. The right organizational structure is the starting point for success.

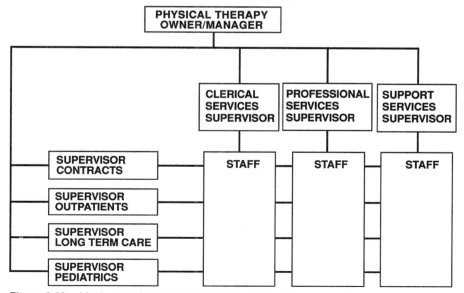

Figure 2.10. Matrix organizational structure for physical therapy practice.

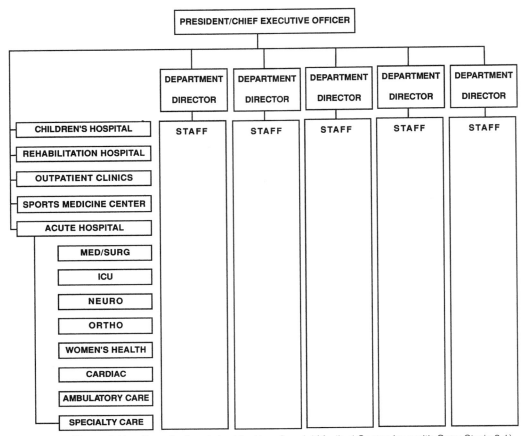

Figure 2.11.   Organizational chart for Very Special Medical Center (use with Case Study 2.1).

CASE STUDY 2.1
Organization Design and Mission Statement

Very Special Medical Center

Very Special Medical Center (VSMC) is a tertiary medical center serving patients within a 500-mile radius. It is a major teaching center with affiliations with Very Special Medical School and several university-based allied health programs. The center includes a children's hospital, a rehabilitation hospital, two large outpatient clinics (off-site), one sports medicine clinic, and a main acute care hospital. The center offers patients access to all general and specialty medical/surgical services. For operational purposes the main hospital has adopted a program line (matrix) organizational structure which is depicted in Figure. 2.11.

The physical therapy department provides services to all programs, hospitals, and clinics of VSMC. Without concern for the actual number of employees, please design (draw) an organizational structure for physical therapy that compliments VSMC's structure and commitment to teaching, research, and the provision of sophisticated specialty care. Briefly explain the rationale behind your design. Finally, write a mission statement for VSMC's physical therapy department.

You may consult Appendix 2.1 to compare your ideas with the authors' suggestions.

References

1. Webster's II new Riverside university dictionary. Boston: Houghton Mifflin, 1984:436,828.
2. Mintzberg H. The structuring of organizations. Englewood Cliffs, NJ: Prentice-Hall, 1979:1–16,18–34,227–248,267–270,431–467.

3. Montague B, McCool BP. Vertical integration: Exploration of a popular strategic concept. Health Care Manage Rev 1986;11:7–19.
4. Timm MM, Wanetik MG. Matrix organization: Design and development for a hospital organization. Hospital Health Serv Admin 1983; Nov/Dec:46–58.
5. Darling LA, Ogg HL: Basic requirements for initiating an interdisciplinary process. Phys Ther 1984;64:1684–1686.
6. MacMillan IC, Jones PE. Designing organizations to compete. J Bus Strategy 1984;4:11–26.
7. MacMillan IC. Corporate ideology and strategic delegation. J Bus Strategy 1983;4(3):71–76.
8. Peters TJ, Waterman RH. In search of excellence: Lessons from America's best-run companies. New York: Harper and Row, 1982:234–291.
9. Woodward, J. Industrial organization, "theory and practice." Oxford: Oxford, 1965:36–39.

CHAPTER 3

Personnel Management Theory

OVERVIEW

The physical therapy manager is responsible for retaining sufficient numbers of capable staff (human resources) so clients can be treated efficiently and effectively. Put another way, effective management of human resources will lead to an acceptable degree of productivity. Answers to the question "How can a manager best meet the needs of staff and the organization?" have been offered by numerous authors because the question and the answer are of interest to managers regardless of their business. This chapter contains a concise overview of historically important and current personnel management theories to assist in answering the preceding question. The role of the manager is defined according to each of the theories. The anticipated responses of those being supervised under each theoretical approach are discussed. A framework for selecting a managerial style appropriate to a particular situation is presented. Practical suggestions based on both theory and practical experience are discussed. Also, with practical settings in mind, strategies for dealing with conflict are addressed. A case study challenges the reader to choose a means to solve several clinical management problems from the options presented in this chapter.

Introduction

As health care providers, physical therapists provide a service to the customers (clients) that they serve. Although the availability and use of machine technology is on the rise, physical therapy remains a human resource (people)-intensive business. In other words, when the costs of delivering physical therapy services are analyzed, there are more costs related to the employment of the people who provide the service than to the buildings and equipment that they use in the course of providing the service. Because human resources account for such a significant portion of the cost of providing physical therapy, the effective management of these resources becomes the key to controlling the cost and quality of physical therapy services. Organizations evaluate the effectiveness of human resource management in terms of productivity. Effective management of human resources will result in high productivity. Ineffective management will result in low productivity.

The goal of human resource management is to maximize the productivity of human resources. Higher productivity means fewer employees and lower costs. Human resource management is the focus of personnel management theory. Often referred to as management or motivation theory, this body of knowledge attempts to provide models which can help managers effectively manage the people for whom they are responsible. This chapter will provide insight into the historical development of personnel management theory, present the theoretical implications of personnel management theories as they relate to the development of an effective management style, and discuss the application of negotiation strategies for successful resolution of conflict in the workplace. Should this last topic area appear divergent, the reader is reminded that almost all of the interactions of the individual employee and manager could be "I want, you want" situations. Only through effective application of negotiation strategies will these potential conflicts result in "I win, you win" outcomes.

Concept of Productivity

To fully appreciate a discussion about personnel management theory it is necessary to understand the concept of productivity. Simply put, productivity is the relationship between the input of resources and the output of a product. It can be defined as the ratio between the amount or cost of resources used and the resulting amount or value of the output produced using those resources. In the case of physical therapy, human resources account for a large portion of the input. The output is primarily the service that we provide our clients. The concept of productivity can be expressed by the equation:

$$\frac{\text{Output}}{\text{Input}} \times 100 = \text{Percent Productivity}$$

There are a number of factors that can influence the productivity of any given input. The reader should consult Chapter 5 for a more detailed discussion of productivity and the practice of physical therapy.

Management Theory: Indications for Employee Motivation

ROLE OF THE MANAGER

In Chapter 2 we defined the role of the manager to be the coordination of the activities of others toward the achievement of organizational goals. In the simplest organization, coordination could be achieved through the use of mutual adjustment. As the complexity of the organization increased, coordination relied increasingly on the use of direct supervision and task standardization (1). So, with increased organizational complexity comes an increased need to manage human activities. The manager is challenged to meld the demands of the organization and the needs of the workers into a functioning whole. Miles (2) proposes that it is through the integration of organizational and human variables that the manager can create an effective and efficient sociotechnical system. He reviews several mechanisms that managers use to integrate these different and sometimes conflicting variables. These mechanisms include direction, organizational design, job design, personnel selection and training, personnel development and appraisal, communication, control, and reward systems. These mechanisms, in fact, describe the role of the manager. How an individual manager approaches the implementation of these integrating mechanisms is the focus of personnel management theory.

CONCEPTUAL FRAMEWORK

Personnel management theory seeks to determine the impact of human aptitudes, attitudes, and behaviors on the motivation to perform in the workplace. As with any body of knowledge, theories about personnel management come from a variety of sources and have evolved over time. Evolution of personnel management theory has occurred as research and experience provide additional insight into the complex and intriguing subject of human behavior in the workplace. Miles provides an excellent conceptual framework for understanding the evolution of management theories (2). He identifies three basic models of management theory and suggests that with a little manipulation most, if not all, management theories will fall in line with one of these basic models. His models of management theory are the traditional model, the human relations model, and the human resource model. Each model is characterized by a specific set of assumptions about human attitudes and behaviors. Inherent in the model assumptions are indications for the way managers should direct the work of others to achieve high levels of productivity. Finally, each model predicts the response of the workers who are managed under the model's assumptions. Following Miles' conceptual framework, we will review some of the most commonly cited theories about personnel management.

TRADITIONAL MODEL

Miles' traditional model finds its origins in the writings of Social Darwinists (2). Applying Darwinist theories about survival of the fittest to the organizational setting, Miles adopts a perspective that applies the concept of superior fitness to the organizational setting. Those with superior ability should use their abilities to lead those of lesser ability. A second group of writings which contribute to Miles' traditional model of management are those of classical economists. Classical economists portrayed man as being in a natural state of leisure. Man would leave this natural state of leisure only when forced to work to make enough money to survive. When man's economic needs were met, he would revert back to the leisure state. Miles' traditional model was also derived from the works of Fredrick Taylor and Max Weber.

Fredrick Taylor: Scientific Management

Fredrick Taylor (3) was instrumental in the development of the scientific management movement. The scientific management movement sought to improve worker productivity through scientific observation and analysis of tasks. Taylor based his works on observations of shop-floor activities. He postulated that even skilled workers could not perform at optimum levels unless guided by supervisors in the performance of standardized tasks. Workers were not capable of independently determining the most efficient way of performing a given task. Workers were to be closely supervised and rewarded for performing standardized tasks through adequate pay.

Max Weber: Bureaucracy

Another writer who contributed to Miles' traditional model (2) was Max Weber (4). Weber, a sociologist, applied the concept of task standardization and job specialization to all levels of the organization, including management. He promoted the segmentation and departmentalization of knowledge, skills, and expertise. Each organizational segment or specialized office was referred to as a bureau. Bureaus were to be arranged in a hierarchical structure. Weber's theories form the basis for the organizational structure known as the bureaucracy. In Weber's bureaucracy, authority and responsibility were attributed to the office, not the individual in the office.

Taken together, the theories that contribute to Miles' traditional model (2) solve the problem of managing workers by providing them with a limited number of rules and techniques which can be learned and repeated. The consistency of the performance is maintained by close supervision. The organization provides reasonable working conditions, equitable treatment, and fair pay. In return, the worker provides a reasonable level of performance. Authority is the central means of control. The "human" needs of the employee are ignored (2). Employees performing the work of the organization have no input into the way their work is performed. In fact, they are considered to be incapable of designing or directing their own activities.

HUMAN RELATIONS MODEL

Theories that contribute to what Miles calls the human relations model (2) began to emerge as early as 1920. They were theories that began to recognize the negative impacts of standardization to the extent that the needs of the individual were ignored. These theories argued that "management must deal with the whole man rather than just his skills and aptitudes" (2). They promoted a concerned and considerate management style and the use of rewards other than money.

Hawthorne Experiments

Major support for the human relations model came from a set of social science studies which began in the late 1920s. These experiments took place at the Western Electric Company in Hawthorne, Illinois. The intent of the researchers was to evaluate the impact of changing work conditions on worker performance. The experiments involved the observation of worker reactions in response to adjustment of the lighting levels in a production area. During the course of the experiments the researchers noted that worker performance was not dependent on variations in the lighting levels. The workers performed at high levels of productivity whether the lighting was raised or lowered, even when the lighting was lowered to substandard levels. The researchers proposed that the important element for maintaining high levels of performance was the attention paid to the workers by the researchers. The fact that management considered them important enough to be concerned about their working conditions and ask for their input led to high productivity levels (5). Today, this worker reaction to management attention is often referred to as the Hawthorne Effect.

Miles considers the human relations model of management an extension of the traditional model with the exception of management's efforts to provide each individual worker with a sense of belonging and importance (2). Management can accomplish this by keeping workers informed, listening to their feedback, and allowing some self-control and self-direction in routine matters. Given an individual sense of belonging and importance workers will accept authority and provide a reasonable level of cooperation and performance.

HUMAN RESOURCE MODEL

Like the human relations model, the human resource model recognizes the worker's need to have a sense of belonging, feel important, and have recognition. It goes beyond the human relations model in recognizing that workers also want the opportunity to develop and apply all of their skills in the performance of their work. People "gain satisfaction from achieving demanding, worthwhile objectives" (2). The satisfaction comes not from an external reward but from the accomplishment itself. The human resource model argues that the organization can benefit if it supports and encourages full participation of all workers. The works of Abraham Maslow and Fredrick Herzberg are among those most frequently cited

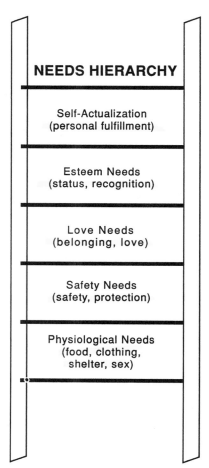

Figure 3.1. Maslow's hierarchy of needs.

in discussions regarding the relationship of human need to worker performance (2, 6, 7).

Abraham Maslow: Hierarchy of Needs Theory

Abraham Maslow (8, 9) argues that all men have a number of wants and needs arranged in an ascending hierarchy from the most basic to the intangible (Fig. 3.1). The driving force behind an individual's activities is the lowest need in the hierarchy which, at that time, remains unmet. As each lower level need is met, the next higher level need becomes the driving force behind the individual's activities. The most basic needs are physiological needs: food, shelter, and clothing. Ascending the hierarchy, the next level of need is safety: security and protection. The third level of need is love: to belong and to be loved. The forth level of need is esteem. Esteem needs represent the need to have status and to be recognized for achievements. At the top of Maslow's hierarchy of needs is the need for self-actualization, the need to achieve the fulfillment of personal goals and objectives. Maslow's theories suggest that performance is driven by

Table 3.1.
Herzberg's Theory of Job Satisfaction

Dissatisfiers	Satisfiers
Administration	Achievement
Benefits	Advancement
Interpersonal relations	Growth potential
Job security	Interpersonal relations
Organizational policy	Power
Salary	Recognition
Supervision	Responsibility
	Salary
	Status

the desire to fulfill unmet human needs. The driving need changes as soon as it is fulfilled. Under the hierarchy of need theory, to maximize worker performance, jobs must be designed to assist the individual's growth and development in a way that satisfies these changing needs.

Fredrick Herzberg: Two-Factor Theory

Herzberg's theories (10, 11) are frequently cited in discussions about the role of management in motivating worker performance. Herzberg suggests that job satisfaction and worker motivation are enhanced by the presence of reasonable working conditions, equitable treatment, and fair pay. These three items, however, are not sufficient to encourage optimal worker performance. In other words, they are only half of the picture. Herzberg theorizes that there are two categories of job attitude factors which influence performance. He refers to these categories of factors as dissatisfiers and satisfiers. Factors that lead to job dissatisfaction are considered hygiene factors (health and safety related). If absent, hygiene factors would result in job dissatisfaction. However, the presence of hygiene factors would not necessarily result in job satisfaction. Job satisfiers, if present, are motivators. The more satisfied the workers, the more cooperative and productive they become. Table 3.1 provides a listing of the types of factors which Herzberg would categorize as dissatisfiers and satisfiers.

There are some definite similarities between Maslow's hierarchy of needs (8, 9) and Herzberg's dissatisfiers and satisfiers (10, 11). Figure 3.2 presents a comparison of Herzberg's and Maslow's concepts.

Miles' human resource model, reflecting the works of authors such as Maslow and Herzberg, defines the manager's role as that of facilitator (2). The goal of the manager is to tap into the full potential of each worker through the development of his/her abilities. Workers are to be fully involved in the control and direction of their activities. In response to facilitation and autonomy, workers will provide a high level of performance. Additionally, they will be satisfied because they are afforded the opportunity to utilize their abilities to the fullest. This is in contrast to the human relations model where employee participation is used as a "means of improving morale" (2).

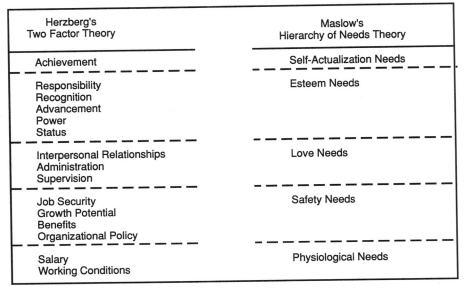

Herzberg's Two Factor Theory	Maslow's Hierarchy of Needs Theory
Achievement	Self-Actualization Needs
Responsibility Recognition Advancement Power Status	Esteem Needs
Interpersonal Relationships Administration Supervision	Love Needs
Job Security Growth Potential Benefits Organizational Policy	Safety Needs
Salary Working Conditions	Physiological Needs

Figure 3.2. A comparison of human needs theories.

McGREGOR'S THEORY X AND THEORY Y

McGregor (12) developed a conceptual framework for a management theory from the works of traditionalists and management theorists previously discussed. He saw the worker as an asset with the potential to make a contribution in the work setting if given the opportunity. Theory X was McGregor's interpretation of the traditionalist view of the average worker. Theory Y, by contrast, was McGregor's interpretation of theories that recognized the worker as an asset. Theory Y presents an image of the average worker which is similar to the assumptions made under Miles' human resource model (2).

McGregor's Theory X assumes that the average person:

1. Inherently avoids work because he dislikes it;
2. Needs firm direction with the threat of punishment to achieve work-related goals;
3. Lacks ambition, has an aversion to responsibility, and firmly desires direction;
4. Values job security.

Theory Y is in direct contrast to Theory X. Theory Y presumes that:

1. The average person finds work a natural activity to engage in.
2. There are other options for obtaining goal-directed behaviors than punishment.
3. Job satisfaction is an important means of securing worker acceptance of work-related goals.
4. Given the opportunity, most people will accept as well as seek responsibility.
5. The attributes needed to solve work-related problems are dispersed among the members of an organization (12).

McGregor, commenting on authority in the workplace, stated, "The assumptions of Theory Y do not deny the appropriateness of authority, but they do deny that it is appropriate for all purposes and under all circumstances" (12).

OUCHI'S THEORY Z

There has been much discussion in recent years about the seemingly unprecedented success of Japanese organizations to motivate workers to consistently achieve high levels of productivity. Ouchi (13) formulated Theory Z based on his observations of Japanese organizations. He contends that the success of Japanese organizations is due to their collaborative style of management. Under the Japanese management style workers are trusted members of the organization. As such, they are consulted on issues that affect them and the product. The assumption is that workers have good ideas. The organization that listens to and implements workers' ideas will have a satisfied, motivated work force. The Japanese system of management creates trust and open communication by providing employees with:

1. Stable employment;
2. Written philosophy;
3. Job enrichment by rotation;
4. De-emphasis on rank;
5. Prescribed career paths and slow advancement;
6. Decision by consensus;
7. A collective value system.

Through the use of this system Japanese companies achieve low turnover of staff, a strong commitment to the organization, and high productivity.

Quality Circles

Under Theory Z type of management, worker participation is achieved through the use of "quality circles" (13). Quality circles are groups of workers from all levels of the organization who meet routinely to identify and solve organizational problems. Through the use of these groups organizations encourage and support a participative decision-making process. Quality circles are committed to the improvement of the performance of the organization. Group members, with the support of management, review policies and procedures of the organization. These groups have the authority to make managerial decisions. When the need for a change is identified, the group will work on the change until it reaches a consensus of opinion on how the change should be made. Proponents of the use of quality circles note that the need for consensus results in a time-consuming decision-making process. However, they balance this against potential negative effects caused by a dissatisfied minority which remains when other forms of participative decision-making processes are used (7). The management approach thought to be so effective in Japanese companies has many similarities to Miles' human resource model (2). Most notably, it recognizes the value of encouraging and supporting the involvement of all workers in the direction and control of organizational activities.

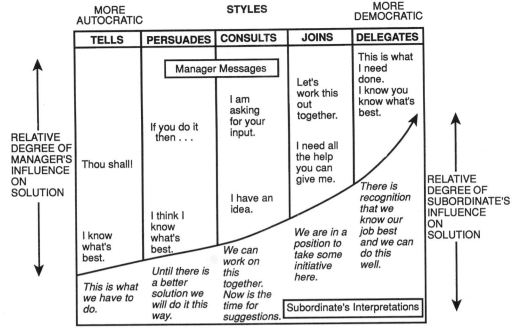

Figure 3.3.   A continuum of management style. (Modified from: Tannenbaum R, Schmidt WH. How to choose a leadership pattern. Harv Bus Rev 1973; May–June: 163–180).

Continuum of Management Style

Management style can vary along a continuum from one of total control to one which allows for subordinate autonomy within limits set by the manager (14). The management styles along this continuum have received many labels. The manager in total control has been labeled dictatorial, authoritarian, traditional, autocratic, and directive. The human relations manager who falls somewhere in the middle of the continuum has been labeled as supportive, nondirective, and laissez faire. The manager who truly allows employee participation in decision making has been referred to as collaborative, participative, and democratic (15). The less than complimentary descriptors for the human relations manager may relate to the adage that actions speak louder than words. Managers whose statements about employee participation and importance are not matched by actions to involve employees in the decision-making process may be perceived as weak and ineffective. A continuum of management style is presented in Figure 3.3.

CONTINGENCY THEORIES

As our discussion about management theory reveals, efforts to explain the relationship between management style and human performance continue. The search for the "best" approach has not yet revealed one approach that has been effective for all managers in all situations. This had led to the development of what are referred to as contingency or situational theories. These theories all postulate that management style is

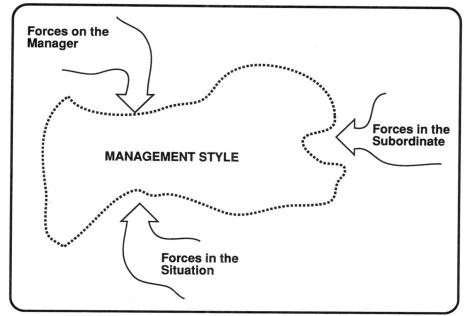

Figure 3.4. Forces influencing choice of management style.

contingent on three sets of variable factors: the manager, the group, and the situation (14).

Forces Influencing Management Style

Tannenbaum and Schmidt (16) discuss variables in terms of forces acting to influence the style of the manager. They categorize these as forces on the manager, forces in the subordinates, and forces in the situation (Fig. 3.4).

Forces on the Manager.   These forces include the manager's value system, confidence in subordinates, leadership tendencies, and security. A manager's value system refers to the assumptions the manager holds about employees' abilities and performance expectations, concerns about employee development, and so on. Managers will hold different levels of confidence in the abilities of their employees to perform different tasks. Leadership style will vary along a continuum (Fig. 3.3) from the need for total control to the ability to share tasks and duties with subordinates. Security refers to the manager's ability to tolerate ambiguity. Managers who can tolerate unpredictable behavior will be able to allow more divergence in employee behaviors. They will be more tolerant of differing ways to achieve similar outcomes.

Forces in the Subordinate.   These are all of the factors that shape an employee's personality, i.e., all of the external and internal forces that come together to define an employee's needs. In addition, it includes the employee's expectations of how a manager should perform.

Forces in the Situation.   These forces are the organization, the effectiveness of the work group, the tasks to be performed, and the time available. Organizational factors include its fundamental principles, environment, technology, competitive strategy, size and age, history, and ownership. These organizational factors may encourage or limit the manager's choice of style. The effectiveness of the work group would consider factors such as the experience, relevant education and training, willingness and ability to coordinate member efforts, past history of achievement, and motivation for future achievement. The more experienced and effective members of the work group are, the more effective they might be under a participative management style. Tasks may vary from routine to highly complex. The group's capability in relation to the tasks will influence the amount of direction and control required for effective performance. Time may limit the amount of participation possible. Decisions that need to be made quickly will allow less time for the involvement of others. Each of these situational forces will play a part in determining the style of leadership which an individual manager will exhibit in a given situation.

Life Cycle Theory

A second contingency theory is Hersey and Blanchard's Life Cycle theory (17). This theory focuses on the "maturity" of those managed as the key indicator for leadership style. Worker maturity is defined in terms of achievement motivation, task-relevant education, experience, and an ability and willingness to take responsibility. A leader will provide varying degrees of both task structure and socioemotional support as the worker matures. At the lowest level of maturity, the leader would provide a high level of structure and low level of support. At an intermediate level of maturity, the effective leader will shift to high structure and high support, and then to low structure and high support. For the mature worker, the leader will provide low structure and low support. The maturity of the followers may also be influenced by the situation. When undertaking a new or poorly defined task even a mature worker or work group may require the leader to return to a high structure approach until the situation is fully understood.

Contingency theories about management attempt to address the importance of the situation on management style. The manager's challenge under contingency theory is to use the style which will be most successful in that specific situation. To do this, the manager must first understand the nature of the forces which affect that situation. There is no single style that will be right in every situation. The style a manager adopts will be influenced by the work group, the situation, and the manager's beliefs about what it will take to get the job done.

Management Theory: Implications for Action

The problem associated with most theories about managing people is translating them into practical strategies in the workplace (2, 18). This section will be devoted to providing suggestions for making the transition and for the development of a practical and effective management style.

WHAT COMES BEFORE MOTIVATION?

Effective management should result in good performance. So, it would seem that a reasonable starting point in the development of an effective management style is the development of reasonable performance expectations. Performance is not dependent on effort alone. Performance has three components. This is presented well by Schermerhorn's theory of High Performance Management (18). This theory proposes that to achieve high levels of performance people must have the right abilities and support and must be motivated to exert the necessary level of effort.

Staff Selection, Training, and Development

The High Performance theory suggests that effective management starts with the selection, training, and development of employees (18). Performance expectations should be consistent with the abilities of the people doing the work. No matter what the level of motivation, employees cannot perform tasks for which they have been inadequately prepared. "An effective manager creates the capacity for high performance by staffing the jobs that need to be done with capable people" (18). This also points out the need for validating our perceptions of an employee's knowledge and skill level through an objective performance evaluation process.

Supportive Environment

Support relates to the employees' work environment. Support is a very tangible factor. It relates to "having the right tools, equipment and facilities; sufficient resources; proper goals and direction; freedom from unnecessary work constraints and performance obstacles; and market-competitive wages or salaries" (18). The concept is simple. Even with the right skills, an employee will be hindered in achievement of maximum performance levels without the proper tools. An effective manager will provide all of the support required to maximize performance.

Motivating for High Performance

An important quality needed to attain high performance is effort. Schermerhorn defines effort as "the willingness to perform" (18). The manager's job is to create the conditions which will increase the chances of employees choosing to work hard. The first step to developing a management style which motivates employees is to recognize and accept the fact that people are not rational, consistent entities; they are full of ambiguities and paradoxes. Of greatest importance are the contradictions which are fundamental to human nature. Peters and Waterman (19) identified several areas of contradiction, which, when taken into account, will improve the manager's ability to motivate employee performance:

1. While responding to positive reinforcement with a drive to do better, the response to negative feedback may be worse performance.
2. "Does it feel right?" is at least as important as "Can I prove it?"
3. As information processors, we can hold only a few facts explicitly in mind, while our unconscious minds can hold and process vast amounts of information.
4. While being sensitive to external rewards and punishments, we are also driven by our own needs.

5. While we say that words are important, we believe that actions speak louder than words.
6. We have a need to be independent but we will sacrifice some degree of independence to an organization that can give us meaning in our lives.

It will help to keep these contradictions in mind during the following discussion of motivation.

Competency Counts

An extension of the High Performance theory relates to the motivational properties of employee competence. Schermerhorn (18) notes that too often competence is overlooked as a motivator. He postulates that a sense of a job well done will increase an employee's desire to do the job. It will result in a self-driven desire to work harder. A sense of competence can be fostered by a manager who makes sure that employees have the abilities and support needed to achieve a high level of competence.

Keep the Door Open

In order to fully participate in and contribute to the performance of the work group, employees need a forum to be heard. This forum could be formal, like quality circles or a weekly staff meeting. It could be informal, such as a standing invitation to come into the manager's office whenever the need arises. In either case, the success of an open door policy depends on three things. First, the manager must make members of the work group aware of the opportunity and encourage them to contribute. Some employees will need more encouragement than others; some may never use the opportunity. All employees will appreciate the fact that they have the opportunity to be heard. Second, employees should never receive negative feedback for speaking out. That does not mean that a manager cannot use feedback to shape "how" an employee communicates or that a manager has to agree to everything that is said. It does mean that employees must be given the latitude to raise any issue they believe to be important in relation to the performance of the work group. Third, employees must be able to see that their contributions are considered important and make a difference over time.

Keeping the door open has some real benefits for the manager as well. In today's complex work environments managers need all the information they can collect. Information is the key to making the right decisions. Managers cannot be everywhere at the same time. Employees can contribute to the effectiveness of the manager's decision-making process by keeping him/her informed. Generally, all they need is the invitation of an open door.

Listen

There is a difference between hearing and listening. In hearing we perceive sounds. In listening, we give our attention to what we are hearing. Managers have many demands on their time. Sometimes, it is very difficult to stop and give full attention to someone who is talking. In not giving a speaker full attention a manager may convey an impression of disinterest and impatience. This kind of reception will most certainly convey that the messenger and the message are not important. Poor listening will not encourage the speaker to share the intended information. It will probably discourage future communication. Listening requires courteous attention. If you cannot stop and listen at the time you are approached, schedule a later time to talk.

Communicate

Keep employees informed. Employees should know both why they are doing things and what they are doing. The goal is to help employees make the connection between their efforts and the success of the organization. To do this they must first be aware of the goals of the organization. They should understand how the efforts of the work group are needed to meet the goals. In addition, they should receive feedback on how they and the organization are doing.

Play Fair

Treat everyone equally and fairly. Do not play favorites. In the authors' experience, nothing can destroy the interpersonal relationships of a work group faster than the perception of inequitable treatment of its members by a manager. Favoritism in the workplace can result in resentment, envy, and, sometimes, sabotage of the group effort.

Create Opportunity

If we are to believe in the concept of man in pursuit of fulfillment, then we will want to create within the work environment the opportunity to fulfill a changing set of needs. Most basic are the opportunities to earn an adequate living and feel safe and protected through the availability of benefits such as health and life insurance. Involvement in a cohesive work group will create the opportunities for belonging. Career ladders, special assignments, public recognition, and committee assignments are all opportunities which the manager can create to meet higher level needs. The ability to develop special interest areas and to be recognized as the group expert on a topic are opportunities for fulfillment of personal ambition. Often, a manager must apply extra creative effort to provide growth opportunities. Mostly, the outcome is worth the effort.

Positive Reinforcement

Positive reinforcement is a way of rewarding employees for a job well done—a way to give credit where credit is due. Research has shown that positive reinforcement will result in a repetition of the behavior rewarded. Therefore, positive reinforcement can be used to shape behaviors toward desired activities. To be most effective, positive reinforcement should be specific to a particular situation, it should occur as close in time to the occurrence of the desired behavior as possible, and it should be unpredictable and intermittent because regular reinforcement loses impact (19).

Know the Individual

To understand the situation fully, a manager must be knowledgeable about the individuals in the work group. Managers should take the time

EXAMPLE 3.1
A Problem That Can Cause Conflict Yet Result in a Win-Win Situation

A close associate of the hospital's President, Mr. Hyerup, has recently fallen and injured a wrist. Mr. Hyerup has just called the Physical Therapy Manager to request that the department schedule his associate for outpatient therapy starting tomorrow. Mr. Hyerup was unaware that the department currently has a two-week waiting time between referral and the start of outpatient services. The waiting time has occurred as a result of a recent increase in referrals coupled with a hospital-wide ban on hiring and the use of overtime. Mr. Hyerup has already given his associate assurances that there will be no problem getting an appointment. He does not seem too excited about the prospect of calling his associate back. The Physical Therapy Manager has promised to "see what he can do and to let Mr. Hyerup know what happens."

Manager: "Mr. Hyerup has requested that we give scheduling priority to this outpatient. He would like to start tomorrow. Can we squeeze her onto the schedule?"

Physical Therapist: "I have a cancellation for tomorrow, but what about all of the clients on our waiting list? In fairness, shouldn't they come first?"

to learn as much as possible about each individual. They should be familiar with their education, experience, ambitions, strengths, and weaknesses. Often, it is helpful to be aware of their personal responsibilities, avocational interests, as well as personality traits. Interest on the part of the manager also sends a message that the individual is an important part of the organization.

Negotiation for Conflict Resolution
ORGANIZATIONAL CONFLICT

For most of us the concept of conflict has a negative connotation. We immediately think of two or more opposing forces locked into a winner take all encounter. Conflict is therefore something to be avoided. Some may think that those who cause conflict are disturbed and should get help. However, conflict within the organizational structure is inevitable. We have already discussed the fact that the organization of effort leads to the subdivision of activities. The larger the organization, the greater the number of divisions and subdivisions. The greater the number of subdivisions, the greater the potential for conflict. Furthermore, organizational conflict does not need to be negative. Organizational conflict can stimulate problem-solving efforts and productive competition. Organizational conflict can benefit the organization if it is managed in a way that minimizes losses and maximizes gains (20).

Conflict can occur between work groups, within work groups, or between managers and those who are managed. Organizational conflict can occur whenever there exists the potential for differing viewpoints or competition for limited resources. Limited resources might include things such as space, equipment, personnel, responsibility, opportunity, or access to management (20). Differing viewpoints can exist any time more than one person is involved in an activity. Example 3.1 describes a hypothetical interaction between a hospital president, the manager of its physical therapy department, and a staff physical therapist.

The Physical Therapy Manager has pressure from all sides. If he schedules the outpatient visit, there is potential conflict between himself and the staff physical therapist. If he tells the President he cannot schedule the treatment, there is the potential for a different conflict situation. So, what is the manager to do?

TYPES OF NEGOTIATION

Organizational conflict can be managed through the effective application of negotiation strategies. There are three types of negotiation. They are 1) the value-exchange negotiation, 2) the power-based negotiation, and 3) the collaborative negotiation (21, 22). The value-exchange negotiation is the type of negotiation that might be used to purchase an expensive piece of equipment or to hire a staff member. The parties involved both want to do business and want to exchange something of value. The power in this negotiation comes from both parties' ability to walk away and not make a deal. The power-based negotiation occurs when one party is deadlocked and the other has the power to force the process forward. The collaborative negotiation occurs when the mutual goal is to reach an agreement through the collaborative efforts of the parties involved. Managers will use all three types of negotiation; however, negotiation with employees will most often involve power-based and collaborative negotiations.

Power-based negotiation occurs in the presence of a deadlock when one party has the power and the need to force the process forward. Power-based negotiation techniques should be the last choice for solving manager-employee conflicts. Power-based negotiations result in win-lose outcomes. People resent the use of power. "It makes them feel threatened, angry, and resentful" (21). Power-based negotiation can also be costly. "It encourages people to function in covert, competitive ways with self-interest the primary concern" (23). In situations where power-based negotiations offer the only viable alternative, it should be applied using a graduated power model. The rules for the graduated power model are to use the power first, to use as little power as possible, and to steer back to a collaborative approach whenever possible. A graded three-step progression in power-based negotiation is:

1. Methods negotiation, which is a discussion of the deadlock and how to proceed;
2. Use the threat of using power to get action;
3. The actual use of power to solve the conflict.

Even in this last step the degree of power should be the least possible to achieve a desired change from the deadlock situation.

Collaborative negotiation techniques are aimed at achieving win-win outcomes. In collaborative negotiation both parties exert power over the situation. This is very different from one party exerting power over another. Collaborative negotiation recognizes that conflict is inevitable, conflict is desirable, and that the stress of conflict is usually due to a mismatch between expectations and the reality of the situation (23). Satisfactory outcomes of the collaborative negotiation process are a mutually satisfying agreement, efficient and timely deliberations, an amicable process that preserves the relationship of the parties involved, and a lasting agreement (22).

GUIDELINES FOR SUCCESSFUL NEGOTIATION

Levenstein (24) provides "ten commandments for negotiators" which will lead to win-win outcomes. These are:

1. "Clarify the common purpose." It becomes a lot easier to compromise on issues if both parties recognize that they share a common goal. In the situation described earlier all parties might agree that the common goal is service to clients.
2. "Keep the discussion relevant." Define the real issues. The parties must agree on their points of disagreement. The second point is to attack the points of disagreement, not each other.
3. "Get agreement on terminology." Make sure that the parties are talking the same language. They could be using different words for the same thing or the same words for different things.
4. "Avoid abstract principles: concentrate on the facts." Along with the principles both sides must consider the realities. Our staff physical therapist in Example 3.1 may feel strongly that executive promises, no matter how well-intended, should not determine the order in which clients are scheduled for treatment. But what are the practical realities?
5. "Look for potential trade-offs." What are the parties willing to give to get their needs met? Are there short-term giveaways for long-term gains?
6. "Listen." To reach agreement the parties must make the effort to concentrate and listen to each other.
7. "Avoid debating tactics: use persuasive tactics." Debating techniques widen the differences between the parties' positions. Persuasive tactics attempt to bring the parties closer together.
8. "Keep in mind the personal element." Try to identify the needs, goals, personal interests, feelings, achievements, and background of the other party. People are more willing to cooperate when they get to know each other.
9. "Use logic logically." Present a logical argument that flows from a need to achieve the common purpose.
10. Look for "integrated solutions." Integrated solutions are solutions that try to satisfy the needs of both parties. To do this parties must look beyond the stated "position" of the other party and identify the "real" purpose of the conflict.

It is easy to see that power-based negotiation techniques have many similarities to a traditional, Theory X type of approach to personnel management. Collaborative negotiation techniques are similar to the human resources, Theory Y type of approach to encouraging performance. The collaborative approach when applied to conflicts between manager and employee will lead to efficient, mutually satisfying, and durable solutions while leaving the relationship between the parties intact. With this additional information in mind let us continue developing our hypothetical interaction from Example 3.1.

> Manager: "I agree, it shouldn't take special attention from the President to get timely physical therapy."
> Staff Physical Therapist: "I understand that you are under pressure to get this client into treatment. I know our President's credibility is important, but it doesn't seem fair."

Manager: "Although it seems unfair in the short run, maybe we can use the situation for the long-term benefit of all of our clients."

Staff Physical Therapist: "How do we do that?"

Manager: "First, we agree to schedule the client to accommodate Mr. Hyerup's immediate need but request some overtime hours to make sure we deliver quality service. Second, we use the situation to demonstrate the importance of timely service and our current service problems. Third, we request him to consider a departmental proposal for additional staff hours to benefit all of our clients."

Staff Physical Therapist: "Sounds like it's worth a try. Let me know if there is anything I can do to back you up."

In fact, Mr. Hyerup may not agree to the manager's requests. It may take patience and time to obtain more staff hours. The real outcome of the negotiation was that the manager and staff therapist have joined forces to negotiate with Mr. Hyerup for what they believe is required to achieve a common goal, timely service for all clients.

CASE STUDY 3.1
Management Style

Outpatients Unlimited, Incorporated (OUI)

Iona Lott is the owner of a multisite outpatient physical therapy practice, OUI. OUI currently employs 30 physical therapists. This is an increase from the 10 physical therapists OUI employed two years ago. At present, all of the therapists and support staff are supervised directly by Iona. Because of the increased size of OUI, communication and coordination are becoming increasingly difficult. If Iona practices a traditional (Theory X) style of management, what actions might she take to resolve OUI's communication and coordination problems? If she practices a participative style of management, what course of action might she follow?

You may consult Appendix 3.1 to compare your efforts with the authors' suggestions.

References

1. Mintzberg H. The structuring of organizations. Englewood Cliffs, NJ: Prentice-Hall, 1979:1–16.
2. Miles RE. Theories of management: Implications for organizational behavior and development. New York: McGraw-Hill, 1975.
3. Taylor, F. The principles of scientific management. New York: Norton, 1967.
4. Gerth HH, Mills CW. From Max Weber: Essays in sociology. New York: Oxford Press, 1958:196–244.
5. Mayo E. The social problems of industrial civilization. Boston: Harvard Graduate School of Business Administration, 1945.
6. Davis GL, Bordieri JF. Perceived autonomy and job satisfaction in occupational therapists. Am J Occup Ther 1988;42:591–595.
7. Strader MK. Adapting theory Z to nursing management. Nursing Manage 1987;18:61–64.
8. Maslow A. Towards a psychology of being. Princeton: VanNostrand, 1968.
9. Maslow A. A theory of motivation. Psych Rev 1943;50:370–396.
10. Herzberg F, Mausner B, Snyderman B. The motivation to work. 2nd ed. New York: Wiley, 1959.
11. Herzberg F. Work and the nature of man. Cleveland: World, 1966.
12. McGregor D. The human side of enterprise. 2nd ed. New York: McGraw-Hill, 1960:1–4.
13. Ouchi W. Theory Z: How American business can meet the Japanese challenge. Reading, PA: Addison-Wesley, 1981.
14. Gibson JL, Ivancevich JM, Donnelly JH. Organizations: Behavior, structure, processes. 3rd ed. Dallas: Business Publications, 1979:207–230.

15. Smith HG. Supervision: Friend or foe? Clin Manage 1984;4:16–17.
16. Tannenbaum R, Schmidt WH. How to choose a leadership pattern. Harv Bus Rev 1973;May–June:162–180.
17. Hersey P, Blanchard KH. Management of organizational behavior. Englewood Cliffs, NJ: Prentice-Hall, 1972.
18. Schermerhorn JR. Improving health care productivity through high-performance managerial development. Health Care Manage Rev 1987;12:49–55.
19. Peters TJ, Waterman RH, Jr. In search of excellence. New York: Harper and Row, 1982:55–86.
20. Jandt FE, Gillette P. Win-win negotiating. New York: Wiley, 1985:24–37.
21. Schatzki M, Tamborlane TA. Negotiation strategies for conflict resolution. Caring 1988;April:56–68.
22. Roseman E. Collaborative negotiation: Getting agreements that last. Med Lab Observer 1986;Feb:71–74.
23. West K. Effective negotiation in the workplace. Bibliotheca Medica Canadiana 1989;10(4):181–183.
24. Levenstein A: Negotiation vs. confrontation. Nursing Manage 1984;15(1):52–53.

Personnel Management: Practical Applications

OVERVIEW

Personnel management theory provides a manager with potentially useful suggestions for motivating employees to perform quality work while maintaining a specified level of productivity. It remains the manager's task to select from among the theoretical options appropriate strategies to meet the demands of real life in the clinical setting. This chapter integrates theoretical ideas from several sources with insights derived from clinical settings to present a practical framework for dealing with personnel matters. Within an organization a personnel manager has the role of standardizing personnel-related policies and procedures throughout the organization. This role results in frequent contact with departmental managers. Common areas of interaction between physical therapy and personnel managers include identifying manpower needs, recruitment, staff development, appraising employee performance, and employee benefits. Suggestions are offered which can facilitate development of a mutually beneficial relationship with the personnel manager. An important area of collaborative effort between the physical therapy and personnel managers is designing a position or "work design" as the process is called. Work design is a process whereby position content, functions, relation-

ships, and personal needs are taken into consideration in organizing work. This process is important to managers and employees because the outcome is a set of reasonable position performance expectations. A position description also results from the work design process. Insufficient numbers of qualified physical therapists and competition for those who are available contribute to a strong employment outlook for physical therapists. An abundance of employment opportunities contribute in part to job turnover. The shortage, turnover, and new programs all make the search for prospective physical therapists a year-round endeavor. Considerations for designing and marketing positions, interviewing, hiring, and appraising employee performance are dealt with in depth. A preference is indicated for performance criteria-based methods of appraising an employee's work. Suggestions are given for developing and implementing this type of appraisal system along with means of dealing with discrepancies identified between expected and actual employee performance. Options for improving performance are addressed as well as the issue of terminating an employee who does not meet performance expectations. Management actions which may enhance retention of competent, productive, and experienced staff are offered. Case studies in this chapter focus on work design and performance appraisal.

Introduction

Personnel management theory clearly indicates that the success of a service organization is dependent on management's ability to organize, direct, and motivate the efforts of the staff. This is as true for physical therapy practice as for any other type of business. To guide the activities of management, organizations routinely adopt policies and procedures. These might be called personnel policies, human resource policies, or administrative policies. Regardless of their title, these policies establish parameters within which managers may direct, reward, and punish employees. They are intended to insure fair and equitable management of all people employed. The amount of latitude allowed the manager by organization policies will vary both by topic and by organization. For example, an organization with very rigid salary administration policies may allow managers little latitude in adjusting salaries for the purpose of recruitment and retention. The same organization may provide managers with wide parameters and significant latitude for the design of the department's organizational structure, career ladder, and position (job) descriptions. For this reason, physical therapy managers will have varying degrees of responsibility for the development of personnel policies and procedures. The manager of a private independent practice will have full responsibility and much latitude. The manager of a physical therapy practice which is part of a larger organization may have limited responsibility and latitude.

In recognition of the variable responsibilities of physical therapy managers for the development and implementation of personnel policies

Table 4.1.
Examples of Personnel Professionals' Responsibilities within Service Organizations

Recruitment and hiring process
New employee orientation
Employee benefits policy administration
Set policies regarding use of benefits
Manage employee health care programs
Develop and monitor performance appraisal practices
Management training and development
Manage employee grievance and disciplinary practices

and procedures, this chapter will provide practical information about personnel management starting with topics related to work design; it will progress from the point of employee recruitment and hiring to personnel development, performance appraisal, and personnel retention. Some basic legal considerations related to employee recruitment, hiring, and management will also be discussed. The goal of this chapter is to provide the reader with a practical resource to guide personnel management activities.

ROLE OF THE PROFESSIONAL PERSONNEL MANAGER

Many organizations rely on personnel professionals to establish organization-wide policies and procedures for personnel management. Personnel professionals have a variety of educational backgrounds. Many have degrees in business administration or psychology while some have obtained their knowledge and expertise through on-the-job training. Organizations utilize personnel professionals to manage institution-wide employee-related programs such as those listed in Table 4.1.

Often, the physical therapy manager will work together with the personnel professional to make sure the special needs of the physical therapy department are met. To work effectively in this situation the physical therapy manager may find the following considerations helpful.

1. Personnel professionals view the organization as a whole. Their goal is to standardize personnel management practice. Deviations from standard practice are not encouraged. To be acceptable, deviations must be important to the organization as a whole.
2. The personnel professional and the physical therapy manager each have knowledge and expertise in their respective specialty areas. They will need to make an effort to understand the key features of the other's specialty if they are to work together effectively. It may be up to the physical therapy manager to provide the personnel professional with information about the physical therapy department and to learn the basic concepts of personnel management.
3. The physical therapy manager should take a leadership role in identifying special personnel issues related to the department. For example, the physical therapy manager may need to investigate and report on current trends in physical therapist recruitment to gain the personnel manager's support for a competitive recruitment package. A proactive approach to personnel management will help avoid long-term personnel problems.

Figure 4.1. Relationships between plans, employee performance, and eventual achievement of desired organizational goals.

Work Design
GENERAL CONSIDERATIONS

Work design refers to the way in which an organization structures and regulates the activities of its employees. Work design is a process. The outcome of the work design process is the creation of a set of employee performance expectations that is unique to the organization and to the specific job. The intended outcome of the work design process is the regulation of employee behavior in the workplace.

Work design is important to both the organization and the employees. Effective design can influence the "success" of the organization and employees alike. For employees, work design translates into performance expectations. Frequently, performance is tied to the employee's organizational reward system. Pay raises, promotions, recognition, and autonomy are all rewards which can and are routinely tied to performance that meets or exceeds expectations. Loss of employment can result from poor performance. The employer and employee should be concerned that the work design process leads to performance expectations that are meaningful, understandable, consistent, fair, and achievable. The organization's performance is dependent on the collective performance of its employees. In other words, an organization is only as successful as its employees. Organizations succeed because they plan for success. The relationship between organizational plans and employee performance is displayed in Figure 4.1.

The organization's plans may be dependent on increased customer satisfaction without an increase in cost of services provided by the organization. Expected outcomes from employee performance would include satisfied customers or a specific quantity of service provided within budgeted levels of resources. Unmet performance expectations on an individual basis translate into unmet organizational goals. Unmet goals may easily affect an organization's ability to survive. A good work design process therefore should be important to the organization and the people it employs.

An organization's work design process is influenced by most of the factors discussed in Chapter 2 which impact on the choice of organizational structure. These factors include the organization's values, mission, goals, and objectives which all determine the work of the organization. Environmental factors such as the diversity of markets and government regulation determine if the work should be geared toward stability or flexibility. Technology and professional standards will influence the skill and training as well as performance standards of some positions. Manpower shortages may also influence job content. Management style and the organization's view of employee characteristics will influence the degree of standardization and control desired.

All of these organizational factors will impact on the performance needed from employees. Once set, performance expectations may affect an organization's ability to respond to changing organizational conditions. For that reason, work design should remain a dynamic process.

WORK DESIGN PARAMETERS

The focus of most information on work design is the relationship between design parameters and employee motivation, satisfaction, and performance (1). The work design process has three parameters. These parameters are position specialization, behavior formalization and training, and professional socialization (2). How these parameters are applied to the design of a position will be influenced by management beliefs about the aptitudes, attitudes, and behaviors of employees (3).

Position Specialization

Position specialization has been described in two-dimensional terms (2). One dimension of specialization which relates to position content is called horizontal specialization. Horizontal specialization deals with the breadth or scope of the position. A position which has a high degree of horizontal specialization will involve only a few, narrowly defined tasks. The less tasks involved in the work and the more narrowly defined each task is, the more specialized the position. The second dimension of position specialization relates to position autonomy and is referred to as vertical specialization. Vertical specialization deals with the depth of the position. Depth relates to the degree of control the employee has over the tasks performed. Vertical specialization separates the performance of the task from the management of the task. The more vertically specialized the position, the less control or autonomy the worker will have over the work.

Horizontal Specialization. The most common type of position spe-

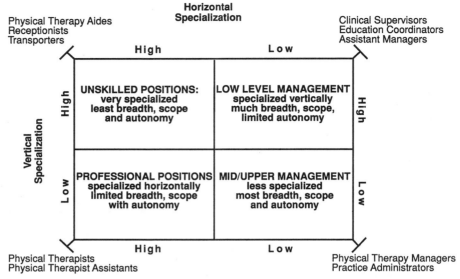

Figure 4.2. The job specialization concept as it applies to physical therapy practice. (Modified from: Mintzberg H. The Structure of Organizations. Englewood Cliffs, NJ: Prentice-Hall, 1979:80.)

cialization is horizontal specialization. Organizations divide and subdivide tasks between employees, specializing jobs to increase worker productivity. According to Smith (4), productivity increases with specialization because of increased dexterity, the savings of time lost in switching tasks, and development of new methods due to specialization. The key factor is repetition. Repetition facilitates standardization and learning.

Vertical Specialization. Vertical specialization separates work performance from work management. Mintzberg (2) states that organizations specialize positions vertically because they believe that a different perspective is required to determine how the work should be performed. At times, positions must be specialized vertically because they are specialized horizontally. Horizontal specialization results in narrow task performance. This may reduce the worker's opportunity to develop a perspective of the whole task. Also, it may reduce the worker's ability to determine how best to perform his/her part of the task as a part of the whole task.

Position specialization should be viewed as a continuum. At one end of the continuum there is position specialization and at the other end there is position enlargement. The degree of specialization may vary by position and by organizational part. Figure 4.2 presents the position specialization concept in relation to a physical therapy practice which is a division of a larger organization.

Position Specialization: Solution or Problem? Although position specialization is intended to enhance performance, it can also create performance problems. Problems created by specialization are related to communication, coordination of work, and balancing of work loads (2). As specialization increases, each position contributes a smaller amount to the completed product or service. To ensure a good outcome, more attention, effort, and time must be devoted to communication and coordination of specialized tasks. Take, for example, a client whose physical therapy treatment involves the delivery of moist heat, electrical stimulation, stretching, and exercise. In a physical therapy practice where jobs are specialized, this client's treatment may require coordination of the activities of a receptionist, a physical therapy aide, a physical therapist assistant, and a physical therapist. It also takes time and effort to coordinate the activities of several individuals. In a less specialized setting, the physical therapist may perform all of the tasks involved in providing this client's treatment.

Work load balancing becomes an issue if one specialized task takes longer than another or the demand for a task fluctuates. Either situation could potentially result in underutilization of personnel or, conversely, work backlogs.

Another form of specialization that is common in physical therapy practice is specialization by client type. This usually takes the form of staff assignment to inpatient versus outpatient, orthopedics versus cardiac, or pediatrics. This type of position specialization is particularly susceptible to work load imbalances.

Position Specialization and Employee Satisfaction. A review of the literature coupled with the authors' experiences lead to the following view of the relationship between position specialization and employee satisfaction. Horizontal specialization can have a positive or negative effect on employee satisfaction. The result depends on whether specialization eliminates position activities that are perceived to be unenjoyable and unchallenging and/or whether the employee views position specialization as an acceptable mechanism for the development of desired skills. Champoux and Howard (5) examined the interaction between position design and work context for 115 medical technologists. They showed that medical technologists with strong growth needs responded more positively to nonroutine or complex activities than did medical technologists with weak growth needs. Conversely, we would expect the employee with low growth needs to respond less positively to work which is nonroutine or highly complex. The effect of horizontal position specialization on employee satisfaction seems to depend on the needs of the individual employee.

Vertical specialization is frequently correlated with position satisfaction (1). Davis and Bordieri (6) studied the relationship between perceived autonomy and position satisfaction in occupational therapists. They found perceived autonomy to be positively related to overall position satisfaction. Ferris and Gilmore (7) studied the relationship between position characteristics, position context (work climate), and position satisfaction. Their findings suggest that challenging work, characterized by autonomy and task identity, can compensate for a poor work environment. Cordery and Wall (1) proposed that autonomy and feedback are critical work design elements which are particularly sensitive to supervisory influence. In other words, the degree of autonomy which is reflected in the work design process is influenced by management's beliefs about worker aptitudes, attitudes, and behaviors in the workplace.

Behavior Formalization

Another parameter of the work design process is behavior formalization. Formalization of behaviors results in the standardization of the organization's work. The purpose of this parameter is to increase efficiency and consistency of work performance. Mintzberg (2) describes three methods which organizations use to formalize behaviors. These are formalization by position, by work flow, and by rules. Because of the critical nature of their services and the potential cost of even small mistakes, health care providers rely heavily on all three ways to formalize behavior and standardize performance to ensure equitable service to all clients.

Formalization by Position. Formalization by position occurs when performance expectations are assigned to the position itself. This is most typically accomplished through the use of a formal position description. The formal position description enhances formalization of position duties because it defines responsibilities, decision-making authority, minimum knowledge, and skill requirements as well as the relationship of the position to other workers and the organization.

Formalization by Work Flow. Under this method, performance expectations are attached to the work itself. In physical therapy practice the work order has been the written referral. The information on the referral creates expectations for the treatment of that specific client.

Formalization by Rules. Rules that define performance expectations are generally issued in written form and collected into a policy and procedure manual. Policies and procedures can create expectations for how, by whom, and under what circumstances work will be done.

Training and Professional Socialization

Training. The third parameter of work design is training and professional socialization. Training is the process by which position-related skills are taught. The more complex and nonroutine the skills needed, the more training is required. The specification of knowledge and skill needed to perform a position is a method of standardizing the performance. Training can take place both inside and outside of the organization. The more training that is required outside of the organization, the less control the organization has over work methods.

In physical therapy practice, training is provided both inside and outside the organization. The basic work methods are determined by the educational program within parameters established by the Commission on Accreditation in Physical Therapy Education/American Physical Therapy Association. After employment, the basic work methods are modified and expanded upon by the organization that employs the physical therapist. Physical therapy aides receive on-the-job training. Their work methods are more easily controlled by the employing organization. Physical therapy managers might receive their business education from an outside source or may receive on-the-job training. The expectation is that basic work methods obtained from an outside source will be modified by the practices of the employing organization.

Professional Socialization. Professional socialization, sometimes referred to as organizational socialization, can be described as the process whereby a member of an organization acquires an understanding of the organization's value system and behavioral norms (2). Feldman (8) expands on this description, noting that for the individual this process also involves the acquisition of new knowledge, the development of skill, and adjustments to the norms and values of the work groups. Feldman conceptualizes a three-stage model of the professional socialization process. The stages are anticipatory socialization, encounter-accommodation, and role management.

Anticipatory socialization occurs before an individual joins an organization (8). For a physical therapist, this would include all of the preparatory education and training, and preconceived expectations about the organization and the roles associated with the position. The entire socialization process can be facilitated if preconceived expectations are as close as possible to reality. The provision of realistic information about the organization and roles during the recruitment process will help avoid the development of unrealistic expectations (9).

Feldman's encounter-accommodation stage (8) is the period when the individual encounters the actual organization and begins to accommodate to its needs and expectations. During this period, clear expectations, adequate training, and feedback can facilitate the socialization process (9).

The role management stage is one of acceptance. In this stage, the individual has learned the position-related roles, has become competent, and can contribute to the achievement of organizational goals (9).

POSITION DESIGN IN PHYSICAL THERAPY

General Considerations

The goal of work design is to develop realistic performance expectations. The three channels used to communicate performance expectations are the position description, policies and procedures, and the referral. Attention will be given to the first two channels as they are primarily under the control of the physical therapy manager. The following discussion focuses on the position description. Later, in Chapter 6, policies and procedures will be dealt with in depth.

During the process of position design, the physical therapy manager must be aware of the internal, external, and practical constraints that may influence performance expectations. Several examples of each category of constraint are listed in Table 4.2.

Any or all of the above constraints may influence the performance expectations which can be assigned to a particular employee or employee classification. For example, professional standards, government regulation, accrediting agencies, customers, medical staff, organizational norms, and manpower shortages may all influence the client care duties assigned to a physical therapy aide. At times, the direction of constraints may be in conflict. For example, the constraints presented by manpower shortages might run contrary to the constraints presented by organizational norms or professional guidelines.

Table 4.2.
Sources of Constraints Influencing Performance Expectations

Internal Constraints

Standardized Personnel Practices
Expectations from Other Parts of the Organization
Administration
Finance
Medical staff
Expectations, Values, and Norms of the Therapy Staff

External Constraints

Government Regulations
Accrediting Agencies
Consumers of Health Care
Clients
Payers
Professional Standards of Practice

Practical Constraints

Practice Size
Manpower Shortages
Skills and Interests of Current Employees

Position Description

Position descriptions are used by organizations to formalize basic performance expectations. They are used by employees to understand the organization's expectations of their position. To meet the needs of the organization and the employee, the position description should contain the following information:

1. A listing of the basic duties of the position. Duties should be described in as much detail as is needed to make performance expectations clear. The description of duties should reflect the values of the organization.
2. A description of the decision-making authority of the position. This could be incorporated into the description of basic duties or written separately. The degree of autonomy in specific duties should be clear.
3. A description of the minimum level of knowledge, skill, and training required to perform the position duties. This should include a delineation of equipment used in the performance of the basic duties of the position.
4. A description of the extent to which the position is responsible for the work of other employees. The extent of that responsibility should be clearly defined. Is the responsibility complete or limited to specific situations such as the delivery of a treatment?
5. A description of the physical demands of the position. This should be quantified if possible.
6. The organizational and supervisory relationships of the position. This would include the position title, organizational component (i.e., department, division), and title of the position's supervisor.
7. Any other pertinent information required to provide a clear understanding of the duties of the position should be included in the position description.

A useful format for a position description is presented in Example 4.1 which is a sample description for a staff physical therapist.

EXAMPLE 4.1
Position Description

Milwaukee Memorial Hospital

POSITION DESCRIPTION

POSITION TITLE: Physical Therapist—Staff

DEPARTMENT: Physical Therapy

DIVISION: Rehabilitation Services

REPORTS TO: Physical Therapy Manager

I. BASIC DUTIES:

   1. Interprets medical information and physician referrals.
   2. Performs comprehensive physical therapy evaluations.
   3. Develops physical therapy treatment goals and plan of care based on and consistent with the results of the physical therapy evaluation.
   4. Schedules all routine and special treatments required by assigned clients to ensure maximum client benefit, timely service, and smooth department operation.
   5. Schedules the work of physical therapist assistants and aides for assigned clients.
   6. Makes arrangements for service delivery by community service providers such as the orthotist and prosthetist.
   7. Ensures the performance of all scheduled physical therapy services.
   8. Provides necessary family teaching in accordance with the client's plan of care.
   9. Determines client care assignments for physical therapist assistants and aides.
   10. Completes all required documentation in accordance with departmental policy and the needs of third party payers.
   11. Performs client equipment needs assessments and orders required equipment in a timely manner to prevent unnecessary discharge delays.
   12. Verifies client insurance coverage for equipment rental and purchase. Refers problems and questions to client and/or family.
   13. Participates in departmental planning, program development, and the development of departmental policies and procedures.
   14. Attends and provides hospital inservice education and continuing education in accordance with departmental policy.
   15. Completes client billing on a timely basis.
   16. Maintains good interpersonal relationships with clients, family members, other employees, the medical staff, management, administration, and other community professionals.
   17. Complies with all departmental and hospital policies and procedures.
   18. Other duties as assigned by the supervisor.

II. DECISION MAKING:

   1. Determines the initial and continuing goals for physical therapy treatment.
   2. Determines the physical therapy plan of care including service and equipment needs.
   3. Determines the client care activities of the physical therapist assistant and aide.
   4. Contributes to decision making regarding client activity level, supervision of client mobility on the nursing unit, client discharge placement, and the need for client services before and after discharge.

III. EQUIPMENT USED:

   1. All equipment routinely used in physical therapy evaluation and treatment including assistive devices, transfer aids, exercise equipment, modalities, hydrotherapy, cardiac monitoring devices, and splinting and casting equipment.

continues

EXAMPLE 4.1 *Continued*

IV. MINIMUM KNOWLEDGE AND SKILL:

    1. Bachelor of science degree in physical therapy or a bachelor's degree and a certificate in physical therapy from an accredited educational program.
    2. Four to six months of clinical affiliations as part of entry level preparation.
    3. State licensure.
    4. CPR certification within three months of employment.

V. RESPONSIBILITY FOR THE WORK OF OTHERS:

    1. Responsible for directing the clinical performance of physical therapist assistants, students, physical therapy aides, and volunteers.

VI. PHYSICAL DEMAND:

    1. Frequent heavy lifting in excess of 70 pounds.

APPROVED BY: _____ DATE: _____

EMPLOYEE SIGNATURE: _____ DATE _____

Recruitment and Hiring
OVERVIEW

Recruitment can be looked upon as the search for talent. It is the process of seeking out position candidates who possess the training, skills, expertise, and characteristics necessary to perform specific duties within the organization. The hiring process is one of mutual evaluation and selection. The process of mutual evaluation involves the joint sharing of information between the position candidate and the organization. The goal of mutual evaluation is to determine if a beneficial employer-employee relationship can be developed. Hiring decisions are considered by many to be the most important decisions that a manager will make. This is because the quality of employees strongly affects the future performance and success of the organization.

Physical therapy managers are routinely involved in the recruitment of department personnel. Depending on the practice structure, there may be need to recruit both professional, skilled, and unskilled employees. The position, the organization, and the community all influence the ease or difficulty of recruiting personnel. The difficulty of recruitment can be judged by the time spent and energy and expense incurred during the recruitment process.

Difficulty in the recruitment of physical therapists is largely attributed to a nationwide shortage of physical therapy personnel (10–12). It has been reported that for every one physical therapist there are three positions available (10). A recent report states that "Calculating the difference between the annual growth in physical therapist jobs and growth in the number of physical therapists available, the best estimates are that there will be an annual deficit in the supply/demand equation of approximately 1351 physical therapists" (11). Put another way, there will be an

87% growth in the number of physical therapy positions by the year 2000. This is an increase of 3800 new positions per year (11). The magnitude of the manpower shortage which faces the physical therapy manager in the pursuit of qualified candidates makes it clear that control of time, effort, and expense related to recruitment requires a well-designed recruitment plan.

RECRUITMENT PLAN

Staff recruitment in the face of severe manpower shortages is very similar to consumer product marketing in a highly competitive market. First, there has to be a marketable product from which the candidate can differentiate among similar products. In this case the product is a physical therapy position, with all of its present and future value for the candidate clearly defined. Next, there has to be a promotional plan which will attract potential position customers' attention to the product long enough to get them interested. Once the customer is interested, it becomes the manager's position to close the sale or to determine that the product and the customer are not a good fit.

Defining a Marketable Position

The starting point then is to determine if the position is marketable. To determine this the physical therapy manager must have a clear definition of the position, know the competition, and know the customer.

Define the Position. For the purposes of recruitment, positions should be defined in terms of position content and position context. Position content refers to all of the information which is contained in the position description. Position context refers to aspects of the surrounding work system (5, 7). Aspects of the work system that should be considered to be important include supervisory style, coworkers, pay and benefits (5), opportunity, security, and organizational climate (7).

In the authors' experiences, specific aspects of the work system which are frequently discussed during the recruitment process include:

1. Compensation. Position candidates are interested in market-competitive salaries and potential for salary increases in the future. Other common forms of compensation include interview reimbursement, relocation reimbursement, hire bonuses, incentive compensation, and payment of professional dues.
2. Benefits. The most common benefits are paid vacation, personal and sick days, holidays, and health, dental, life, and disability insurance.
3. Growth Opportunities. Growth opportunities come in a variety of forms. Common opportunities include access to tuition reimbursement, continuing education, involvement in student education, exposure to a variety of experienced staff, and promotional opportunities such as a career ladder.
4. Position Expectations. Most candidates are interested in the type of work they will be asked to perform. A new graduate may be most interested in the types of clients they will treat. A more experienced candidate will frequently inquire about workload and productivity expectations.
5. Work Schedule Flexibility. Work schedule flexibility may relate to the employee's schedule, the number of hours worked, or the ability to shift work hours due to changing personal needs. The number of female phys-

ical therapists continues to exceed the number of male physical therapists by nearly 3:1 (13). Often, female physical therapists seek opportunities which offer the flexibility to balance family and professional demands. Employers can meet the needs of these candidates through the creation of part-time positions, position sharing, provision of promotional opportunities that are not dependent on full-time employment, and other nontraditional incentives.

6. Community. Candidates from outside of the employer's immediate geographical area will likely ask basic questions about the community. The physical therapy manager should be prepared with information about such things as housing (be careful about any discriminatory comments or practices), recreation, arts, universities, even the weather. A brochure on the community may be helpful.

Know the Competition.   Physical therapy managers should understand that they must compete with all other employers for a limited number of qualified candidates (12). From an economic perspective potential employers of physical therapists are seeing the law of supply and demand at work. To compete successfully, physical therapy managers must know how the position, content, and context of their position stacks up against the competition. They also must be willing to redefine the position should they discover that their position is not as attractive as the competition's position. We do not mean to imply that a physical therapy manager can or should do everything the competition does. In many cases that just is not feasible. A hospital department may not be able to offer the same salary as the private practice across town. However, it may be possible to define the position to make it more attractive in other ways. It is to the manager's advantage that different people have different needs.

Know the Customer.   Successful recruitment requires familiarity with the needs of the candidate. Harkson et al. (14) studied the relationship between position factors and turnover in physical therapists. From analysis of 567 completed questionnaires these authors concluded that settings which offer a variety of client populations and expanded professional opportunities such as continuing education, student education, and research may be better able to retain physical therapists. Fifty-two percent of the respondents identified a "desire to pursue a different area of physical therapy" as an important motivator for leaving a position. The investigators reported that physical therapists look for autonomy in direct patient care, opportunities for advancement, and salaries commensurate with education and experience. They also noted differences based on therapist education and experience. New graduates were more interested in opportunity and financial assistance with continuing education. Physical therapists with master's degrees were more interested in involvement with organizational policy making. The importance of salary varied with years in the profession and sex. Salary issues were more likely to motivate therapists with three to nine years experience to seek new positions. Male therapists were more likely to be motivated by salary than were female physical therapists.

The challenge is to identify the needs of a specific candidate. Physical therapy managers can accomplish this during the employment interview. Interview questions should be directed at determining the needs of the candidate. Where do you see yourself in three to five years? What are your professional objectives? What did you like best about your last position? What did you enjoy least? Probing questions will help managers identify and point out how their position and organization can help the candidate meet his/her needs. It will also go a long way in demonstrating the organization's interest in the individual and not just in filling an open position.

The physical therapy manager must represent the position honestly. An employee's socialization to the organization begins before employment. Expectations about the organization are largely developed during the recruitment and interview process. Unrealistic position expectations resulting from overzealous "selling" by the interviewer can result in adjustment difficulties and dissatisfaction after employment (9).

Recruitment Promotion and Advertising

There are a variety of ways to attract the attention of position candidates. As the difficulty of attracting qualified candidates has increased, physical therapy managers have become increasingly creative in the advertising and promotion of vacant positions. The following methods have been used.

Advertising. Recruitment advertising in print media is likely the most frequently used method of attracting position candidates. This includes monthly physical therapy publications, the Sunday classified section, and a growing number of mass-mailed professional recruitment materials. A problem for employers is how to make their advertisement stand out in the crowd. The following suggestions for successful advertisements have been made by advertising specialists (15).

Design the advertisement to attract attention. Advertisement size, color, set-up, and placement will all contribute to its noticeability. The advertisement will hold interest if it can demonstrate how the features of the position can meet the needs of the candidate. The advertisement must present information in a manner which will establish the credibility of the position and the organization. The advertisement must positively differentiate the position from positions offered by competing advertisers. Finally, the advertisement should motivate the reader to respond and indicate to them how and where to respond (15).

The development of an effective advertisement is not easy. The physical therapy manager should consider obtaining guidance from professionals experienced in print advertising. Possible sources of help are a personnel professional or advertising specialist. In our experience, the cost of obtaining professional guidance is money wisely spent.

Complimentary forms of advertising frequently used are recruitment brochures, publications, newsletters, and videos. These materials are often designed to attract attention without looking like advertisements. Sometimes called collateral materials (15), they are used to provide candidates with more detailed information about the position content and context.

Involvement in Physical Therapy Student Education. Involvement in physical therapy student education is another way to attract the attention of potential position candidates. Involvement in physical therapy education offers an organization the opportunity to develop relationships with future candidates before or at the point when they are looking for employment. There are several ways that an organization can participate in physical therapy education. The most common way is to become a clinical education site. If clinical affiliates are scheduled year-round, the organization could have a constant pool of candidates from various schools to recruit. On the other hand, recruitment of clinical affiliates from schools geographically distant from the organization may yield fewer viable candidates.

A second method used to develop relationships with physical therapy students is to host some form of a class outing. For example, the organization can invite the entire class of students to a brunch or evening buffet coupled with an educational program. The educational program could be provided by the organization's clinical staff or a noted outside speaker. Opportunities to socialize with the clinical staff and management should be included. Financial sponsorship of the event can sometimes be shared with the school if it fulfills a curriculum requirement.

The third method for involvement is to encourage clinical staff to teach in the physical therapy school curriculum. This activity vicariously increases the credibility of the organization. It may also provide access for the recruitment of future therapists.

Recruitment Incentives.   It is becoming more common for organizations to provide recruitment incentives. Some examples of recruitment incentives are payment of interview expenses, offers of gifts in return for coming to the facility for an interview, and hire bonuses. Recruitment incentives are used to differentiate a position from other opportunities. Unfortunately, it takes little time for the competition to adopt any effective recruitment incentive.

Another recruitment incentive which has met with a degree of success is the provision of a student "scholarship" in return for an employment commitment. Physical therapy students are offered scholarships to defer the costs of their education. In return, they sign an agreement to become an employee of the funding organization for a specific period of time after graduation. A variation of this concept is the offer to reimburse a candidate for all or part of the cost of their professional education upon accepting employment. There is usually a minimum employment time stipulated as part of the offer. In most cases there is a repayment clause should the funded student decide not to meet the original terms of the agreement. The sponsoring institution is also obligated to provide employment in the type of clinical environment negotiated for with the funded student.

Recruitment Fairs.   Recruitment fairs are generally sponsored by schools or professional organizations. If well planned, they will offer an organization the opportunity to come in contact with a large number of potential candidates at one time. Success at recruitment fairs is largely a matter of image. The organization that presents a professional, credible image will obtain maximum benefit. The use of quality promotional materials is essential. The use of promotional giveaways is a plus. If the fair is on a university campus, staffing a booth with current employees who graduated from the school hosting the fair may enhance the attention students give to that booth.

Social Events. Sponsorship of professional social events is another way of attracting the attention of potential position candidates. The goal is to increase candidate awareness of the organization's professional strengths and opportunities. These events can be linked with educational activities, professional meetings, or community events such as a health fair. The appropriate setting for social events may vary between professional communities.

Prospect File. One of the more creative concepts which has been presented in recent literature is the use of a prospect file (10). This is an adaptation of a well-tested marketing approach. It involves the tracking and periodic contacting of potential candidates through the use of a newsletter, education announcements, and so on. The goal is to maintain a relationship. Periodically, the organization will determine if the prospect is in the market for a new position.

Professional Recruitment Firms. More often, physical therapy managers are turning to professional recruitment firms for assistance. These firms can be hired on a contingency basis for the recruitment and placement of physical therapists. Although effective, and at times the only option, the use of professional recruiters can be costly. The average fee charged by these agencies can be from 20 to 30% of the employee's first year salary. Frequently, fees are payable upon employment and refundable only if the candidate remains in the position for less than six months.

In our experience students frequently fail to understand the implications of giving even the most casual sign of interest to recruiters. Since there is no cost to the student, when approached by a recruiter they may be courteous enough to listen and may show interest in being represented. If the recruiter has the slightest reason to think that they represent a student they will make every effort to find a match with a potential employer. Should the student find a position on their own, the recruiter may pursue the employer to collect the recruitment fee. Some employers are unable or unwilling to pay the additional recruitment cost which means the employer may choose not to hire this particular new graduate.

In summary, an effective recruitment plan has two components: first, the definition of a marketable position and, second, the development of a plan to get the attention of qualified candidates long enough to "sell" them on the position. In practice, recruitment efforts are often sporadic. Sporadic recruitment refers to the practice of recruiting only when an open position exists. This approach has many drawbacks. In the face of a severe manpower shortage this usually results in longer turnaround time to fill a vacant position. The costs associated with vacant positions include lost revenue, lost business due to customer dissatisfaction, loss of additional staff due to excessive work loads, costs of using temporary help at high hourly rates, and manager frustration at being unable to prevent these costs from occurring. It is the opinion of the authors that to be effective a recruitment plan must be continuous. Physical therapy managers should be recruiting as a part of their routine activities. Recruitment efforts should be organized into a formal recruitment plan.

HIRING THE BEST CANDIDATE

Recruitment efforts should attract candidates who are qualified for the position. Then comes the task of hiring the best possible candidate. First, the manager needs to select the best candidate. This is accomplished by screening and interviewing the candidate. After making a selection the manager has to close the sale. Often in physical therapy recruitment a manager will have only one candidate for the open position. Still, the candidate should be screened and interviewed. With one candidate, the manager may have to determine whether the practice would be better off with an open position for the moment and whether to continue the search.

Screening

The selection process involves the comparison of one candidate's qualifications against another's (16). To perform this comparison the manager will need to screen the candidate. Screening involves evaluation and verification of education, previous employment history, and professional affiliations. In addition, the manager will want to assess the candidate's reasons for seeking the position, the fit between the candidate's and the organization's philosophy, goals, and expectations, and the fit between the candidate's personality and those of other members of the work group. Appearance, dress, and hygiene may be factors to consider depending on the nature of the work.

Interview

An interview can be a stressful experience for both the manager and the candidate. Both want to get good information and make a favorable impression. The candidate needs to rely on the manager to create the situation in which mutual goals can be achieved. This means paying attention to the interview setting, preparation, and process.

Setting. The interview setting should be comfortable and conducive to private discussion, which means no interruptions. If the manager is aware of a potential interruption then the candidate should be informed in advance. Refreshments can help to relax the candidate. If the interview extends into the lunch hour, it can continue over luncheon. The setting for luncheon should dictate the topics discussed at that time.

Preparation. The manager should be prepared to discuss the specifics of the position in terms of position content and context. All supporting documentation, such as position descriptions, should be available. Rooms should be scheduled. If the candidate is to meet with more than one person a written schedule with appointments, names, titles, and responsibilities should be provided. Be sure to allow enough time for each interview. If the schedule is lengthy, schedule breaks. Decide in advance what information needs to be gathered, how it will be recorded, and by whom. A standard form may be helpful to appraise the same qualities from different interviewers' perspectives.

Process. The information obtained and the impression of the facility will depend largely on the process of the interview. The interview process should:

1. Encourage give and take discussions related to future working relation-ships;
2. Include the use of open-ended questions to allow the candidate to provide needed information and not simply answer "yes and no" questions;
3. Allow the candidate enough time to think about and answer questions completely (16).

The manager's goal is to pinpoint the needs of the candidate which can be met by the organization and the position. These will only come to light if the candidate is provided the opportunity and encouraged to express him/herself.

LEGAL CONSIDERATIONS

There are federal and state laws which protect position candidates from discriminatory recruitment practices. Title VII of the Civil Rights Act, as amended by the Equal Employment Opportunity Act of 1972, prohibits discrimination on the basis of race, color, religion, sex, or na-tional origin in any term, condition, or privilege of employment. The Rehabilitation Act of 1973 prohibits employment discrimination against the handicapped. The Employment Act of 1967 makes unlawful any em-ployment practices which discriminate against any individual because of the individual's age. It applies to individuals between the ages of 40 and 70. An exhaustive discussion of these and other laws which prohibit employment discrimination is beyond the scope of this text. It is, however, important for the physical therapy manager to recognize the existence of these legal constraints. Furthermore, it is important to recognize that it is the manager's legal responsibility to avoid discriminatory practices during the recruitment and hire process. Table 4.3 is intended to help the manager understand situations in which discrimination may seem to exist and to recognize statements which position candidates might construe to be dis-criminatory. Additional employment-related laws are summarized in Chapter 10.

Personnel Development

Personnel development was discussed earlier as part of the process of professional socialization. An orientation and training period can fa-cilitate the socialization of the employee into the organization and the work group. Because personnel development is important to the recruit-ment, satisfaction, performance, and retention of physical therapy staff, it merits further discussion.

A Conceptual Model

We propose that personnel development should be viewed as a two-phase process. The first phase includes orientation and the development of minimum level skills. This initial phase will take different amounts of time depending on the aptitudes and previous experience of the employee. Broadly speaking, the first phase will take from 6 to 12 months. The

Table 4.3.
Legal Considerations for the Recruitment and Hire Process

Sexual and Marital Discrimination

Positions may not be restricted for any of the following reasons:
Assumptions related to the applicant's sex.
Preferences of coworkers, employers, clients, or customers.
Position was traditionally restricted to members of the opposite sex.
Position involves heavy physical labor, manual dexterity, late-night hours, overtime, isolated working conditions, or unpleasant surroundings.
Position involves travel, or travel with members of the opposite sex.
Physical facilities are not available for both sexes.
Position requires personal characteristics not exclusive to either sex, such as tact, charm, or aggressiveness.

Questions to avoid:
Do you get along well with other women?
Do you have children?
Who takes care of your children while you work?
What is your marital status?
Do you plan to have children?
Will your family responsibilities prevent you from traveling?
What do you do when your children get sick?

Race Discrimination

It is unlawful to deprive an applicant of a position because of his/her race.

Questions to avoid:
Will you have problems working with members of a different race?
Your supervisor will be white, will that bother you?
How do you feel about black militancy?
Did you or your family ever receive public assistance?
Do your parents work?

Discrimination Due to National Origin

It is unlawful to deprive an applicant of a position because of his/her national origin.

Questions to avoid:
You don't mind Polish jokes, do you?
That's an unusual name. What nationality are you?
Were you born in this country?
Your name is difficult to pronounce. Have you considered changing it?
Where does your family live?

Religious Discrimination

It is unlawful to deprive an applicant of a position because of his/her religion.

Questions to avoid:
What religion are you?
What church do you go to?
Are you active in any church groups?
Will you miss work because of religious holidays?

employee's role in the first phase is to be receptive and to make the necessary effort to learn. The manager must assume responsibility for design and implementation of the development plan. This includes assessing the employee's skill level and development needs, designing the appropriate training experiences, providing the time and opportunity to learn, and providing feedback.

The second phase is growth beyond the initial level of skill. Ideally, this phase continues throughout the period of employment. The intensity and rate of development will be dependent on both the employee and the employer. In this phase the employee should assume more responsibility for the development process. It remains the manager's role to provide opportunity and feedback. The identification of needs, setting development goals, and implementation should be done collaboratively. The manager and the employee should assume joint responsibility for the employee's continued growth and development.

Performance Appraisal
PURPOSE

As in the case of work design, the performance appraisal system is important to the employer and the employee. For both, the primary objective of performance appraisal is to compare actual employee performance against expected employee performance. An effective performance appraisal system can also achieve some important secondary objectives.

An effective performance appraisal system can enhance employee understanding of performance expectations and how the employee relates to the organization's goals (17, 18). This can be achieved through the use of objectively defined performance expectations which are clearly and formally related to the organization's goals and objectives. The employee wants to know what behaviors will meet the organization's expectations. The relationship between the employee's needs and achievement of the organization's expectations should be clear.

A performance appraisal system can improve communication between employee and employer. Formal requirements for performance feedback create the environment and the opportunity for communication. Employees want ongoing feedback. Feedback given infrequently is not likely to improve performance. Feedback that is immediate, specific, unpredictable, and intermittent is expected to maximize performance. Recall that negative feedback is seldom received well (19). Nobody wants to be told they are not doing a good job. To be effective, negative feedback should be specific, constructive, and confidential. It should be accompanied by a description of behaviors which would meet expectations.

An effective performance appraisal system can be used as the basis for an equitable application of an employee reward system. Raises, promotions, and development opportunities can be tied directly to the outcome of an objective performance appraisal system. From this perspective it is important for the employee to believe that the performance expectations are reasonable and the performance appraisal system truly measures performance of their work.

Employee motivation can be improved by an effective performance appraisal system. A system that relates improved performance to rewards has the potential to motivate employee performance. If, however, the employee believes that the performance expectations are unreasonable or the system is incapable of measuring performance, it could decrease employee motivation.

A well-planned performance appraisal system has the potential to facilitate organizational compliance with federal and state equal opportunity employment directives. "It is possible that if improperly designed and unvalidated appraisal instruments are used to hire and evaluate employees, these instruments may inadvertently discriminate against an individual or group of individuals; . . . . Well developed appraisal systems have demonstrated their ability to protect health care agencies from discrimination litigation" (17). The final value of a sound appraisal system is that it can assist the organization in planning its human resource requirements (17).

REVIEW OF METHODS

There are many methods of performance appraisal utilized by health care organizations. The following analysis of the various methods will identify the useful aspects and pitfalls associated with each method.

Essay Appraisal Method

Under this type of appraisal system the manager is required to write an essay describing the strengths and weaknesses of the employee. This method is time consuming for the manager. The quality of the information and its presentation are dependent on the writing skills of the manager. This essay appraisal method allows for an in-depth review of the employee's performance, but the information may be subjective. It is likely that relevant information will be missed and that irrelevant information will be included (17).

Graphic Rating Scale

Here, the manager will evaluate the employee against preestablished standards using a five- to seven-point visual scale. The points on this type of ordinal scale are assigned labels from exceptional to unsatisfactory (17). Figure 4.3 presents a five-point scale. This method is thought to have poor interrater reliability. It also fails to provide any useful feedback to the average performer (17).

Critical Incident Method

Under the critical incident method the manager keeps an ongoing record of incidents of positive and negative performance. This record is used at the end of the evaluation period to judge overall performance. The critical incident method is weakened by a human tendency to note

Figure 4.3.   A graphic performance rating scale.

and record negative incidents more readily than positive incidents. This method is difficult to maintain when a large number of employees are supervised by one manager. Some of this method's weaknesses can be balanced if employees as well as managers are allowed to record notable incidents. Employees are more likely to record positive incidents which may aid the manager's recall (17).

Comparison Method

This method requires the manager to rank members of a work group according to some standard of efficiency and effectiveness. For example, physical therapists could be ranked according to production of billable increments of service. This method has limited value for use with jobs that require skills other than providing direct care and recording charges. In other words, there is more to performance than level of productivity. Because the manager ranks work group members against one another, first to last, this method can cause negative peer pressure within the work group. The comparison method as described here does not address the quality of the services performed (17).

Management by Objectives

In a management by objectives system employees are evaluated based on their success at achieving specific, previously agreed upon, performance goals. This approach is individualized. It focuses on outcome, but not on method. It may penalize employees who fail to achieve goals due to factors outside of their realm of control such as an increased work load due to staff shortages (17).

Performance Criteria Based Method

A recent appraisal trend in health care is to use performance appraisal methods that are based on specific objective performance criteria. The Performance Criteria Based Method (PCBM) comes from the employee's position description. The major functions of the position are defined in terms of performance indicators. These performance indicators are stated in terms of specific behaviors (16, 20). The behaviors are evaluated in terms of a performance rating scale. Performance goals flow automatically from the evaluation process. Just as there is a unique description for each position there should be a unique set of performance criteria for each position.

Performance Indicators. To be suitable for use with a PCBM, the position description must be divided into distinct functional areas. Example 4.2 is the position description reviewed earlier as Example 4.1 but rewritten to reflect seven functional areas. Within the functional areas, the performance indicators or position duties must be expressed in specific behavioral terms. In Example 4.2, the position duties listed under each of the functional areas describe specific behaviors that the therapist must exhibit in the performance of the work. The described behaviors are concrete and measurable through observation, incident reports, chart review, and peer review.

Performance Rating Scale. After the position has been described in functional and behavioral terms, the manager must develop examples of performance that meet, exceed, or fall short of minimum performance expectations. Each performance indicator should be described in this manner according to the same ordinal scale. Example 4.3 relates to performance indicator IA2 "Performs comprehensive physical therapy evaluations" (see Example 4.2). Note that the behaviors described in Example 4.3 are observable and with experience the manager can evaluate these behaviors with a high degree of reliability.

The greater the number of distinct functions and performance indicators identified and defined, the more specific and objective the performance appraisal process. Employees should be involved in this process. Involvement will ensure that skills and performance expectations are appropriately defined. Employee participation will also contribute to the credibility of the PCBM in terms of reasonableness of the expectations and accuracy of the measurement tool. To be effective, there must be a shared belief between the manager and the employee that the position performance criteria define reasonable and achievable expectations. The employee must also believe that the PCBM will result in a fair and equitable evaluation of all employees within their specific position classification.

Setting Performance Goals. It is easy to see how performance goals flow from the PCBM. For each performance indicator the employee will have a current performance level based on the appraisal and a clear description of what needs to be done to perform at the next highest level.

EXAMPLE 4.2
Position Description Expanded to Include Observable Performance Criteria

Milwaukee Memorial Hospital

POSITION DESCRIPTION

POSITION TITLE: Physical Therapist—Staff

DEPARTMENT: Physical Therapy

DIVISION: Rehabilitation Services

REPORTS TO: Physical Therapy Manager

I. BASIC DUTIES:

A. EVALUATION AND TREATMENT:

1. Interprets medical information and physician referrals.
2. Performs comprehensive physical therapy evaluations.
3. Develops physical therapy treatment goals and plan of care based on, and consistent with, the results of the physical therapy evaluation.
4. Performs client equipment needs assessments and orders required equipment in a timely manner to prevent unnecessary discharge delays.
5. Maintains treatment and evaluation skills through attendance at inservice education and continuing education progress in accordance with departmental policy.
6. Promotes staff and client safety at all times.

B. OPERATIONAL PLANNING:

1. Schedules all routine and special treatments required by assigned clients to ensure maximum client benefit, timely service, and smooth department operation.
2. Schedules the work of physical therapist assistants and aides for assigned clients.
3. Makes arrangements for service delivery by community service providers such as the orthotist and prosthetist.
4. Ensures the performance of all scheduled physical therapy services.
5. Determines client care assignments for physical therapist assistants and aides.
6. Participates in departmental planning and program development.
7. Performs all evaluation and treatment procedures within the time frames and in a manner consistent with department policies and procedures.

C. PROBLEM SOLVING:

1. Verifies and documents client insurance coverage for equipment rental and purchase. Refers problems and questions to client and/or family.
2. Participates in the development of departmental policies and procedures.
3. Identifies and manages problems with client care, discharge planning, and department operations within the scope of the position's decision-making authority.

D. COMMUNICATION:

1. Provides necessary family teaching in accordance with the client's plan of care.
2. Completes all required documentation in accordance with departmental policy and the needs of third party payers.
3. Completes client billing within 24 hours of service.
4. Provides hospital inservice education and continuing education in accordance with departmental policy.
5. Maintains open lines of communication with clients, families, other employees, the medical staff, management, administration, and other community professionals.

continues

EXAMPLE 4.2   *Continued*

E. INTERPERSONAL RELATIONS:

1. Maintains good interpersonal relationships with clients, family members, other employees, the medical staff, management, administration, and other community professionals.
2. Complies with all departmental and hospital policies and procedures.

F. OTHER:

1. Other duties as assigned by the supervisor.

II. DECISION MAKING:

1. Determines the initial and continuing goals for physical therapy treatment.
2. Determines the physical therapy plan of care, including service and equipment needs.
3. Determines the client care activities of the physical therapist assistant and aide.
4. Contribute to decision making regarding client activity level, supervision of client mobility on the nursing unit, client discharge placement, and the need for client services before and after discharge.

III. EQUIPMENT USED:

1. All equipment routinely used in physical therapy evaluation and treatment including assistive devices, transfer aids, exercise equipment, modalities, hydrotherapy, cardiac monitoring devices, and splinting and casting equipment.

IV. MINIMUM KNOWLEDGE AND SKILL:

1. Bachelor of science degree in physical therapy or a bachelor of science degree and a certificate in physical therapy from an accredited educational program.
2. Four to six months of clinical affiliations as part of entry level preparation.
3. State licensure.
4. CPR certification within three months of employment.

V. RESPONSIBILITY FOR THE WORK OF OTHERS:

1. Responsible for directing the clinical performance of physical therapist assistants, students, physical therapy aides, and volunteers.

VI. PHYSICAL DEMAND:

1. Frequent heavy lifting in excess of 70 pounds.

APPROVED BY: _____ DATE _____

EMPLOYEE SIGNATURE: _____ DATE _____

Given to an employee at the time of hire, the PCBM clearly describes the position expectations in behavioral terms.

Use of the PCBM may provide performance goals for the physical therapy manager. As discussed in Chapter 3, performance is based on ability, support, and effort (20). As a result of the use of PCBM the manager may identify needs for training and support. For example, the staff may require inservice education to become proficient in a specific type of client evaluation. They may require equipment or materials which are currently unavailable to perform an advanced evaluation. In that case, the manager

EXAMPLE 4.3
Performance Criteria for Performing Comprehensive Physical Therapy Evaluations

I. BASIC DUTIES:

A. EVALUATION AND TREATMENT:

2. Performs comprehensive physical therapy evaluations.

Rating: Description of Performance:

Level 5   Exceptional Performance

Independently and appropriately selects, performs advanced physical therapy evaluation procedures, or recommends medical evaluation procedures.

Level 4   Exceeds Expectations

Recognizes the need to perform advanced physical therapy evaluation procedures. Seeks input from others on the appropriate implementation of unfamiliar procedures such as pediatric evaluation, quality of movement evaluation, advanced orthopedic evaluation, etc.

Level 3   Meets Expectations

Completes all basic physical therapy evaluations independently and in a timely manner. Refer to department policies for a description of basic evaluation procedures.

Level 2   Meets Some Expectations

Occasionally requires assistance to select appropriate basic evaluation procedures. Sometimes requires assistance with the performance of basic evaluation procedures.

Level 1   Unsatisfactory Performance

Consistently requires assistance to select appropriate basic evaluation procedures and assistance with the performance of these procedures.

must assume responsibility, along with the employee, for improving performance.

Implementation of PCBM.   For practical reasons, the PCBM should be implemented at the beginning of an evaluation cycle. However, many organizations tie the employee appraisal system to the fiscal year. Staff should be fully aware of the performance indicators from the beginning of the appraisal period. Feedback on performance should be given throughout the appraisal period. The annual review of performance should be a summary of all of the feedback which has come before. There should be no surprises. It is often helpful to have an employee do a self-appraisal before the formal evaluation process. This will help to identify discrepancies between the perspectives of the manager and the employee being appraised. The performance appraisal should involve mutual discussion of the employee's performance. The objective is to reach a shared perception of the employee's performance.

MANAGING PERFORMANCE DISCREPANCIES

Performance discrepancies can be defined as anything that an employee is doing or not doing that is different from the expected performance. An effective performance appraisal system will identify performance discrepancies. Once identified, the manager and employee contribute to the analysis and resolution of the discrepancy. Early in the resolution process it becomes necessary to determine the cause of the performance discrepancy. Does it relate to ability, support, and/or effort? (21). Figure 4.4 provides the manager with a process for the evaluation of performance discrepancies. The process starts with a shared understanding of performance expectations and identified discrepancies and then goes on to determine the status of ability, support, and effort. Effort is first evaluated in terms of incentives and consequences related to performance or non-performance. Incentives and consequences are under the manager's control and are addressed first. Then effort is evaluated from the employee's perspective. Does the employee desire to exert the needed effort? The results of the discussion lead the manager and employee to the appropriate response.

EMPLOYEE COACHING

When organizational obstacles to performance have been eliminated, the manager's next alternative is coaching. Coaching is a face-to-face process used to analyze and improve performance. Effective performance coaching involves the following steps:

1. The manager must accurately identify and describe in detail the performance discrepancy observed.
2. The manager must help the employee understand why the discrepancy is of concern. This should include a discussion of the negative consequences of the performance discrepancy.
3. The manager and the employee must agree that the performance discrepancy exists. Mutual problem solving is dependent on the employee acknowledging the existence of the performance discrepancy.
4. The manager and employee together should identify and discuss alternative solutions.
5. The manager and employee must mutually agree on the action to be taken. The manager must gain the employee's commitment to the plan.
6. A follow-up should be scheduled to evaluate the outcome of the action taken.
7. The manager must recognize any improvement that occurs.

Coaching can be a time consuming and expensive process. The success of any coaching effort is dependent on the commitment of both the manager and the employee. If the employee fails to follow through on the agreed upon action plan then the next alternative is disciplinary action.

EMPLOYEE DISCIPLINE

To protect itself from liability due to inappropriate disciplinary action an organization should have clear and concise policies and procedures to guide the disciplinary process. Managers must follow those policies and procedures. Most large organizations have well-established policies and procedures to guide managers through the disciplinary process. A common progression of disciplinary actions is presented in Table 4.4.

Lachman (22) indicates that an effective disciplinary process starts with the presentation of a clear description of the behavior that is lacking

Identify Performance Discrepancy:

Does the employee know
performance is unsatisfactory?

        Yes   No →   Provide feedback to the employee.
        ↓

Does the employee know and
understand performance
expectations?

        Yes   No →   Provide employee with clear, concise
        ↓   information about performance
                              expectations.

Does the employee have the ability
to meet performance expectations?

        Yes   No →   Provide the employee with training
        ↓   and/or practice.

Does the employee have the
organizational support required to
meet performance expectations?

        Yes   No →   Determine what support is required
        ↓   and provide it.

Do incentives motivate employee
to exert effort to meet performance
expectations?

        Yes   No →   Provide incentives which motivate the
        ↓   employee to exert required effort.

Do negative consequences follow
nonperformance? Do positive
consequences follow
performance?

        Yes   No →   Change consequences.
        ↓

Could the employee meet
performance expectations if he or
she wanted to?

        Yes   No →   Transfer or terminate employee.
        ↓

Provide coaching to redirect
employee's behavior etc.

Begin the entire process again by
looking for new performance
discrepancies.

Figure 4.4. A performance discrepancy analysis decision tree. (Modified from: Lachman VD. Increasing productivity through performance evaluation. J Nursing Admin 1984;12(12):11.)

or unacceptable. The discussion should focus on performance discrepancies, not on the individual. This information is shared with the employee. Previous actions taken to correct the performance discrepancy should be reviewed. The employee and manager should discuss the situation and the employee should be given the chance to provide an explanation for the performance discrepancy. Ultimately, the manager should

Table 4.4.
Progression of Management Responses to Employee Noncompliance with Policies and Procedures

Occurrence	Management Action
Initial	Private oral warning
Second	Written warning
Third	Probation period for improvement
Fourth	Suspension
Recurrence	Termination

indicate what action should be taken by the employee and why. A follow-up date should be set. The consequences of nonperformance should be clearly understood by the employee. In all cases the manager should document actions taken and responses observed. Documentation should be objective and factual, not judgmental.

LEGAL CONSIDERATIONS

There are federal and state laws to protect employees from discriminatory application of opportunities, rewards, or any other privilege of employment. Because organizations use the outcomes of performance appraisal to apply rewards and other privileges they must be sure that their practices are nondiscriminatory. This means that care must be taken to ensure that the appraisal process deals with matters solely related to employee performance of the work. Metz (23) suggests nine elements of a performance appraisal system which, if taken into consideration, will stand up well under most legal challenges. These elements are:

1. A performance appraisal system should be based on clear, position-relevant performance standards.
2. Employees should be aware of the performance standards before they are evaluated.
3. Criteria for applications of rewards, promotions, and other privileges should be clearly communicated to employees and consistently applied.
4. Performance discrepancies should be clearly documented on appraisal forms.
5. Performance-related feedback should be given to employees in both oral and written form.
6. A mechanism should be in place which employees can use to dispute or comment on appraisal outcomes.
7. Personnel decisions should be congruent with employee evaluations.
8. Employees should be encouraged and given organization-supported opportunities for development.
9. A manager's appraisal decisions should be audited by the organization.

Personnel Retention

Seasoned employees are an asset to any organization. They represent a significant investment in financial resources, time, effort, and, often, management enthusiasm (24). For these reasons it is particularly frustrating for a physical therapy manager when a valuable employee intends to leave the organization. With severe manpower shortages, turnover is disrupting to services and replacement difficult at best. The costs associated with turnover can be significant. First, there are the costs of unmet service demands. These include lost revenue, lost business opportunities, decreased client satisfaction, and compromised quality of care. Second, there is the cost of decreased staff satisfaction caused by disruption of the work group and increased work loads.

A study of turnover among physical therapists found that 26% of physical therapists who had been in the field less than two years had had two to five jobs. Of the 446 physical therapists in the study who had been in the profession more than two years, 73% reported having had between two and five jobs (14).

Traditionally, turnover has been related to a variety of factors such as the demographic characteristics of age, seniority, and family responsibility. It has also been related to personal factors such as fulfillment, employee satisfaction, organizational commitment, and position tension (24). Traditional efforts to manage turnover have focused on decreasing turnover of all employees, including both good and poor performers. More recent thought has addressed the concepts of functional and dysfunctional turnover.

Is Turnover Always Bad?

Abelson (25) feels that in some cases turnover can benefit the organization. "Departure of a poor performer is functional" (25). Organizations can also view turnover as a comparison of costs associated with the turnover of an employee. These are the cost of the employee's departure in terms of lost revenue or the cost of recruiting a replacement versus the cost of retaining the employee. Retainment costs might come from meeting demands for higher pay or lowered employee morale due to the presence of a dissatisfied employee. There will be occasions when the cost of retaining a valued employee will outweigh the costs associated with their departure from the organization.

Is Turnover Controllable?

An experienced manager will soon realize that in many cases turnover is not controllable. Satisfied employees often leave for reasons unrelated to their employment situation. Family responsibility is a common reason for young professional women to leave a satisfying position. Dual career families also contribute to turnover (25). Dual career families are especially common in professions such as physical therapy because of the high proportion of women in the field. Physical therapy managers must accept that some turnover is beyond their control. They should concentrate their efforts on preventing turnover that can be controlled.

Factors Influencing Turnover

Factors influencing turnover can be categorized as individual factors, organizational factors, and environmental factors (24, 25). Factors at the individual level which are thought to contribute to employee turnover are listed in the first column of Table 4.5. Strategies for management to

Table 4.5.
Turnover Factors and Management Actions Encouraging Employee Retention

Factors Encouraging Turnover	Management Actions Encouraging Retention
Poorly defined position responsibilities.	Clearly define performance expectations.
High stress position.	Management support to provide needed resources and remove obstacles which interfere with performance.
Unchallenging work that does not utilize employee skills.	Clearly define employee roles prior to employment. Create clinical and management opportunities for advancement. Design positions with performance expectations that match required skills.
Unfair performance expectations.	Involve employees in setting performance expectations.
Lack of development opportunities.	Provide frequent development opportunities which meet both organizational and employee development goals.
Lack of recognition for work accomplishments.	Provide recognition for good performance.
Lack of opportunity to express work related dissatisfaction.	Provide formal mechanisms and encourage employees to express dissatisfaction.
Low flexibility.	Allow for flexible hours and working arrangements.
Pay inequities.	Provide employees with financial compensation which reflects market conditions. Avoid internal pay inequities.
Lack of advancement opportunities.	Provide opportunities for clinical and management advancement whenever possible.
Low levels of autonomy.	Adopt a participative style of management which allows employees autonomy based on ability.
Competitive environment.	Competitive position content and context.
Undesirable geographic location.	Provide social support to new employees. Recruit employees who are comfortable with the size and environment of the community.

deal with these individual factors to improve retention are listed in the second column of Table 4.5.

Organizational factors associated with turnover include not giving attention to the individual factors. Examples of such oversights are failure to acknowledge employee contributions, lack of opportunity for employees to provide feedback, little flexibility for accommodation of personal demands (e.g., flexible scheduling, part-time hours), lack of advancement opportunities, low levels of employee autonomy, and an unfavorable work climate. Environmental factors related to turnover include a competitive environment which increases position opportunities, undesirable geographic location, metropolitan size, and minimal cultural opportunities in the community.

Turnover of physical therapists has been associated with many factors. These include the desire to pursue a different area of physical therapy, insufficient salary, no opportunity for promotion, lack of independence in decision making about patient care, and little feeling of accomplishment (14). In most settings, these factors could be modified in a way which would enhance employee retention.

SUMMARY

Table 4.5 draws attention to the interrelationships among an effective work design process, employee recruitment, the performance appraisal process, and employee retention. A properly implemented work design process will yield reasonable performance expectations and a match between employee skills and position duties. Work design determines the amount of autonomy an employee will have in the performance of the work. It will provide for a clear understanding of position responsibilities. Effective work design will also result in an employee training program designed to develop each employee into a contributing member of the organization. An employee recruitment plan will lead to competitive work design, competitive salary ranges, and position flexibility. It should also result in a good match between position requirements and employee expectations. The performance appraisal process will allow for employee recognition. The outcome of the appraisal process will provide a basis for rewards and promotions and it will provide the employee with the opportunity to express dissatisfaction. Clearly, employee retention is associated with the application of sound personnel management practices.

Case Study 4.1
Effect of Work Design on Retention

Oshkosh General Hospital

Oshkosh General Hospital (OGH) is located in a town with a population of 70,000. OGH has a physical therapy department which employs a manager, seven physical therapists, two physical therapist assistants, and three aides. Oshkosh's size has not interfered with OGH's ability to recruit physical therapists. That is because it is located 60 miles from two large metropolitan areas that boast a physical therapy school. In fact, OGH recruits three to four physical therapists annually to deal with its 50% turnover rate. The average length of employment for its physical therapists is two years. OGH's Physical Therapy Manager and Administrator are very concerned about the department's inability to retain physical therapists. The continual departure and arrival of new therapists has been costly and disruptive. New program development has been virtually impossible.

A task force was formed to review the situation. It was composed of the Administrator,

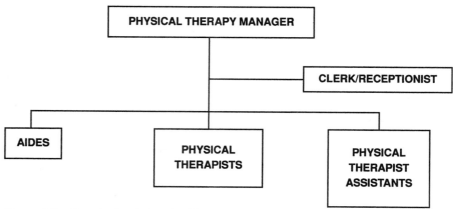

Figure 4.5. Organizational chart for OGH in Case Study 4.1.

the Physical Therapy Manager, the Personnel Manager, the most senior physical therapist, and the most recently hired physical therapist. The report of the task force identified that the major causes of physical therapist turnover were: 1) the high percentage of clerical and support tasks physical therapists were required to perform and 2) the lack of opportunity for advancement.

The first step taken to remedy the situation was the addition of a clerical position and a shifting of support work to aides wherever possible. Department position descriptions were modified to reflect the changes. The second step, providing opportunities for advancement, remains to be dealt with.

Please recommend five methods OGH's Physical Therapy Manager might consider which would not require the creation of more than one additional supervisory position. The department already has one full-time manager for 13 employees.

The current OGH Physical Therapy Department Organizational Chart is presented in Figure 4.5.

Appendix 4.1 provides some suggested answers to this case study.

CASE STUDY 4.2
Defining Performance Expectations in Behavioral Terms

Milwaukee Memorial Hospital

The Physical Therapy Department of Milwaukee Memorial Hospital is moving toward the use of a performance criteria-based performance appraisal system. All department employees have been asked to assist in the process. Using the position description in Example 4.2 and the Performance Rating Scale in Figure 4.3 you have been asked to help define your position's performance criteria in behavioral terms. You have been assigned the following performance criteria:

B2. Schedules the work of physical therapist assistants and aides for assigned clients.

D5. Maintains open lines of communication with clients, families, other employees, the medical staff, management, administration, and other community professionals.

Using Example 4.3 as a reference describe these performance criteria in behavioral terms for each level of performance. Descriptions should be objective and measurable.

Appendix 4.2 will provide you with some alternative considerations to gauge your own responses.

References

1. Cordery JL, Wall TD. Work design and supervisory practice: A model. Hum Relat 1985;38:425–441.
2. Mintzberg H. The structuring of organizations. Englewood Cliffs, NJ: Prentice-Hall, 1979:69–103.

3. Miles RE. Theories of management: Implications for organizational behavior and development. New York: McGraw-Hill, 1975:51–71.

4. Smith A. The wealth of nations. London: Dent, 1910. In: Mintzberg H. The structuring of organizations. Englewood Cliffs, NJ: Prentice-Hall, 1979:70.

5. Champoux JE, Howard, PD. Job design and work context reactions among medical technologists. J Allied Health 1989;18:177–187.

6. Davis GL, Bordieri JE. Perceived autonomy and job satisfaction in occupational therapists. Am J Occup Ther 1988;42:591–595.

7. Ferris GR, Gilmore DC. The moderating role of work context in job design research: A test of competing models. Acad Manage J 1984;27:885–892.

8. Feldman DC. Organizational socialization of hospital employees: A comparative view of occupational groups. Medical Care 1977;15:799–813.

9. Smith DM. Organizational socialization of physical therapists. Phys Ther 1989;69:282–286.

10. Strakal G. The manpower shortage: part one-strategies to reduce its impact. Pyramid 1989;18(4):1–3.

11. Davis K. U.S. demand for physical therapists outweighs supply. Prog Rep 1988;17(2):5.

12. Benanti, JA. Turbulent times call for innovative management. Clin Manage 1989;8(1):14–15.

13. Magistro CM. Twenty-second Mary McMillan lecture. Phys Ther 1987;67:1726–1732.

14. Harkson DG, Unterreiner AS, Shepard KF. Factors related to job turnover in physical therapy. Phys Ther 1982;62:1465–1470.

15. Drake Advertising Limited. Recruitment: filling the ranks. Drake Business Review. Cited in Management Memos, Section on Administration, American Physical Therapy Association, March, 1990.

16. Peringian L, Skeegan S. Attracting and hiring the right person. Clin Manage 1982;2(3):11–12.

17. Wiatrowski MD, Palkon DS. Performance appraisal systems in health care administration. Health Care Manage Rev 1987;12(1):71–80.

18. Bohannon RW. The performance appraisal: Considerations for supervisors and staff. Clin Manage 1987;7(4):10–13.

19. Peters TJ, Waterman RH, Jr. In search of excellence. New York: Harper and Row, 1982:55,67–73.

20. Lindsey D. A model performance appraisal instrument for school physical therapists. Clin Manage 1986;6(5):20–26.

21. Schermerhorn JR. Improving health care productivity through high-performance managerial development. Health Care Manage Rev 1987;12(4):49–55.

22. Lachman VD. Increasing productivity through performance evaluation. J Nursing Admin 1984;14(12):7–14.

23. Metz EJ. Designing legally defensible performance appraisal systems. Training Dev J 1988;July:47–51.

24. Smith HL, Discenza R. Developing a framework for retaining health care employees: A challenge to traditional thinking. Health Care Supervisor 1988;7(1):17–28.

25. Abelson MA. Strategic management of turnover: A model for the health service administrator. Health Care Manage Rev 1986;11(2):61–71.

CHAPTER **5**

Fiscal Management

OVERVIEW

This chapter provides the reader with essential financial management principles applicable to health care organizations. Accountants are the financial professionals responsible for the financial well-being of an organization. Their role in advising physical therapy managers and physical therapists in private practice is discussed. Standard financial terms are defined. The typical types of financial reports that a revenue center manager would contribute to and receive are presented and explained. Relevant examples are used to demonstrate how these reports are used to guide present and future actions. Financial reports have much in common with progress reports written about a client. As a result of the client assessment or the assessment of the financial status of the department changes in strategy may take place, goals may be modified, or a program may be expanded or discontinued. Areas with financial impact that a physical therapy manager is likely to be involved with are discussed in depth. Case studies at the end of the chapter offer the reader the opportunity to apply many of the financial management principles presented.

Introduction

USE OF FINANCIAL INFORMATION

Financial management refers broadly to the use of financial information to evaluate and direct the activities of an organization. Financial information can be used to evaluate an organization's ability to generate revenue through the sale of goods and services. It can be used to determine when and how an organization spends its financial resources. With information about an organization's revenues and expenses, it can quickly be determined whether the organization will sustain a profit or a loss from part or all of its activities. In addition to evaluating current performance, financial information can be used to evaluate an organization's performance over time. Comparison of past and present performance can identify changes or trends that would help predict threats to an organization's survival or opportunities for its future growth. The outcome of financial performance evaluation is an enhanced ability to make good decisions about an organization's current operations and future direction.

Information from a financial management system has many uses. It is used by managers to plan and direct day-to-day operations. This usually takes the form of an annual budgeting process. It can also take the form of a financial assessment for a new product or service an organization might want to provide. Managers use budgets to determine what kind and how much of a resource should be used to produce a desired outcome. Financial information can also help managers identify deviations, often referred to as variances, from what has been planned. Deviations serve as a red flag for managers whose attention may be spread over a wide variety of activities. Because financial information is consistent across time periods, departments, and organizations, it is frequently used to evaluate and solve organizational problems. It may also be used to make nonroutine decisions and to plan for the future. Employees might use financial information to assess the value of profit sharing or bonus plans. Financial information is also used by persons outside of the organization. The government, shareholders, private investors, banks, and philanthropists may all use an organization's financial information. All of these outside parties may affect the success of an organization. They are all possible sources of external funding. An organization will require external funding any time it does not have the cash to buy today what it needs or wants today.

Organizations collect financial information through the use of a financial management (accounting) system. A financial management system will establish procedures for the collection, analysis, and reporting of financial information. Because the information produced by a financial management system must meet the needs of so many different audiences, the methods used by an organization must follow accepted accounting standards. These standards have been established by the Accounting Principles Board and the Financial Accounting Standards Board. That means that anyone who is familiar with standard accounting methods can reliably understand and interpret financial information from any organization.

If physical therapists never had to interact with other professionals, if they never had to be part of an organization or make decisions about their professional practice in an institutional or private practice setting, then they would never need to understand the principles of financial management. The fact is that, if physical therapists are to be effective members of the health care community and if they are going to contribute to the growth of their profession within that community, they will at some time be called upon to understand and/or apply the principles of financial management. The challenge to understand the financial side of physical therapy may come from a variety of sources. It may come from a desire to serve as a leader in a professional association on a state or national level. It may come as an opportunity for advancement into physical therapy management. Or, perhaps, it may come from the drive for independence through involvement in a private practice. Whatever the source, few physical therapists in today's complex health care environment will be able to avoid the use of financial management principles. To accept the challenge without some preparation would be a disservice to ourselves and others who depend upon us to represent their needs.

The purpose of this chapter is to provide the physical therapist with an overview of financial management principles and to familiarize them with the financial management methods commonly used by health care organizations. Special attention will be paid to those financial management system procedures with which the physical therapist would most commonly be involved. Common activities might include such things as interpretation of financial statements, predicting the demand for physical therapy services, budgeting, setting staffing levels, evaluating capital equipment purchases, evaluating productivity, new service planning, and obtaining payment for services.

ROLE OF THE FINANCE PROFESSIONAL

Organizations rely on accountants to establish procedures for the collection, analysis, and reporting of financial information. Like physical therapists, accountants are recognized professionals who are licensed by the state in which they practice. To be eligible for state licensure, an accountant must pass a standardized examination prepared by the American Institute of Certified Public Accountants. A licensed accountant is referred to as a Certified Public Accountant or a CPA. Accountants are usually employed in one of three fields. These are public, private, or government accounting (1). The public accountant offers his services to the general public much in the same way as a lawyer or a physical therapist in private practice. A private accountant is employed by an organization and works only for that organization. The chief accounting officer in a organization is commonly called the controller (1).

In the course of their careers, physical therapists will find themselves in many situations that require them to work with an accountant. For the physical therapist who is employed by a health care organization, this interaction will come in the course of working with a financial services department. Therapists in private practice will require the services of a public accountant to set up a financial information system, to perform annual audits, to prepare annual financial reports, and, many times, to assist them in obtaining loans or credit from a bank or other investors. The public accountant can also provide the private practitioner with advice on issues related to insurance, employee benefits, investments, and pension plans (2). All of these issues will have an impact on the success of a private practice. Therapists, whether employed or in private practice, will have contact with government agencies that control reimbursement for physical therapy services. The policies and procedures of those agencies are often established and administered by finance professionals. To get maximum benefit from the services of finance professionals, the physical therapist should have a basic understanding of financial management.

Financial Statements

Financial statements are reports which describe the financial position and operating results of an organization. Financial statements provide a summary of financial information which has been collected over a specific period of time. The specified time period could be a week, a month, a three-month period, referred to as a quarter, or a year. Yearly reports can also be referred to as annual or fiscal year reports. An organization's business year does not have to follow the calendar year. A fiscal year may start in any month a business chooses to start operations and will end on the last day of the twelfth month. Financial statements are most often produced on a monthly, quarterly, and annual basis.

The two major financial statements are the balance sheet and the income statement. The balance sheet summarizes the financial position of an organization as of a particular date. The income statement demonstrates an organization's profit or loss from operations for a specific period of time. A third type of financial statement is the cash flow statement. The cash flow statement demonstrates what has happened to make available cash increase and decrease during a period of time. Financial statements are the final product of a financial management system and, therefore, are a good place to start to learn about financial management. Familiarity with the balance sheet and the income statement will help the physical therapist understand the types of and uses for financial information that organizations routinely collect. The understanding and use of cash flow statements will be of particular importance to the therapist in private practice.

BALANCE SHEET

The balance sheet is a financial statement of an organization's assets, liabilities, and owner's equity. It summarizes the organization's financial position as of a particular date. That date is usually the last day of a month or the last day of the fiscal year. The balance sheet in Example 5.1 summarizes the financial position of Independent Physical Therapists, Incorporated (IPT, Inc.) as of June 30, 1999.

The balance sheet could be represented by the equation:

$$ASSETS = LIABILITIES + OWNER'S\ EQUITY$$

EXAMPLE 5.1
Balance Sheet

Independent Physical Therapists, Incorporated
Balance Sheet
June 30, 1999

Assets		Liabilities and Owner's Equity	
Cash	$30,000	Liabilities	
Accounts receivable	12,000	Accounts payable	$ 27,000
Land	40,000	Accrued expenses	3,000
Buildings	90,000	Notes payable	100,000
Equipment	50,000	Total liabilities	130,000
		Owner's Equity	
		Partner's capital	92,000
		Total equity	92,000
Total assets	$222,000	Total Liability and Owner's Equity	$222,000

Assets

The assets of an organization always equal the rights to those assets (3). Assets are economic resources that are owned by an organization and are expected to benefit future operations. Assets include such things as cash, investments, buildings, fixtures, furniture, equipment, and money that is owed to the organization from customers who were sold goods or services on credit. Money owed to an organization is referred to as accounts receivable. Cash and other assets that can be quickly converted to cash are referred to as liquid or current assets. Assets that cannot be quickly converted to cash are referred to as fixed assets. An organization can own assets which can no longer benefit future operations. This might occur because a piece of equipment becomes obsolete. It could also occur when a debt owed to the company becomes so old it is doubtful it can be collected. When this occurs, the total assets of the organization would be reduced by the recorded value of that asset.

Liabilities

Liabilities are debts. They can be thought of as the assets of an organization that are owned by its creditors. Accounts payable are amounts owed by the organization to creditors who sold them goods or services on credit. Notes payable are amounts owed by the organization which are evidenced by formal promissory agreements for specific amounts of money plus interest due at a future date (3). In other words, notes payable are loans. Current liabilities are those that must be paid within a short period of time, usually within one year. Long-term liabilities are those that are not due and payable for a longer period of time, generally greater than one year.

Owner's Equity

Owner's equity represents that portion of the organization's assets that are owned by the owners. Owners are the shareholders of the organization. Owner's equity can increase in two ways: first, through invest-

EXAMPLE 5.2
Common-Size Balance Sheet

Independent Physical Therapists, Incorporated
Common-Size Comparative Balance Statement
June 30, 1998 and June 30, 1999

	1999	1998	Common-Size Percentage 1999	1998
Assets				
Current Assets				
Cash	$30,000	$24,000	13.5%	14.2%
Accounts receivable	12,000	15,000	5.4	8.9
Total current assets	$42,000	$39,000	18.9%	23.1%
Property and Equipment				
Land	$40,000	$40,000	18.0%	23.7%
Buildings	90,000	60,000	40.5	35.5
Equipment	50,000	30,000	22.5	17.8
Total Property and Equipment	$180,000	$130,000	81.1%	76.9%
Total Assets	$222,000	$169,000	100.0%	100.0%
Liabilities and Owner's Equity				
Current Liabilities				
Accounts payable	$27,000	$17,800	12.2%	10.5%
Accrued expenses	3,000	2,200	1.4	1.3
Total Current Liabilities	$30,000	$20,000	13.6%	11.8%
Long-Term Liabilities				
Notes payable	$100,000	$60,000	45.0%	35.5%
Total Liabilities	$130,000	$80,000	58.6%	47.3%
Owner's Equity				
Partner's capital	$92,000	$89,000	41.4%	52.7%
Total Owner's Equity	$92,000	$89,000	41.4%	52.7%
Total Liabilities and Equity	$222,000	$169,000	100.0%	100.0%

ment of resources by the owner and, second, through earnings from profitable operations.

Making Comparisons from the Balance Sheet

The balance sheet becomes most valuable when it used for the purposes of comparative analysis. To aid in the comparison of different entries on the balance sheet each entry is listed as both a dollar value and as a percentage of some total of which that entry is a part. When percentages are used to represent the entries on a financial statement it is called a common-size statement. A common-size statement is used for vertical analysis by scanning columns of entries (4). Balance sheets can also present information from more than one date. This would allow for the comparison of the organization's financial position at different points in time. The statement would then be called a comparative balance sheet (5). The comparison of financial information from different periods allows for the identification of trends that might affect the future of the organization. This is referred to as horizontal analysis (4). Both vertical (column) and horizontal (row) analysis can be performed using the common-size comparative balance sheet for IPT, Inc. for June 30, 1999 found in Example 5.2.

EXAMPLE 5.3
Income Statement

Independent Physical Therapists, Incorporated Income Statement Year Ending June 30, 1999		
Revenues		
Service	$391,244	
Supplies sold	11,620	
Equipment rental	8,940	
Total Revenue		$411,804
Expenses		
Salaries	$207,200	
Benefits	55,800	
Supplies, general	8,320	
Supplies sold	8,900	
Equipment	4,560	
Education	4,300	
Recruitment	11,549	
Advertising and sales	26,896	
Environmental services	4,290	
Utilities	6,194	
Purchased services	4,330	
Depreciation	18,667	
Travel	1,085	
Total Expenses		$362,091
Net Income (Loss)		$49,713

INCOME STATEMENT

The income statement is a financial report used to evaluate the performance of an organization through the comparison of money spent (expenses) to money earned (revenue) for a specific period of time. The income statement demonstrates the net income or loss for the period. The term net income refers to income remaining after expenses have been subtracted from total revenue for the period. A net loss indicates the expenses were greater than total revenue for the period. The income statement can be represented by the equation:

REVENUE + EXPENSES = NET INCOME (LOSS)

Alternate titles for the income statement are Earnings Statement, Statement of Operations, and Profit and Loss Statement. Regardless of the title used, these statements will always contain the same information. The income statement in Example 5.3 summarizes the performance of IPT, Inc. for the year ending June 30, 1999. IPT, Inc. made a profit for the year ending June 30, 1999. If they had lost money for the period the loss figure at the bottom of the statement would have been enclosed in parentheses. By convention, financial statements use parentheses instead of a negative symbol to indicate a loss or negative balance.

Revenue

Revenue is the income received by an organization for the goods and/or services sold during a specific period in time. Revenue is calculated by multiplying the volume of services and goods sold by the selling price of the good or service. Revenue is credited to the period in which the sale is made, not in the period the money is received. This is done to make sure that the expenses connected with the production of a good or service are accounted for in the same period as the revenue from the sale of the good or service. Discounts or items sold at sale prices would result in a reduction in revenue.

Expenses

Expenses represent the amount of money spent by an organization to produce goods and services during a specific period of time. Generally, an organization has more expense categories than it does revenue categories. Organizations which spend a large percentage of total expense dollars on equipment are referred to as capital intensive. When the greatest percentage of total expenses is related to salary and benefits, the organization is referred to as labor intensive. Physical therapy departments or practices are considered to be labor intensive.

USING FINANCIAL STATEMENTS
Comparative Analysis Using Income Statements

Income statements can be prepared for time periods in the past, present or future. Statements prepared for the future are referred to as pro forma statements or budgets. Income statements are also of most value when used for comparative analysis. As with the balance sheet, the income statement can be used to compare the relationships between statement entries and performance from one time period to another. Example 5.4 is an example of a common-size comparative income statement.

Because it is a statement of financial performance, the income statement can also be used to compare actual performance with planned (budgeted) performance. Example 5.5 allows a comparison between projected or budgeted performance and actual performance for the fiscal year ending June 30, 1999.

Use of an income statement that compares what was planned with what actually occurred allows for the identification of areas of operation that may require special attention. Through use of the comparative statement in Example 5.5, some observations can be made regarding the performance of IPT, Inc. during fiscal year 1999. This comparative income statement is called a statement of operation. It compares the projected income statement with the actual income statement for a period of operation. It presents the outcome of this comparison in the form of operating variances. Negative variances are presented in parentheses. First, revenues exceeded budget levels by $16,244. Upon initial review this may appear beneficial. Upon further review it can be seen that while revenue exceeded budget by $16,244, expenses incurred to produce total revenue exceeded budget by $37,024. Most of this negative variance is related to disproportionately high salary, benefit, purchased services, and recruitment costs. The net result is an income level that is $37,887 below budgeted levels. We can speculate that IPT, Inc. was not adequately prepared to provide the additional demand generated by its marketing efforts. It is obvious that an increased demand for services was not beneficial to this organi-

EXAMPLE 5.4
Common-Size Income Statement

<table>
<tr><td colspan="5" align="center">Independent Physical Therapists, Incorporated
Common-Size Comparative Income Statement
Years Ending June 30,1999 and June 30, 1998</td></tr>
<tr><td></td><td></td><td></td><td colspan="2" align="center">Common-Size Percentages</td></tr>
<tr><td></td><td align="center">1999</td><td align="center">1998</td><td align="center">1999</td><td align="center">1998</td></tr>
<tr><td>Revenues</td><td></td><td></td><td></td><td></td></tr>
<tr><td>Services</td><td>$391,244</td><td>$302,500</td><td>95.0%</td><td>95.1%</td></tr>
<tr><td>Supplies sold</td><td>11,620</td><td>8,715</td><td>2.8</td><td>2.8</td></tr>
<tr><td>Equipment rental</td><td>8,940</td><td>6,705</td><td>2.2</td><td>2.1</td></tr>
<tr><td>Total Revenues</td><td>$411,804</td><td>$317,920</td><td>100.0%</td><td>100.0%</td></tr>
<tr><td>Expenses</td><td></td><td></td><td></td><td></td></tr>
<tr><td>Salaries</td><td>$207,200</td><td>$189,760</td><td>57.9%</td><td>59.0%</td></tr>
<tr><td>Benefits</td><td>55,800</td><td>47,440</td><td>15.6</td><td>14.8</td></tr>
<tr><td>Supplies, general</td><td>8,320</td><td>6,249</td><td>2.3</td><td>1.9</td></tr>
<tr><td>Supplies sold</td><td>8,900</td><td>6,675</td><td>2.5</td><td>2.1</td></tr>
<tr><td>Equipment</td><td>4,560</td><td>15,300</td><td>1.3</td><td>4.8</td></tr>
<tr><td>Education</td><td>4,300</td><td>3,500</td><td>1.2</td><td>1.1</td></tr>
<tr><td>Recruitment</td><td>11,549</td><td>8,000</td><td>3.2</td><td>2.5</td></tr>
<tr><td>Advertising and sales</td><td>26,896</td><td>10,000</td><td>7.5</td><td>3.1</td></tr>
<tr><td>Environmental services</td><td>4,290</td><td>4,000</td><td>1.2</td><td>1.2</td></tr>
<tr><td>Utilities</td><td>6,194</td><td>5,850</td><td>1.7</td><td>1.8</td></tr>
<tr><td>Purchased services</td><td>4,330</td><td>6,525</td><td>1.2</td><td>2.0</td></tr>
<tr><td>Depreciation</td><td>18,667</td><td>17,767</td><td>.5.2</td><td>5.5</td></tr>
<tr><td>Travel</td><td>1,085</td><td>500</td><td>0.0</td><td>0.0</td></tr>
<tr><td>Total Expenses</td><td>$362,091</td><td>$321,566</td><td>100.0%</td><td>100.0%</td></tr>
<tr><td>Net Income</td><td>$ 49,713</td><td>($3,646)</td><td></td><td></td></tr>
</table>

zation at this time. The cost of the resources needed to provide the additional services outweighed the revenue generated.

RATIO ANALYSIS

Financial statements also allow comparisons to be made between one piece of financial information and another. This is called ratio analysis. In comparing one piece of financial information with another, ratios can be used as guides for the analyst to rate the performance and financial condition of the organization. An organization's performance and condition can be rated over time or it can be rated in comparison to the performance and condition of similar organizations. Commonly used ratios are the current ratio, the quick ratio, debt ratio, receivables turnover ratio, revenue productivity ratio, and the rate of return on assets (3, 5, 6).

Current Ratio

The current ratio compares current assets with current liabilities. The current ratio is calculated by dividing current assets by current liabilities. The higher the ratio the better the organization's ability to pay its current bills. This ratio is important to would be creditors and investors.

Quick Ratio

The quick ratio compares liquid assets with current liabilities. Liquid assets include cash and those assets that can be quickly converted to cash.

EXAMPLE 5.5
Comparative Income Statement

Independent Physical Therapists, Incorporated
Statement of Operations
Period Ending June 30, 1999

	Actual	Budget	Variance
Revenues			
Services	$391,244	$375,000	($16,244)
Supplies sold	11,620	10,000	(1,620)
Rentals	8,940	9,000	60
Total Revenue	$411,804	$394,000	($17,804)
Expenses			
Salaries	$207,200	$190,000	($17,200)
Benefits	55,800	45,000	(10,800)
Supplies, general	8,320	8,000	(320)
Supplies sold	8,900	9,000	100
Equipment	4,560	4,500	(60)
Education	4,300	4,300	00
Recruitment	11,549	8,000	(3,549)
Advertising and sales	26,896	25,000	(1,896)
Environmental services	4,290	4,000	(290)
Utilities	6,194	6,000	(194)
Purchased services	4,330	2,000	(2,330)
Depreciation	18,667	18,667	0
Travel	1,085	600	(485)
Total Expenses	$362,091	$306,400	($37,024)
Net Income	$49,713	$87,600	($37,887)

The quick ratio is similar to the current ratio except it excludes current assets such as inventories which cannot be quickly converted to cash in the event that cash reserves are inadequate to cover current bills.

Debt Ratio

The debt ratio compares total liabilities to total assets. Debt ratio is calculated by dividing total liabilities by total assets. This ratio gives the percentage of the organization's assets that are financed through borrowing. It is used to determine if the organization is a good credit risk. The lower the percentage, the less money borrowed from creditors to purchase currently owned assets.

Receivable Turnover Ratio

The receivables turnover ratio tells the average number of days it takes to convert accounts receivable (credit sales) into cash. It is calculated by dividing the annual credit sales by the current receivables. This ratio is used to evaluate an organization's credit policy. Is it too lenient or restrictive? It can also be used to evaluate the quality of the receivables. Generally, the older the debt the less likely it can be collected. The receivables turnover ratio is also used to determine future cash flow and cash requirements.

Revenue Productivity Ratio

The revenue productivity ratio indicates the amount of revenue generated for each dollar of salary expense. It is calculated by dividing total revenue from services by related salary expenses. In a labor-intensive organization like a physical therapy practice, this ratio can be used as an indicator of staff productivity (5).

Return on Assets

The rate of return on assets is used to evaluate an organization's ability to earn a return on funds supplied from all sources. It is calculated by dividing net income plus interest expenses by total assets. The higher the return, the better the performance (3).

The above ratios are likely to be the most frequently used and important for the physical therapist in both institutional and private practice settings. There are many other ratios that are often used by the finance professional to evaluate an organization. The physical therapist should utilize available public or private accountants to determine the best ratios to use to obtain information needed to assess the performance of their department or practice.

CASH FLOW STATEMENT

The cash flow statement demonstrates how an organization's cash balances change over a specific period of time. It does this by identifying both the sources and uses of cash during a specific period. An organization's cash flow is important to creditors, owners, and investors because it impacts on its ability to pay bills, replace equipment, buy new equipment, and, generally, to grow in the future. As with other financial statements, cash flow statements can be prepared for past, current, or future time periods. The cash flow statement begins with the cash balance as of the beginning of the time period. It then reviews actual or projected sources and uses for cash throughout the period. It ends with the cash balance at the end of the time period. Example 5.6 provides a review of sources and uses of cash by IPT, Inc. for fiscal year 1999.

The cash flow statement in Example 5.6 indicates that the sole source of cash during this year is from operations. Other sources of cash for an organization might be investment of cash by the owner, sale of assets, or outside financing. In addition to the purchase of assets and withdrawal by the owner (pay dividends), cash can be used to pay off creditors or to fund unprofitable operations. An organization can use a pro forma cash flow statement to project future cash sources, uses, and balances. This is done to ensure that available cash will meet future cash requirements. Cash flow projections allow management to delay planned expenditures or arrange for credit to cover projected shortfalls.

Financial Planning

One of the most important uses of financial information is for planning. Planning implies an orientation to the future. Financial planning can take the form of an annual budgeting process or it can be used to make decisions about new directions for the future. In the first case, the plan is often referred to as an operating budget. It guides the operation

EXAMPLE 5.6
Cash Flow Statement

Independent Physical Therapists, Incorporated Cash Flow Statement Year Ending June 30, 1999		
Cash balance, July 1, 1998		$24,000
Sources of Cash		
Cash from operations	$49,713	
Accounts receivable	350,000	
Total Sources of Cash		$399,713
Uses of Cash		
Purchase of equipment	$5,000	
Building expansion	5,000	
Owner withdrawal	37,713	
Accounts payable	88,000	
Payroll	262,000	
Total Uses of Cash		$397,713
Increase in Cash		2,000
Cash Balance, June 30, 1999		$26,000

by outlining the types and levels of expenditures that all or part of an organization plans to make during a specific period of time. An operating budget typically covers a one-year period, subdivided into monthly and quarterly increments. When the financial plan is used to make decisions about new or future activity, the plan is frequently referred to as a business plan. It should be noted, however, that the financial analysis is only part of the total business planning process. A business plan typically projects financial performance for three to five years into the future. It is subdivided into yearly increments. Budgeting, whether for the continuation of current operations or new activities, requires the development of pro forma financial statements. The following discussion of financial planning will cover the basic principles of budget and business plan development. The physical therapist manager may be involved in both types of financial planning activities.

TRENDS IN FINANCIAL PLANNING
Traditional Financial Planning

The changes faced by health care organizations have had a major impact on the methods they use to develop financial plans. Traditionally, health care organizations have used an extrapolation method to project future activity. The extrapolation method uses historical information as a starting point. This method assumes that all factors influencing demand for health care services will remain unchanged except for the demographic profile of the organization's market (service) area. Once the changes in demographic profile were identified, the impact on future activity was projected. The financial plan reflected the projected changes. Demographic changes tended to occur slowly and activity levels were fairly stable over long periods of time. In that environment, an organization could feel confident in the accuracy of financial plans that extended years into the future. The operating budgets used by health care organizations were fixed for the upcoming period. These operating budgets could be relied upon to realistically represent actual activity in terms of revenue and expenses. While the extrapolation method was adequate in the past, it is less than adequate in today's environment where there are numerous forces influencing the demand for health care services provided by a specific organization and from the health care industry in general. For that reason many health care organizations are adopting a flexible financial planning process (7).

Flexible Financial Planning

Flexible planning methods allow for changes in the demand for services during the budget period. This is done by separating the expenses that are influenced by level of activity from those that remain the same regardless of level of activity. As a result of the trend toward flexible budgeting effective financial management will depend on a good understanding of the relationships between expenses and level of activity.

CHART OF ACCOUNTS

To produce accurate financial statements an organization must collect information about how money is spent and earned. It must also keep track of the value of its assets, liabilities, and owner's equity. To accomplish this the organization adopts specific policies and procedures that direct the collection of information into distinct categories. These categories of expense, revenue, assets, and liabilities are called accounts. The total listing of these accounts is called a chart of accounts. The chart of accounts lists accounts that are used by an organization by account title and their identifying account number (3). The number and type of accounts used by an organization will vary with its size, its business, and how much detailed information is desired by management and outside parties. Example 5.7 is a listing of accounts that could be used to collect information about expenses in a physical therapy department or practice.

REVENUE BUDGET

Revenue is the income received by an organization for goods or services sold during a specific period of time. Revenue is calculated by multiplying the volume of goods and services sold by the selling price of those goods and services. Revenue can be represented by the equation:

$$\text{REVENUE} = \text{UNITS SOLD} \times \text{SELLING PRICE PER UNIT}$$

To develop a revenue budget an organization must decide how it will measure the amount of goods and services it sells. It must also decide what it will charge for the unit of goods and services it sells. Finally, it must project the amount of goods and services it will sell during the budget period. For the well-established organization, this may simply be based on previous experience with adjustments made for increasing costs and changing demand. For the new organization or an organization facing new competitive pressures it can be a lengthy and important process. In either case, it will be important to understand the basic principles of revenue

EXAMPLE 5.7
Chart of Expense Accounts

Independent Physical Therapists, Inc.
Chart of Expense Accounts[a]

0010	Salaries	0080	Dues and Subscriptions
0011	Administrative	0090	Education
0012	Professional	0100	Travel
0013	Technical	0110	Recruitment
0014	Clerical	0120	Purchased Services
0015	Benefits	0121	Physical therapy
0016	FICA	0122	Accountant fees
0020	Supplies, General	0123	Legal fees
0021	Medical	0124	Other
0022	Office	0130	Rent/Lease
0023	Small tools	0131	Building
0030	Supplies Sold	0132	Equipment
0040	Equipment Repaired and Replaced	0133	Miscellaneous
0050	Dietary	0140	Accrued Expenses
0060	Environmental Services	0141	Payroll
0061	Maintenance and grounds	0142	Taxes
0062	Housekeeping	0143	Depreciation
0063	Linen service		
0070	Utilities		
0071	Heat		
0072	Electrical		
0073	Telephone		

[a]The above list of operating expense accounts is meant to be a representative sample only. A finance professional should be consulted to develop a list of expense accounts for any specific application.

budget preparation. This will ensure that the most reliable and effective budget is adopted. Remember that budgets are used to guide future operations. Large organizations are often divided into segments for the purpose of developing revenue budgets. The segments of a large organization which produce revenue are often referred to as profit centers.

Measuring Goods and Services for Sale

Goods and services for sale must be defined by some unit of measure in order to determine what the buyer should be charged. A unit is the measure that an organization uses to define the amount of goods or services it sells to its customers. A unit refers to the way the item is packaged for sale. The unit of measure for a service can be based on time or activity. A time-based unit might be a minute, an hour, or a day. The unit of measure for a good is based on some amount of the good sold. A unit of measure based on an amount might be a single item, a dose, a pair, or a packaged weight of something. In physical therapy practice there are generally three categories of activities that will need to be defined by some unit of measure. These are services, equipment, and supplies sold and equipment rented.

Physical therapists use a variety of ways to define units of measure. Possible activity-based units for measuring services include visits, procedures, or a course of treatment. Occasionally, activity-based units will be further defined by the total number of units provided. When this approach is used the customer may be charged a different price for initial and additional units of service. Time-based units are based on some increment of time. Often a 15-minute increment will be used. The current trend is toward selection of a unit of measure for services that is time-based. This trend is most likely related to the fact that the greatest expense of providing any type of physical therapy service is professional salaries. The use of a time-based unit of measure allows for monitoring of staff productivity.

Units of measure for supplies and equipment sold vary with the item. Items can come prepackaged or they might require adjustment or modification. The cost of supplies may be included in the cost of a procedure or be a separate charge. In the authors' experience, prepackaged equipment sold to patients is sold as an item with the price proportionally related to its cost to the organization. Supplies that are required for the delivery of a treatment, have a low per treatment cost, and whose cost cannot be easily allocated to individual treatments are included as part of the treatment cost. An example of this would be the antibacterial additives that might be used in a sterile hydrotherapy procedure. Supplies that are used to make something for a specific patient, have a high cost, and whose cost can be easily allocated to an individual treatment are assigned a specific unit of measure and billed as a separate charge. An example of this type of supply would be the casting and fabrication materials used in a serial casting or splinting procedure.

Units of measure for equipment rental are generally time based. The time increment varies by rental item but generally reflects the average amount of time the equipment is used or longer periods of time such as a week or a month.

Units of measure will vary greatly from one organization to another. There are a number of factors that should influence the choice of which unit of measure to adopt. First, the unit of measure should represent a logical increment of service or goods. An item that comes in packages of two and is always used in pairs should be sold as a pair. If all of the services provided to a patient are not billed as a single charge, they should be subdivided by different activities or in standard increments of time. Second, the unit of measure should be such that the cost associated with its production can be calculated accurately. This will be essential to setting prices and budgeting expenses. Third, units of measure should be standardized within an organization for like goods and services. If physical therapy services were measured by time increment and occupational therapy services were measured by procedure, it would be very confusing to patients who use both services. It would also make comparisons between these similar departments very difficult for management. Finally, when selecting units of measure an organization should consider what their competitors are using. Adopting like units of measure will enhance communication with customers who compare prices and will allow for comparisons between like services provided by different organizations.

Price Setting for Physical Therapy Goods and Services

The selling price of goods or services is based in the unit of measure selected. Price setting is an important decision-making process. The goal of the price-setting process is to set prices at a level that will maximize the difference between total expenses and total revenue. Although this might sound simple enough, in fact it can be very complicated. The complications arise from the interdependence among price, volume of sales, cost of goods and services, and income from sales. Price very often influences the number of units of services or goods sold. It always influences the income per unit of goods or services. The volume sold influences the cost of producing a unit of goods and services. The difference between the price and the cost of producing a unit is the net income. If the price causes a decrease in sales volume, the cost of producing a unit of goods or services will most likely increase and the income per unit will decrease.

The interdependence of these factors can be demonstrated through the use of a hypothetical, but not impossible, example. IPT, Inc. spent $4,000.00 to purchase hydrotherapy equipment. They anticipated providing 400 hydrotherapy treatments per year for the 10-year life of the equipment. If their predictions were correct, the equipment cost per treatment would be $1.00 [$4,000.00 − (400 × 10)]. Their labor, supplies, and other related costs equaled $10.00. They decided to charge $25.00 for a hydrotherapy procedure. At that charge they anticipated a $14.00 (+ 127%) profit per procedure! After a year it was realized that the original predictions had been optimistic. A competing physical therapy service was providing hydrotherapy treatment for $18.00 and that service was getting all of the hydrotherapy referrals. IPT, Inc. had provided only 20 hydrotherapy procedures and there was no indication that utilization would increase in subsequent years. At that rate, the equipment cost per treatment would be $20.00 [$4000.00 − (20 × 10)] and the total cost per treatment would be $30.00. At a charge of $25.00 per treatment, IPT, Inc. would be losing $5.00 (− 17%) per treatment. A wiser pricing decision may have resulted in a better outcome.

Pricing Strategies

There are many pricing strategies that organizations use to maximize income. When selecting a price setting strategy there are a number of factors to consider: first, the cost of producing the goods or service to be sold; second, the revenue required per unit to meet expenses and achieve a net income; third, the organization's capacity to produce units of goods and service; fourth, competitors' prices; and, finally, the effect of price on consumption of the product. It will be helpful to keep these factors in mind during the following review of pricing strategies commonly used by health care organizations.

Cost Plus Pricing.   In this approach the price setting simply takes the total expenses associated with the production of a product plus the desired net income and divides by the projected volume of units sold to arrive at the selling price per unit. Although commonly used, this method has some drawbacks. It relies on the organization's ability to accurately calculate the cost of producing a unit of a good or service. This is particularly difficult in service organizations. The cost plus method ignores both competitors' prices and the perceived value of the product. As a result, a product could be overpriced or underpriced.

Market Share Pricing.   This approach to price setting is often used by new businesses. Under this method, the price is set low to attract high volumes of sales. The immediate result is a low per unit income. The goal is to achieve a high total income by selling more units of product. To effectively use the method, an organization must be able to support operations at a low income level until a high sales volume is achieved.

Going Rate Pricing.   This approach to setting prices seeks to keep prices at the average levels charged by the industry and/or competitors. This is a common strategy among health care providers. This approach ignores the individual organization's costs and income requirements and pays sole attention to external factors.

Capitation Pricing.   This approach to price setting is gaining in popularity in the health care industry. Under capitation pricing, the organization sets a price for goods or services that might be delivered to a customer or a group of customers during a specific period of time. The amount charged is based on projections of probable utilization and cost of goods or services during that period. If the utilization is lower than expected, the organization will make a higher income. If the utilization is higher than expected, the organization may break even or experience a loss. This method requires that an organization be able to accurately project both its costs and potential utilization to be successful.

When making pricing decisions, the organization must be mindful of the requirements of the Robinson-Patman Act. This act prohibits charging different prices to comparable customers unless the price differences are based on ". . . differences in the cost of manufacture, sale or delivery resulting from the differing methods or quantities in which commodities are to such purchasers sold or delivered" (4). Simply put, price differences must be based on real cost differences.

Fee Schedules for Physical Therapy

In physical therapy practice prices for goods and services are usually set forth in a fee schedule. The fee schedule is a list of all possible goods and services which could be sold by a particular physical therapy department or practice. Example 5.8 gives examples of the types of charges that might be included on a typical physical therapy fee schedule. Note that the fee schedule includes a description of the charges, the charge for each good or service, and a numeric code for each charge. This numeric code is essential to automation of the billing system. Price differences between customers for the same unit of good or service are provided in the form of discounts off standard charges listed on the fee schedule (4).

Forecasting Volumes of Sales

Sales volume forecasting is a process of predicting how many units of goods or services an organization will sell during a specific period of time. Sales volume forecasting is done whenever an organization develops an annual budget or plans to start a new activity. To predict future sales an organization must rely on indicators of future conditions that may affect the demand for the goods or services in question. Commonly used indicators include past experience, changes in service area demographics, economic conditions, competitors' activities, current market share, and

EXAMPLE 5.8
Schedule of Charges

<table>
<tr><td colspan="3" align="center">**Physical Therapy Department**
Schedule of Charges</td></tr>
<tr><td>Code</td><td>Description</td><td>Charge per Unit</td></tr>
<tr><td>47001</td><td>Evaluation/15 min.</td><td>$30.00</td></tr>
<tr><td>47002</td><td>Individual treatment/15 min.</td><td>25.75</td></tr>
<tr><td>47003</td><td>Group treatment/15 min.</td><td>16.00</td></tr>
<tr><td>47004</td><td>Ultrasound/15 min.</td><td>15.60</td></tr>
<tr><td>47005</td><td>Hot packs/15 min.</td><td>15.60</td></tr>
<tr><td>47006</td><td>Electric stimulation/15 min.</td><td>26.40</td></tr>
<tr><td>47007</td><td>Traction—cervical/15 min.</td><td>20.00</td></tr>
<tr><td>47401</td><td>TENS rental/week</td><td>15.00</td></tr>
<tr><td>47402</td><td>Wheelchair rental/week</td><td>35.00</td></tr>
<tr><td>47501</td><td>Home traction unit</td><td>56.00</td></tr>
<tr><td>47502</td><td>Crutches—auxiliary</td><td>45.00</td></tr>
<tr><td>47503</td><td>Ace wrap—3 in.</td><td>20.00</td></tr>
<tr><td>47504</td><td>Velcro—wide/inch</td><td>1.30</td></tr>
<tr><td>47505</td><td>Cast material/ankle</td><td>150.00</td></tr>
</table>

planned marketing activities. An organization should also try to anticipate changes which might affect internal operations and the ability to meet demand for services. This is particularly important in physical therapy practice where chronic manpower shortages may make it impossible or impractical to meet all of the demands for service. Once forecasted, total sales volume can be multiplied by the charges for goods and services on the fee schedule to forecast total revenue for the budget period.

EXPENSE BUDGETS

Expenses represent the amount of money spent by an organization to produce goods and services during a specific period of time. In order to accurately project expenses to be incurred in the future, an organization must estimate the volume of future sales for the period and it must be able to project the cost of producing a unit of good or service during the same time period. Cost projection requires a good understanding of both the types and the characteristics of different expenses. Expenses can be classified into two types. These are operating expenses and capital expenses. Both types of expenses can be related to the production of an organization's goods and services. Operating expenses can be related to the day to day operation of the organization. Salaries and supplies are examples of operating expenses. Capital expenses are associated with the purchase of large items which will be utilized over an extended period of time. Capital expenses are generally related to the purchase of equipment, buildings, and land which will be used to produce a good or service. Operating and capital budgets are usually prepared separately. Expenses can also be characterized by the way they respond to changes in organizational activity. Based on their response to activity level, they can be classified as variable, semi-variable, or fixed. Expenses can also be directly or indirectly related to the production of a specific unit of goods or services. Large organizations are also divided into segments for the purposes of preparing operating expense budgets. Segments of a large organization that incur expenses are referred to as cost centers.

Operating Expense Budget

The foundation of the operating budget is the chart of expense accounts. An organization will develop a chart of expense accounts to categorize projected and actual expenses. Each type of expenditure will be consistently assigned to a specific expense account. Example 5.7 represents a chart of expenses that might be used by a physical therapy practice. When physical therapy is one of many services provided by a larger organization (i.e., a department of a hospital), the chart of expenses used to budget for the future and monitor actual expenditures will be much shorter. It is likely to reflect only those expense accounts over which the department manager has direct control.

Salary and Benefits Budget.   The provision of physical therapy services and related goods is labor intensive. This means that salary and benefit expenses account for a major portion of total operating expenses. Accurate calculation of salary and benefit expenses is key to successful budgeting in physical therapy practice. Salary budgets are usually calculated on the basis of full time equivalent (FTE) positions. An FTE represents the equivalent of one 40 hours per week position. A single FTE is equal to 2080 (40 hours per week × 52 weeks per year) man-hours per year. An FTE does not have to represent just one employee. It may represent two or more part-time positions. Important in the budgeting process is the number of man-hours that must be paid to produce the projected volume of revenue.

In its simplest form, the salary budget is calculated by multiplying the number of man-hours (FTEs) that are required by the hourly rate of pay. This can be represented by the equation:

$$\text{SALARY} = \text{MAN-HOURS PAID} \times \text{RATE OF PAY PER HOUR}$$

Because rate of pay varies by the type of job and by experience and/or seniority within the same job classification, these calculations should be done by individual employee or by job classification. When calculating salary cost by employee, the employee's actual or projected rate of pay is used as the base. When salary costs are calculated by job classification, the average of all pay rates of the employees in that classification is used as the base rate. Salary budgets should reflect projected salary increases. Salary budgets can be prepared for any increment of time. It is common to prepare salary budgets on a monthly and annual basis. This allows adjustments for seasonal trends. In practice, the terms salary budget and payroll budget are used interchangeably. Example 5.9 shows the annual salary budget for IPT, Inc. Note that salary costs are higher during summer months and during the month of December. This is due to the utilization of extra man-hours to replace employees who are absent on paid vacation time. IPT, Inc. uses job classifications to calculate salary costs. Methods for determining the number of FTEs required to meet projected demand for services are discussed under "Productivity."

Benefit expenses are determined by the type of benefits the organization will offer its employees. Benefits include costs related to providing

EXAMPLE 5.9
Monthly Salary Budget

Independent Physical Therapists, Inc.
Monthly Salary Budget
Fiscal Year 1999

FTE per Position	1	2	3	4	5	6	7	8	9	10	11	12
Manager	1.0	1.0	1.0	1.0	1.0	1.0	1.0	1.0	1.0	1.0	1.0	1.0
PT	2.0	2.0	2.0	2.0	3.0	3.0	3.0	3.0	3.0	2.0	2.0	3.0
PT Asst	1.0	1.0	1.0	1.0	1.	1.0	1.0	1.0	1.0	1.0	1.0	1.0
Aide	2.0	2.0	2.0	2.0	2.0	2.0	2.0	2.0	2.0	2.0	2.0	2.0
Clerk	1.0	1.0	1.0	1.0	1.0	1.0	1.0	1.0	1.0	1.0	1.0	1.0
Total	7.0	7.0	7.0	7.0	8.0	8.0	8.0	8.0	8.0	7.0	7.0	8.0

Salary per Position

	1	2	3	4	5	6	7	8	9	10	11	12
Manager	5,000	5,000	5,000	5,000	5,000	5,000	5,000	5,000	5,000	5,000	5,000	5,000
PT	6,667	6,667	6,667	6,667	10,000	10,000	10,000	10,000	10,000	6,667	6,667	10,000
PT Asst	2,083	2,083	2,083	2,083	2,083	2,083	2,083	2,083	2,083	2,083	2,083	2,083
Aide	2,500	2,500	2,500	2,500	2,500	2,500	2,500	2,500	2,500	2,500	2,500	2,500
Clerk	1,667	1,667	1,667	1,667	1,667	1,667	1,667	1,667	1,667	1,667	1,667	1,667
Total	17,917	17,917	17,917	17,917	21,250	21,250	21,250	21,250	21,250	17,917	17,917	21,250

Annual Salary Expense: $235,000

employees with paid time off, insurance, memberships, discounts on services or products, child care, education, entertainment, etc. The list of possible benefits is almost endless. The important point to keep in mind is that benefits may cost an organization 20 to 30% of total salary cost. When calculating the cost of manpower, benefit costs must be taken into consideration.

Capital Expense Budget

Capital expenses are associated with the purchase of equipment, buildings, and land. Expenses associated with the start-up of a new business or new venture of an existing business can also be classified as capital. Capital expenditures continue to contribute to the production of goods and services beyond the period of purchase. The exact definition of a capital expenditure varies between organizations. It is usually defined by some dollar amount. For example, any piece of equipment which costs over $200 will be considered a capital expenditure.

Calculation of Capital Expenditures. Capital cost includes more than the purchase price of an item. It could include capital lease costs for items purchased on installment, delivery costs, installation costs, and interest expenses if money had to be borrowed to make the purchase. It would also include the cost of any start-up training.

Depreciation of Capital Expenditures. Capital expenses are kept separate from operating expenses because of the way they are accounted for on the income statement. As you recall, the income statement presents both revenues and expenses for a specific period of time. The expense associated with a capital purchase will contribute to revenue produced in several periods of operation. To fairly evaluate the performance of an organization the expense of a capital purchase should be allocated across all of the periods it will effect. This is done through the use of depreciation.

Depreciation cost is the amount of capital expense which can be allocated to a specific operating period as an offset against revenue for that period. Depreciation costs can be calculated by dividing the total amount of the capital expenditure by the item's useful life. This can be represented by the equation:

$$\text{ANNUAL DEPRECIATION} = \frac{\text{CAPITAL EXPENSE}}{\text{USEFUL LIFE (YEARS)}}$$

Useful life is usually defined as a specific number of years. The annual depreciation cost is then listed as an expense each year during the capital item's useful life. At the end of its useful life an item is said to be fully depreciated. This is called the straight-line method for calculation of annual depreciation expenses. There are several other methods that an accountant might use to calculate depreciation.

The useful life of a specific capital item can be estimated using industry norms, manufacturer's guidelines, and past experience. In health care, the useful life of buildings and fixed equipment would range from 10 to 15 years. The useful life of movable equipment would range from 5 to 10 years. Small tools have a useful life of about 2 years.

Evaluation of Capital Expenditures. Capital expenditures usually require the long-term commitment of significant financial resources. Often, because of limited financial resources, an organization will have to choose between or prioritize capital expenditures. There are two methods that are frequently used to evaluate the future contribution of potential capital expenditures. The first is payback period. Payback period is the length of time required to recover the entire cost of a capital investment from the annual net cash flow which results from the investment. The shorter the payback period, the better the investment. Net cash flow refers to income after related operating expenses have been covered (1). Payback period can be represented by the equation:

$$\text{PAYBACK PERIOD (YEARS)} = \frac{\text{AMOUNT TO BE INVESTED}}{\text{PROJECTED ANNUAL NET CASH FLOW}}$$

The second method is rate of return on average investment (ROI). This is the average net income from an investment expressed as a percentage of the average amount invested. ROI can be represented by the following equations:

Step 1

$$\text{AVERAGE INVESTMENT} = \text{ORIGINAL COST} \div 2$$

Step 2

$$\text{ROI (\%)} = \text{AVERAGE PROJECTED NET INCOME} \div \text{AVERAGE INVESTMENT}$$

In comparing alternative investments, the higher rate of return is better. The application of this method may be more easily understood in the context of personal finances. If choosing between two alternate savings accounts, one offering a 5.5% interest rate (rate of return) and the other offering a 6.5% interest rate, all other factors being equal, we will choose the savings account offering a 6.5% return. The use of this evaluation method allows an organization to make the same type of decision related to capital expenditures (1).

Cost Characteristics

Cost characteristics refer to the way costs respond to changes in the activity level of the organization. It also refers to how a specific cost can be related to the production of a specific good or service. When describing how a cost responds to changes in level of activity we refer to them as variable, semi-variable, or fixed. A cost can be either directly or indirectly related to the production of a specific unit of good or service. The understanding of cost characteristics and their application to the financial planning process allows a manager to relate the cost of producing a good or service to the revenue produced at any level of output. This is the foundation of flexible budgeting. The technique is often referred to a cost-volume-profit or breakeven analysis.

Variable Costs.   Any cost that increases or decreases in direct proportion to the volume of activity is a variable cost. In order to be variable with total volume, a cost must be constant on a per unit basis. In physical therapy practice, the cost of linen and labor are examples of variable costs. The costs of these resources are constant for the delivery of a specific treatment. The total cost of these resources increases or decreases with the number of treatments performed. For example, a modality treatment requires the use of one patient gown, two sheets, and four towels at a cost of $2.00 per treatment. To project the total linen cost for a period, you would multiply the projected number of modality treatments times the $2.00 per treatment cost. The more treatments provided, the greater the total cost. The per unit of treatment cost remains constant. Some resources are only available in preset increments. For example, labor may only be available by the hour or by the eight-hour day. In that case it is considered a step-variable cost. With step-variable costs the goal is to maximize the productivity at each step before adding more resources.

Semi-Variable Costs.   These are costs that are in part related to level of activity and in part based on some other factor such as time. Telephone service is a good example. There is a cost associated with having access to telephone service. There is an additional cost which results from the use of the accessible telephone service. Part of the cost would be incurred even if the telephone were never used. In a simplistic sense, the components of semi-variable cost can be looked upon as the cost of availability and the cost of usage.

Fixed Costs.   These are costs that remain unchanged despite changes in volume of activity. A cost is fixed when the total cost of the resource remains unchanged, but the per unit cost increases with decreases in level of activity and decreases with increases in level of activity. The cost of

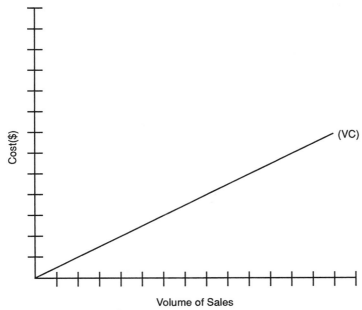

Figure 5.1.   Variable costs (VC).

air conditioning is a good example of a fixed cost. If it costs $10.00 per hour to air condition the physical therapy department and 10 units of service are produced every hour, the cost per unit is $1.00. If 20 units of service are produced every hour then the cost per unit drops to $0.50. If the activity level drops to 5 units of service per hour, then the cost per unit increases to $2.00. Fixed costs can be committed for long periods or discretionary on an annual basis. Committed fixed costs include investments in land, buildings, and equipment. Discretionary fixed costs are related to annual decisions to spend in certain areas. Discretionary fixed costs may be adjusted in times of financial crisis.

These cost characteristics can be presented graphically. Figures 5.1, 5.2, and 5.3 display the responses of the various cost characteristics to increases in level of activity. Figure 5.4 presents the interaction of these different types of costs as parts of the total cost of producing goods and services. Total cost can be represented by the equation:

$$\text{TOTAL COST} = \text{FIXED COST} +$$

$$\text{VOLUME (VARIABLE COST)}$$

For the purposes of calculation semi-variable costs are divided into their fixed and variable components.

Cost-Volume-Profit Analysis.   The cost-volume-profit analysis relates cost to revenue. In doing so, this analysis can be used to assess the impacts of varying levels of activity (volume) on net income and the relationship of per unit revenues (price) to cost. Figure 5.5 graphically presents the components of cost-volume-profit analysis. Note that a line representing total revenue has been added. Point A on the graph represents

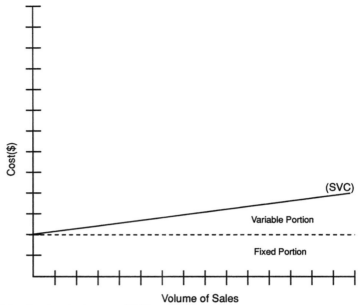

Figure 5.2.   Semi-variable costs (*SVC*).

the breakeven point, the point at which total cost equals total revenue. At breakeven, profit and loss equal zero. An increase in volume will result in a profit from operations. A decrease in volume of activity will result in a loss from operations. If volume is below the breakeven point and can not be increased, the organization will need to decrease costs or increase prices to avoid a net loss from operations (8).

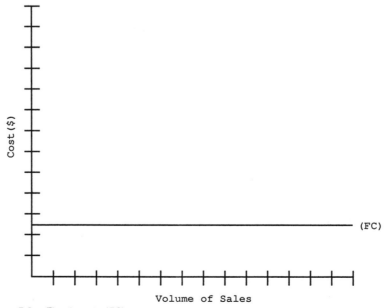

Figure 5.3.   Fixed costs (*FC*).

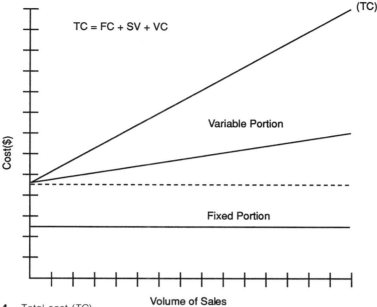

TC = FC + SV + VC

(TC)

Variable Portion

Fixed Portion

Cost($)

Volume of Sales

Figure 5.4. Total cost (*TC*).

Direct and Indirect Costs. Costs that are directly associated with the production of a unit of good or service are called direct costs. Costs that must be incurred in the production of an organization's goods and services but cannot be directly related to the production of a specific unit of goods or service are called indirect costs. Direct costs are generally easy to identify. For a physical therapy practice the cost of salaries for professional staff, treatment supplies, treatment equipment, or education would

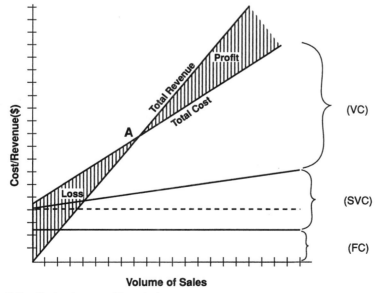

Cost/Revenue($)

Total Revenue

Profit

Total Cost

A

Loss

(VC)

(SVC)

(FC)

Volume of Sales

Figure 5.5. Cost-volume-profit analysis.

EXAMPLE 5.10
Quarterly Cash Budget

Independent Physical Therapists, Inc. Quarterly Cash Budget, Fiscal 1999				
	9-30-98	12-31-98	3-31-99	6-30-99
Beginning Balance	$26,000	$36,000	$33,000	$32,500
Sources of Cash				
Operations	13,000	14,000	15,000	13,000
Accounts receivable	90,000	92,000	94,000	97,000
Total Sources of Cash	129,000	142,000	142,000	142,500
Uses of Cash				
Purchase equipment	5,000	3,000	–	–
Accounts payable	23,000	23,000	23,000	23,000
Payroll	62,500	65,000	67,000	63,000
Owner withdrawal	–	15,000	15,000	15,000
Miscellaneous	2,500	3,000	4,500	3,000
Total Uses of Cash	93,000	109,000	109,500	104,000
Estimated Cash Balance	$36,000	$33,000	$32,500	$38,500

be considered direct costs. Indirect costs can be more difficult to identify. If physical therapy services are provided as part of a larger organization, indirect costs might include the organization's administration, building and utilities, housekeeping, and marketing services. Indirect costs are allocated to the cost of producing a specific unit of goods or service. The basis for allocation may be volume of activity, square footage of space, or any other basis that the organization chooses to select. In a small private practice all of the costs could be classified as direct.

CASH FLOW BUDGET

The cash flow budget will demonstrate how an organization's cash resources are projected to change during the budget period. It does this by projecting the timing for both increases and decreases in cash levels. It presents these changes by source and use of cash over time. A cash budget is used to ensure that available cash will meet cash requirements during the budget period. Example 5.10 is the cash budget for fiscal 1999. In this example, cash flow is budgeted on a quarterly basis. It is not unusual for cash flow to be budgeted on a weekly or biweekly basis to correspond to the payroll cycle. This is done because, in a labor-intensive organization, payroll accounts for the greatest outlay of cash resources, and the inability to meet payroll requirements could seriously hurt an organization.

PRODUCTIVITY

The topic of productivity has gained much attention in the health care industry since the advent of reimbursement changes designed to control the cost of health care. Productivity can be defined as the ratio between the amount or cost of resources used to the resulting amount or value of the output produced using those resources. In the health care environment the output might be defined as a patient day, a treatment, a dose, etc. These are the same measures that organizations use to define their goods and services for sale to clients. The concept of productivity can be applied to any resource used by an organization to produce its output of goods and services. Organizations routinely monitor the productivity of such resources as cash, supplies, physical plant facilities, and, of course, man-hours. If the amount of output increases relative to the amount of input then we can say that there has been an increase in productivity.

There are several ways that the productivity of a given resource can be increased. For example, the layout of a treatment area will impact on the amount of output a physical therapist can produce. The more efficient the layout, the more treatments a physical therapist can provide. If as a result of modifications in treatment area layout a physical therapist can produce more units of service, then their productivity has increased. The same concept can be applied to documentation procedures. If through the use of standardized evaluation and treatment forms a therapist will spend less time in documentation and as a result they can produce more units of direct patient treatment, then their productivity will be increased.

The productivity of a resource can also be increased through increased use of other resources. It usually takes more than one resource to produce a given output. For example, the provision of physical therapy treatment requires the input of several types of personnel, supplies, equipment, and space. If a shortage of equipment is limiting the amount of treatment a physical therapist can provide, then the addition of treatment equipment will increase the productivity of the physical therapist. If a treatment area is underutilized, the addition of a physical therapist providing treatment in the treatment area will increase the productivity of the area. Finally, an increase in knowledge or technology might also result in the increased productivity of a resource. Automation of data collection and analysis following patient evaluation would save the therapist time and result in increased productivity (9).

Productivity measurement related to the use of human resources is referred to as labor productivity. Because the provision of physical therapy is labor intensive, labor productivity is of great concern to physical therapy managers and clinicians alike. A labor productivity system which sets standards and monitors productivity has several purposes. It can be used as a tool for management of employee performance. The use of a productivity standard provides for a shared understanding of performance expectations. A productivity system can be used as a basis for assessment of the efficiency of an organization or segment of an organization. Productivity standards can provide data regarding staff requirements. Productivity monitoring can be used to demonstrate the impacts of workload on quality of service. Productivity standards are also used to determine the costs and prices of output.

The goal of any organization is to maximize the productivity of its resources while maintaining the quality of its output. In the health care industry the following factors may act to constrain an organization's ability to increase labor productivity.

1. Technological constraints. These are inefficiencies which are created by the physical plant and equipment that are used to deliver service. If, in our previous example, the inefficient treatment space layout could not be improved then productivity could not be increased.
2. Constraints related to the operating structure of the traditional large health care institution. Because the exact type and volume of client service needs cannot be predicted in advance, a stand-by capacity to provide services may be required. These are resources that are consumed without generating output.
3. Ideological constraints on increasing labor productivity. Health care workers hold traditional beliefs about how health care services should be delivered. It can be very difficult to increase productivity by changing service delivery patterns. This is especially true if the required change runs counter to these traditional beliefs.
4. Professional constraints that limit labor productivity. Professional constraints come from a variety of sources: licensure laws, accreditation standards, and professional associations. These constraints are designed to ensure the quality of health care services. In doing so, they restrict an organization's control over how and by whom many health care services are delivered (10).

Labor Productivity Standards for Physical Therapy

Productivity standards establish the expected ratio of input of resources to output of goods and services. Use of a productivity standard requires that an organization be able to measure its use of a resource and relate it to the output of a good or service. This can be done by measuring input and output in terms of dollars. A labor productivity standard using dollars would relate the cost of salaries and benefits to the revenue produced. For example, an organization might expect to produce $2.00 of revenue for every $1.00 of cost. The productivity standard would be 200%. Labor productivity can also be measured in terms of time. A labor productivity standard using time would relate the man-hours worked or man-hours paid to the amount of output produced. This is most effective when the amount of output is also measured in terms of time. For example, if the service were sold by units of time such as 15-minute increments a physical therapy department could have a productivity standard of 70% of man-hours worked. This would mean that 42 minutes of every hour worked or 5 hours and 36 minutes of every 8-hour shift should be spent in the provision of client services. Time not spent providing patient care would be spent preparing for clients, documentation, communication, meetings, and other necessary activities. The difference between hours worked and hours paid are all of the hours for which an employee would be paid but not available for work. This would include vacation time, personnel time, holidays, and sick time. It might include time for activities like educational seminars. The use of hours paid relates productivity to the total cost of the resource. The use of hours worked relates productivity to the use of resources which are actually available for the production of goods and services.

The authors are unaware of any specific standards of productivity that are widely accepted or used in the practice of physical therapy. This is most likely due to the different factors which influence productivity and are also specific to the individual organization. To set productivity standards which are specific to the organization the physical therapy manager can choose from three methods. First, if the data base exists, the manager can use information about past operations to establish expectations for future performance. This method assumes that there has been little change in operation over time. It also assumes that past productivity has been at an acceptable level. Second, the manager can use time studies. Time studies measure and evaluate actual practice. Based on the outcome of time studies, practice can be modified and standards set to maximize productivity. Third, when no historical or current information exists, such as in the start-up of a new practice, the manager must estimate standards. The estimated standards would be evaluated and revised as soon as actual operating information is available.

Using Productivity Standards to Calculate Staff Requirements

Once established, productivity standards should be used in the calculation of staff requirements. The steps necessary to arrive at the number of FTEs are presented in Example 5.11 using IPT, Inc. as the information source.

Example 5.11 demonstrates the use of productivity standards in the context of a simple staffing situation. Staffing decisions become more complex when decisions need to be made regarding skill mix of personnel. In our example the use of a physical therapist assistant was not considered feasible. The unexpected absence of the physical therapist would have resulted in a halt in operations. In a larger setting the use of less expensive personnel to increase the productivity of more expensive personnel should be a consideration. In making skill mix decisions the physical therapy manager should weigh the need for flexibility against potential cost savings. A physical therapist can, if needed, perform all of the job duties of an assistant or aide. The use of a physical therapist offers maximum flexibility at a maximum cost. An aide can only perform duties which can be learned from on-the-job training within the restrictions established by legal and professional constraints. The use of an aide offers minimum flexibility at a minimum cost.

SUMMARY

The essential financial information a physical therapist manager or entrepreneur would need to understand and respond to has been discussed from several perspectives. The two most important reasons for dealing with financial information are to guide decisions within an organization and to present the financial status to external entities.

Since physical therapy is a labor-intensive business, productivity becomes an important consideration in the operation of a department. How to establish the appropriate number of FTEs was discussed in detail along with how to determine the appropriate mix of professional and nonprofessional staff members.

EXAMPLE 5.11
Calculation of Physical Therapy Staff Requirements

Staff Requirements for IPT, Inc.

Assumptions
1. A unit of service (UOS) represents 15 minutes of billable service.
2. Projected annual volume of service is 16,000 UOS with delivery evenly distributed throughout the 306 days of operation.
3. Hours of operation are 7 AM to 5 PM (10 hours/day).
4. IPT, Inc.'s productivity standard for physical therapists is 70% billable client care to 30% other activity based on time worked. This equals 2.8 UOS produced for every man-hour worked.

Five-Step Calculation Process

Step One: Total Hours of Operation
306 Days of Operation × 10 Hours of Operation/Day = 3060 Hours of Operation/Year

Step Two: UOS Delivered per Hour of Operation
16,000 UOS/Year ÷ 3060 Hours of Operation/Year = 5.2 UOS/Hour of Operation.

Step Three: Physical Therapist (PT) Hours Worked per Hour of Operation
5.2 UOS Delivered per Hour of Operation (Assumption 4) ÷ 2.8 UOS Produced per Hour Worked = 1.9 PT Hours Worked per Hour of Operation.[a]

Step Four: PT Man-Hours Worked Required per Year
3060 Hours of Operation × 2.0 Man-Hours/Hour of Operation = 6120 Man-Hours Worked per Year

Step Five: Man-Hours Paid per Year
IPT, Inc. provides all employees with a benefit package which includes 232 hours of paid time off. This includes time for vacation, holidays, education days, and sick time. That means for every full time equivalent (FTE) of 2080 hours there are 1848 (89%) hours worked.

6120 Man-Hours Worked ÷ 89% (Percentage of Hours Paid) = 6876 Hours Paid

To convert total hours paid to total FTEs, divide 6876 hours paid by 2080 hours (one FTE). In this example 3.31 FTEs are needed to provide the projected 16,000 UOS.

---

[a]Generally therapists can only be hired for blocks of 4 hours. Therefore, a clinic will need to pay for more man-hours than it actually requires.

CASE STUDY 5.1
Productivity and Salary Budgeting

Good As New Rehabilitation Center (GNRC)

GNRC is planning to open a new sports medicine center. During the first year GNRC projects that the center will treat 250 patients. They expect to provide an average of twenty 60-minute physical therapy treatments per referral. Service volume should build steadily throughout the first year. The projected volume of patients served for the first, second, third, and fourth quarters are 25, 50, 75, and 100 respectively. GNRC uses the standard definition of an FTE to budget and monitor payroll. It has been decided that for the first year the center will require maximum flexibility from the staff of the sports medicine center. For that reason they will hire only physical therapists.

As the physical therapy manager, you have been asked to prepare a salary budget for physical therapists for the first year of the new center. To complete this budget, you must first determine the productivity standards upon which the budget will be based. GNRC uses time-based productivity standards.

After working out your own solutions see Appendix 5.1 to check your work.

CASE STUDY 5.2
Staff Planning: Skill Mix and Cost Implications

Middlesize Memorial (MM)

MM is a 300-bed acute care hospital located in Green Bay, Wisconsin. MM provides the only physical therapy service in the community. It offers both inpatient and outpatient services all in the same central location. The MM Physical Therapy Department provides

41,184 45-minute treatments annually. The department currently employs 30 FTE physical therapists. The average percentage of time paid but not worked, is 10%. A recent time study indicated that much of the work currently done by physical therapists could be performed by physical therapist assistants or by aides trained on the job. The time study indicated that the actual direct care productivity rate, based on hours worked, for the physical therapists was 55%. Of the remaining time, 10% was spent on clerical tasks, 10% was spent on prep and clean-up, and the remaining 25% was spent on indirect patient-related activities, meetings, phone calls, etc. From the time study it was also determined that an average of 20% of a direct treatment could have been provided by on-the-job trained aides under supervision of a physical therapist or physical therapist assistant. An additional 30% of a treatment could have been provided by a physical therapist assistant under the supervision of a physical therapist. The remaining 50% of a treatment required a physical therapist.

Within the limits of the information provided about the activities of MM's physical therapists you are asked to determine if there might be a more effective skill mix for this department. If the clerical staff is paid $7.50 per hour and the average hourly salary rates for a therapist, assistant, and aide are $15.00, $9.00, and $6.00, respectively, determine the cost savings which would result from implementation of your plan. (Hint: All positions do not have to have the same productivity standards. You will need to establish productivity rates for all positions which provide patient treatment. For guidance, refer to the section "Using Productivity Standards to Calculate Staff Requirements.")

When you complete your work, check Appendix 5.2 for feedback.

References

1. Pyle WW, White JA. Fundamental accounting principles. 7th ed. Homewood: Richard D. Irwin, 1975:2–14,786–788.
2. Simmons J. The accountant's role in setting-up in private practice. Physiotherapy 1987:73:622.
3. Meigs WB, Johnson CE, Meigs RF. Accounting: The basis for business decisions. New York: McGraw-Hill, 1977:15,773–798.
4. Garrison RH. Managerial accounting: Concepts for planning, control, decision making. Revised ed. Dallas: Business Publications, 1979:505,640–646.
5. Dillon LR, LaMont RR. Financial statement analysis. Clin Manage 1983;35(4):36–39.
6. Van Horne JC. Financial management and policy. 5th ed. Englewood Cliffs, NJ: Prentice-Hall, 1980:711–730.
7. Hicks LL, Bopp KD, Speck R. Forecasting demand for hospital services in an unstable environment. Nursing Econ 1987:5:304–310.
8. Sellers JH, Sellers JS. Profit planning and control for PTs. Clin Manage 1983:3(2):29–33.
9. Feldstein PJ. Productivity and effectiveness: An economist's viewpoint. Health Matrix 1985–86;Winter:19–23.
10. May JJ. Productivity—the human dimension. Health Matrix 1985–86;Winter:24–30.

CHAPTER **6**

Reimbursement and Documentation

OVERVIEW

Initial, interim, and discharge notes are written by all physical therapists. They are written to communicate pertinent information regarding a client's status, response to treatment, and changes over time. There are many potential readers of notes within a health care organization and external to it. Each reader has a particular focus. Two important external readers are representatives of third party payers and lawyers. The note may be read by a reviewer who will determine if payment will be made. In a court of law a note is taken as evidence of what was or was not done for a client. Since one note may be read by many individuals, there is need for a format that fosters the recording and reporting of important information. Important information is that which is obtained by objective and reliable means. This chapter emphasizes use of a modified Subjective-Objective Assessment Plan (SOAP) note format for reporting clinical information. The use of subjective and objective information in a note is discussed. Two case studies are presented which give the reader opportunities to assess and improve upon existing notes based on the concepts presented in the chapter.

Introduction

A document is "a written or printed paper bearing the original, official, or legal form of something that can be used to provide decisive information" . . . , proof or support of a claim (1). Documentation is a

127

Table 6.1.
Purposes of Documentation (2)

Accountability
Appraisal of quality of care
Communication
Education
Improve care
Legal protection
Management control
Motivation of client and staff
Reimbursement
Research
Third party payer requirement (frequency of notes, content requirements)

process involving systematic gathering of information, recording information in a synthesized form, organizing the synthesized information, and producing a document. Table 6.1 lists many of the purposes that have been expressed for documenting in the physical therapy clinical setting.

Two of these purposes, reimbursement and communication for physical therapy services, will be discussed in this chapter. The medical-legal aspects associated with documentation will be discussed later in Chapter 10.

Reimbursement
CLIENT ADMITTING PROCEDURES

Client care documentation begins when the client is admitted to care of a health care provider. At the point of admission the provider collects basic information about the client. Each health care organization will have in place a policy and procedure for the collection of patient demographic and insurance information as a part of the admitting procedure. Admitting policies and procedures should indicate what information shall be collected, who shall collect it, and how the information should be recorded.

During the admissions process, a client billing account is created. This account will be used to track and bill for all services provided to the client by the health care provider. It will be used to record payments received for services rendered. To facilitate billing, information about health care insurance is routinely collected when a client is admitted. Frequently, the client, or his/her guardian, is requested to sign a statement of financial responsibility. Through the statement of financial responsibility the client assumes ultimate responsibility for payment should his/her insurance fail to cover part or all of the services.

Information collected during the admissions process is used to open the institutional medical record. The institutional medical record contains client-related demographic, insurance, and clinical information. Table 6.1 lists many of the potential uses of the information contained in the client's medical record.

INSURANCE VERIFICATION

Often, health care providers will attempt to verify insurance coverage prior the the delivery of client services. In some cases, prior authorization or approval from the insurance carrier is required as a condition of payment. In other cases, insurance verification is performed as a customer service or out of self-protection. As a customer service, insurance verification helps the client determine the extent of personal financial responsibility for services to be rendered. This may assist them in making decisions about elective procedures or choosing between alternative care locations. As a self-protective mechanism, insurance verification allows the health care provider to comply with coverage requirements, determine financial risk, obtain up-front payments for noncovered services or from uninsured clients, make admission decisions, and otherwise plan to maximize the potential for payment.

Procedures for insurance verification vary between health care providers and between insurance carriers. Generally, it entails a call to the employer, the insurance carrier, or the authorized representative. Because there is little consistency in the way companies handle verification procedures, it can take several calls to obtain authorization. Clients can assist in the verification process by providing good insurance information. In some cases, insurance verification is not necessary because coverage criteria are published and given to clients and providers. This is the case with Medicare and, at times, other government-supported health care coverage programs.

The usual result of the verification procedure is an indication from the insurer that the service is covered under the terms of the client's policy. Insurance verification does not normally guarantee payment. Payment is dependent on availability of coverage, obtaining prior approval when necessary, proof of medical necessity, and delivery of the appropriate services. Proof of medical necessity and delivery are often established through review of clinical documentation from the medical record.

RELATIONSHIP BETWEEN DOCUMENTATION AND REIMBURSEMENT

Documentation in the medical record is the key to demonstrating that health care services were medically necessary, had a reasonable potential to result in significant improvement, and were provided as billed. Review of clinical documentation by payers is directed at these questions. Information is sought in objective terms. If objective information cannot be found in the medical record, the payer will refuse payment. Clearly, from the payer perspective, if it isn't documented, it wasn't done. For this reason, the content of the medical record should be aimed at providing necessary supporting information. Every item documented on the client's bill should have a counterpart in the clinical documentation. The clinical documentation should note why the service or product was provided, when it was provided, and the intended and, if possible, the actual outcome.

For services such as physical therapy, proof of delivery of services

INTERNAL READERS	EXTERNAL READERS
The writer at a later date	Third party payers
Physicians	Case managers
Staff PT coworkers	Physical therapists
PT supervisors	Other disciplines
Other health care disciplines	Accreditation reviewers
Quality assurance reviewers	Quality assurance reviewers
Students	Referral sources
Medical record technologists	Researchers
Researchers	Consumers
Clients	Friends of clients
Family members	Lawyers

Figure 6.1. Potential readership of a physical therapy document note.

is often documented through the use of per visit attendance records. These records record in chart form the date of service and the type of services provided. The therapist's signature or initials are used to verify entries. Other supporting information would be included in the evaluation and treatment documentation.

The cost of such through documentation is an often discussed issue. Health care providers are spending significant portions of their work day documenting. The cost of not documenting is clear. Services will be provided without compensation.

Documentation
WHO READS CLINICAL DOCUMENTS?

Among the responsibilities of every practicing physical therapist is to communicate the status of their clients to others. Periodic written, pictorial, and graphic descriptions of a client, the treatment program, and the responses to treatment are presented in clinical notes. While the term "note" indicates the basic purpose for its formation, to remind or to informally communicate, it does not reflect the other significant purposes a note can serve (2). We will use the word document preceding the word note. Using the terms "document note" together will serve to remind the writer of the scope of potential uses of this type of document. The most common audience for document notes are people within or internal to the health care organization. Other potential readers such as representatives of insurance companies who pay health care bills are outside of or external to the organization. Figure 6.1 identifies the usual as well as potential readership of a document note.

The preceding figure indicates a potentially extensive circulation of a document note. Such a varied readership means the content of the document note can be subjected to analysis from multiple points of view.

Third Party Payers

Someone other than the client receiving physical therapy services usually pays for the services. These payment sources include independent health plans, private insurance companies, and government health care programs. Collectively these payers are known as third party payers (3).

A common motivation of third party payers is to control health care costs (3-5). One method of controlling costs is to require documents which show that services:

1. Meet any nonmedical requirements of coverage;
2. Were ordered by a physician;
3. Were necessary based on clinical findings;
4. Required the skill of the provider;
5. Were performed as billed;
6. Had the potential to or did result in significant benefit.

This approach was adapted by the Health Care Financing Administration (HCFA), the governmental agency that oversees the Medicare program. Eventually, many private insurance companies followed suit and developed similar reimbursement requirements (3).

DOCUMENTS

For reimbursement, three documents are generally provided or requested. These documents are a written physician referral for physical therapy for a client, forms used to record special measurements, and notes. Reimbursement for covered physical therapy services under Medicare and Medicaid require physician referral. Depending on the state, a physician referral may be necessary to evaluate, or to treat, or to evaluate and treat any client. Regardless of state law, some private insurance companies pay for physical therapy services only if a physician referral for the service has been issued (6).

Standard Documents

In the information gathering phase of the clinical documentation process, standard forms are often used for recording and depicting measurements and observations (7–9). The information on these forms is part of the client's official medical record. Completed forms may be maintained in the client's departmental file, in the client's institutional record, or in both places. Any documentation used by external parties must be part of the institutional record. Copies of the institutional record may be requested for review by third party payers and others authorized by the client (Fig. 6.1).

Initial Document Note

An initial physical therapy document note describes the status of a client as seen through the eyes of the therapist before treatment is initiated. Many authors have stressed the importance of taking the time to do a thorough initial examination of the client (2, 9, 10) which includes taking measurements with reliable measurement methods (11, 12). Without complete and reliable initial status data, development of an appropriate treatment plan to meet the client's needs is unlikely. Later, making an accurate appraisal of the early effects of treatment can be hindered, if not made impossible, because of an incomplete initial examination. The same problem is encountered when attempting to appraise the overall effect of treatment. Objective data required to compare the initial status data with the

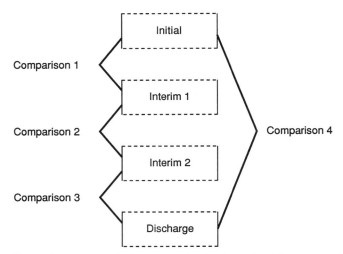

Figure 6.2. Comparisons are made in document notes throughout the course of treatment. Some therapists write the discharge document much like an interim document and make comparisons between the final status and the preceding interim document (*Comparison 3*). Others make a beginning-to-end comparison between the initial status at admission and the final status at discharge (*Comparison 4*).

findings at discharge may be unavailable. Figure 6.2 shows the relationships among the three types of document notes over time.

Interim Document Note

Notes written after the initial note and before the discharge note are interim document notes. Since clients can improve, show no change, or regress, we agree with those who have substituted the name interim note for what has commonly been called a progress note (12). Interim document notes focus on changes that have occurred since the preceding note was written. The preceding note could be the initial or another interim document note. Any change in the client's condition that results in a change in the existing treatment plan is an indication for a reassessment of the client and the production of the next interim document note. In the case of Medicare, the frequency of interim documents is mandated. They must be done daily, at two-week, or monthly intervals depending on the location of care and the type of coverage. For example, Medicare requires home care physical therapy documentation for each therapist visit. The same measurement tools, measurements, and methods should be used throughout the course of treatment. This will allow readers to make meaningful judgments about the achievement of treatment goals at various measurement intervals.

Discharge Document Note

The final written document is the discharge document note. Comparisons are made between the initial and final status of the client (2) as well as with the most current interim document note (12). The discharge document note includes a description of the overall changes achieved as a result of treatment provided throughout the course of therapy. The goals achieved are also listed within the discharge document note. Goals that were not achieved are discussed including the reason(s) for nonachievement. The program at the time of discharge, copies of all educational materials given to the client, equipment list, and follow-up plans are all contained in the discharge document note. The discharge document note may be the only information available to physical therapists who provide continued treatment of the client at a later date. Clarity, exactness, and completeness of the physical therapy discharge document note can enhance continuity of treatment, reduce the need to repeat some examination procedures, and assist in setting realistic short-term goals.

DOCUMENTATION FORMAT
Problem-Oriented Documentation

Almost concurrent with the inception of the Medicare program, Weed (13, 14) developed a problem-oriented medical record (POMR)-keeping system. The key feature of the system was a focus on the client's identified problems. An essential part of the POMR system was a structure and rules for writing document notes. Problem-oriented clinical notes required gathering subjective information (information from a source other than the therapist) and objective information (measurements the therapist obtained during examination). From these two information categories the therapist made an assessment of the client. Within the assessment section of a note the therapist was encouraged to analyze the problem, draw conclusions, and make other professional judgments (10, 12, 15). The assessment was followed by a treatment plan to deal with the identified problem (14).

Subjective-Objective Assessment Plan (SOAP) Documentation Format

The problem-oriented note format gained popularity as an entity separate from the POMR system. The format became known as the SOAP note format (S = subjective, O = objective, A = assessment, P = plan). Pressure for accountability from third party payers was a stimulus which enhanced the popularity of this format with therapists. The organizational guidance provided by the SOAP format for examinations and writing document notes was readily adaptable to any category of client. It is currently believed that the SOAP format is the most common document note-writing format in use (12, 15, 16). This popularity makes it likely that third party payer representatives who review document notes have become familiar with this format. Reviewers may have some expectations about what and where specific information should be contained in a document note. For additional information on SOAP note concepts specifically for physical therapists the reader may consult Refs. 2, 10, 12, and 15.

Subjective and Objective Information and Measurements. Information listed in a document note as subjective and objective can vary among facilities (12). The use of subjective information in a document note has also been questioned. It has been suggested that a document should focus on OAP because subjective data is not reliable. Furthermore, it has been stated that HCFA may not consider subjective information to be meaningful. Starting a note with this kind of information may unfavorably bias a reviewer (9). These arguments are intuitively sound because they relate to a strategy for enhancing payment for services. There is, however, another perspective on subjective information that tempers the preceding arguments. The important consideration regarding the usefulness of data for decision making should not simply be if it is classified as subjective or objective data (11). The major consideration should be whether or not a reliable objective means of measurement was used to collect the data. Subjective variables measured by reliable and objective means can produce data from which to draw reasonable conclusions. To confuse the issue even more, the usual interpretation of what is subjective information in the context of a SOAP note does not always meet the reliable and objective requirements stated above. And, some data often listed under the objective category, i.e., some manual muscle test grades, are subjective data.

The client, everyone related to client care, and third party payers would be better served if unreliable subjective data were not included in a document note. However, there simply is not a sufficient array of clinically usable reliable measurement tools to objectively measure most of the pertinent subjective variables therapists consider useful (16). Currently there is strong encouragement for greater client involvement in treatment planning to enhance participation in and compliance with therapeutic activities (17). Subjective information such as the client's interests, goals, and perceptions as well as useful opinions of other individuals can all contribute insights into how to individualize treatment plans. We suggest that, rather than eliminate subjective information from the SOAP format document notes, the subjective section should be subdivided into two parts: one part for subjective information from the client and other sources and the other part for subjective but reliable measurements. Subjective measurements are measurements which require client or therapist interpretation or judgment (18). Such measurements have degrees of agreement between various therapists. Examples include developmental level assessments, amount of tone present, and capsular tightness. Example 6.1 is a general model using a modified SOAP format which incorporates the divided subjective section based on the preceding definition of subjective measurements.

Table 6.2 contains a list of common measurement methods dichotomized into subjective and objective measurement categories. This table is intended to clarify which reliable measurements we would place in the subjective category and which would be categorized as objective. These distinctions are consistent with measurement concepts applied to research (18).

Document Note Summary

This section on documentation shows that there are many potential readers of a document note. Every reader has a bias and is looking for something in particular. Usually, only one document note is written for all potential readers. For the sake of organization a modified SOAP format was presented. Because of its widespread use, the SOAP format is familiar to experienced third party reviewers. Using this format may facilitate reading the note because certain information should be found in specific sections.

EXAMPLE 6.1
Contents of a General Modified SOAP Format Document

Identification and Demographic Information

Client's name:
Facility name:
Physician's name:
Primary diagnosis:
Secondary diagnosis:
Payment source/insurance information:
Responsible party/client's agent:
Home address and phone number(s):

Clinical Information

Discipline writing note:
Type of note (initial, interim, discharge):
Date:
Past history:
History of current illness/injury:
Referral information:
Other pertinent information:

Subjective Information

From third parties:
   Client interview
   Family interview
   Other care givers
Therapist measurements:
   (see Table 6.2 for examples of subjective measurements)

Objective Information

Therapist measurements:
   Organized by physiological systems/anatomical areas
   (see Table 6.2 for examples of objective measurements)

Therapist Assessment

Analysis of subjective and objective information:
Conclusions based on the above information:
Identified problems listed:
Short-term goals listed:
   Estimate of time to achieve, quality, frequency, etc.
Long-term goals listed:
   Estimate of time to achieve
Potential for achieving stated goals:

Plan of Care

Treatment for each problem identified:
   Parameters of treatment (frequency, intensity, duration)
Referrals to other health care providers:
Instructions/recommendations given:
   To client
   To family
   To care givers
Follow-up plans:

Therapist's signature _____ Date _____

Physician's signature _____ Date _____

Table 6.2.
Categorization of Common Physical Therapy Measurement Variables for Modified SOAP Document Notes

Subjective Measurements	Variables	Objective Measurements
	Cognition	
Measurements dependent on written or verbal communication		Time to respond
		Number of correct performances
		Duration of attention
	Endurance	
Rating on perceived exertion scale		VO^2 maximum
Facial expression		EKG strip
Facial color		Respiratory rate
		Distance covered
	Function	
Minimal, moderate or maximal assistance		Time required to do activity
Percent of effort exerted		Frequency of activity
Quality of effort		Number of conditions the activity can be completed under
Score on functional abilities test		
	Range	
Visual approximations		Goniometric readings
		Chart recorder strips from various exercise devices
		Tape measurements
	Strength	
Manual muscle test grades above fair		Torque values from chart recorder strips of various exercise devices
		Hand dynamometer readings
		Repetitions completed
		Kilograms or pounds lifted

If the data-gathering process has been flawed, the treatment plan will be, to some extent, inappropriate. By striving to obtain appropriate data with reliable measurement methods a competent, conscientious therapist, who is consistent in taking measurements, can gather discriminating data, that is, data which allows comparisons and sound judgments to be made regarding the influence of treatment. Discriminating data presented clearly in a familiar format can facilitate reimbursement. Discriminating data is also the basis for research needed to validate the selection of specific physical therapy treatments to ourselves, third party payers, and others.

Can Documentation Interfere with Communication?

The answer is a definite yes. Consideration should be given to the purpose of clinical documentation. The purpose is to communicate meaningful information to the reader. There are several factors which can interfere with the physical therapist's ability to communicate through clinical documentation. Table 6.3 lists several of these factors.

Each of these factors in Table 6.3 can interfere with communication.

Table 6.3.
Common Factors Causing Communication Problems in Document Notes

Use of physical therapy terminology which is not readily interpreted by the non-physical therapist reader.

Use of abbreviations which are not universally understood.

Inclusion of excessive verbiage or information which is of no value to the reader.

Use of a format, or lack of consistent format, which sends the reader on an often unrewarding search for the desired information.

The resulting poor communication can impact on the quality of client care, negate the therapist's input into the client care process, or result in payment denials, all because the information contained in the documentation was not easily or quickly obtained or understood.

Table 6.4 presents suggestions to maximize the effectiveness of physical therapy document information for non-physical therapist reviewers.

Implementation of the preceding suggestions should increase the communication value of the physical therapist's documentation and, possibly, decrease the time spent documenting.

SUMMARY

Reimbursement for health care services is dependent on quality documentation by care providers. The health care organization

Table 6.4.
Suggestions to Enhance Communication with Non-Therapist Document Reviewers

- Whenever possible, eliminate the use of all but the most universally understood professional terminology and abbreviations. Even regionally acceptable terminology and abbreviations may cause problems as medical review often occurs in a different part of the country. If grades or ratings must be used, provide the norms or averages for comparison. This is most easily done through the use of preprinted charts and forms. Always provide an interpretation of clinical findings which will be meaningful to the non-physical therapist reader. Payers are most often interested in practical functional improvements that result from improvements in strength, coordination, etc.

- Avoid the use of long-winded narratives in favor of outlines, charts, and brief notes. The reader should be able to take in a maximum amount of pertinent information in a minimum amount of time.

- Repetition of information should be kept to a minimum. If previous information is needed for comparison, present the information in a side-by-side manner so it is easier to locate and compare.

- Be consistent in both the information provided and the format used. Response to services can only be judged if the same data variables are measured at intervals of care. Consistently using a format can facilitate the location of specific data elements during review and speed the documentation review process.

can facilitate the potential for timely reimbursement through the use of proper admitting procedures and insurance verification activities. Proof of medical necessity and delivery of billed services comes from the medical record. It is through comprehensive, concise, objective clinical documentation that these things are demonstrated.

CASE STUDY 6.1
Note Writing for Payer Review

But It Was All There!

Shirley Righteous, PT, was outraged when she received a payment denial on a 50-year-old client she had treated for a nonspecific shoulder problem which had caused both pain and dysfunction. Under Shirley's expert care, the client had made a good recovery and was able to return to all former activities. Physical therapy services were provided for a period of three months. The client's treatment had been on hold for a two-week period at the end of the first month due to a family emergency. The client had maintained her status during the interruption through the use of a home exercise program. The payer had denied coverage from the beginning of the second month of care. The denial was based on the payer's inability to determine what part, if any, of the treatment was medically appropriate and required the skills of a physical therapist. After a review of the client's medical record, Shirley felt certain that adequate supporting information had been provided. Shirley decided to call on the Utilization Review (UR) Committee of her State's APTA chapter for assistance. Shirley sent them a copy of the client's treatment attendance records and the following documentation.

The UR Committee recommended that she adopt a new documentation format. You have been asked to rewrite her treatment notes to help her understand the problem. Shirley was right, "it was all there, but . . .".

INITIAL EVALUATION

CLIENT: Nancy Nice
AGE: 50
DIAGNOSIS: Unspecified Shoulder Problem
REFERRAL: Evaluate and treat
DATE: May 15

This 50 yo female has been referred to physical therapy for evaluation and treatment of an unspecified shoulder problem which has resulted in pain and decreased function. The client reports that pain is at a level 8 severity and wakes her at night. Onset of this problem was two weeks ago. No specific incident leading to this problem can be identified. Client was moving furniture prior to onset.

Examination reveals tenderness to palpation on the apex of the shoulder. No discoloration or sign of external injury is evident. Shoulder flex is 0–160°. Client can elevate arm against gravity only with pain. Shoulder add and ext are WNL (B). Horz abd is painful throughout. Abd is 0–120° and painful. Shoulder ER is 0–25°, IR is WNL. Strength could not be evaluated due to pain. Appears to at least F. Muscle tenderness and spasm of (B) rhomboids, traps, cervical spinal muscles was noted.

Client reports that she is unable to perform usual household duties. She has some difficulty dressing, showering, and combing her hair.

Plan to see client 3 × per week for three weeks for ultrasound and therapeutic exercise. Goal is to decrease pain and restore ROM to previous level.

Shirley Righteous, PT

May 30
INTERIM NOTE
Nancy Nice

REIMBURSEMENT AND DOCUMENTATION

Treatment on hold. Client is in Chicago visiting her sister. Will resume treatment when she returns.

S.R., PT

June 15

INTERIM NOTE

Nancy Nice

Treatment restarted on this date. Client reports shoulder pain severity at a level 5. Minimal tenderness to palpation noted. ROM has improved by 5° to 10° in elevation. ER remains unchanged. Client responding well to treatment. Proceed as previously described.

S.R., PT

July 15

INTERIM NOTE

Nancy Nice

Client has been treated 3× per week since last note of June 15. She reports pain at a level 3 severity during the day which increases to a level 5 severity at night. Minimal tenderness to palpation at the apex of the shoulder is still evident. Shoulder ROM has improved 5° to 15° since initial evaluation. ROM deficits and pain continue to interfere with the performance of normal activity. Client performs home exercise program (HEP) independently. Continue as previously described.

S.R., PT

August 15

INTERIM NOTE

Nancy Nice

Client was treated 3× per week from July 15 through August 1st. Treatment frequency was reduced to 1× per week as of August 1st. As of this date, the client is pain free. Shoulder ROM is WFL. Patient has resumed all normal activities. She will continue on a HEP and notify this therapist in the event of further problems. No further treatment is indicated at this time. Client has been discontinued from therapy.

Shirley Righteous, PT

CASE STUDY 6.2
Write a Modified SOAP Format Document Note

Background

Farley Davidson is a 37 yo motorcycle repairman who was involved in a MVA 16 wks ago. He sustained left parietal, clavicle, humeral, rib, and femoral fractures. The humerus was fixed internally at Northwest Community by Dr. Cutter.

Farley has a unique tattoo on his left biceps which was marred in the accident and cut during surgery by Dr. Cutter. Farley, who is left-handed, could animate this tattoo by activating and relaxing his elbow flexors. He is suing the driver of the vehicle and the surgeon for defacing his tattoo and reducing the "tattoo action" he can produce with his elbow flexors. His legal counsel, Wanna, Getcha, and Good, has been authorized to obtain copies of all pertinent hospital documents.

You treated Farley when he was in the hospital. You have since changed positions and are in a partnership with another therapist in a private practice, Hans-Zohn, SC. Farley came to you for continued therapy for strengthening. You suspect this is because you made an effort to deal with his tattoo concerns by maintaining pliability of the scar area, providing extra elbow flexion strengthening, and retraining activities for his left elbow flexor group when he was in the acute facility. You did these activities on your own in addition to the gait training, stretching, and strengthening that he was referred for. You did not record these extra activities in your document notes.

Farley's current physician, Dr. Maxie Care, requested your assessment of Farley's strength, girth, skin condition, and muscle control. Farley brought you copies of your own prior document notes to aid your assessment. Your final document note included the following information: "Functionally normal strength left UE, upper arm girths appear equal bilaterally, surgical area well-healed, left UE range WNL, independent in self-care activities." You find the information inadequate to make comparisons with today's observations.

The task here is to decide what you could have said in your original note documents that would have been more useful to you now. As a start, list the subjective information presented above. Then, suggest which objective measurements might have been taken to better quantify the major areas of concern. Finally, rewrite the subjective and objective portions of a document note including fictitious data derived from your measurement suggestions. Use the model format in Example 6.1.

Appendices 6.1 and 6.2 may be consulted after you have worked on these assignments.

References

1. Webster's II new Riverside university dictionary. Boston: Houghton Mifflin, 1984:394,804.
2. Wessman HC. Records. In: Hickok RJ, ed. Physical therapy administration and management. 2nd ed. Baltimore: Williams & Wilkins, 1982:99−104,109,113.
3. Daulong MR, Nye MF. Issues and trends in reimbursement. In: Mathews J. Practice issues in physical therapy. Thorofare, NJ: Slack, 1989:91.
4. Series: Challenges in physical therapy lesson I: Why documentation spells survival. Bethesda: Professional Health Educators, Inc. 1988:1−11.
5. Phillipi L. A key issue in reimbursement for rehabilitative services in long-term care. Phys Ther Forum 1990;June 18:1,3−4.
6. Burch E. Direct access. In: Mathews J. Practice issues in physical therapy. Thorofare, NJ: Slack, 1989:31.
7. Tomberlin JP, Eggert J, Callister L. The use of standardized evaluation forms in physical therapy. J Orthop Sports Phys Ther 1984;5:348−372.
8. Jette AM. Functional status index: Reliability of a chronic disease measurement instrument. Arch Phys Med Rehabil 1980;61:395−401.
9. Series: challenges in physical therapy lesson II: learning a documentation method. Bethesda: Professional Health Educators, Inc. 1988:2,5−7,9−10,12−14,23.
10. Feitelberg SB. The problem oriented record system in physical therapy. Burlington: University of Vermont, 1975:21−28.
11. Rothstein JM. On defining subjective and objective measurements. Phys Ther 1989;69:577−579.
12. Kettenbach G. Writing S.O.A.P. notes. Philadelphia: FA Davis, 1990:5,29,32,34,39,45,130.
13. Weed LL. Medical records, patient care, and medical education. Irish J Med Sci 1964;6:271−282.
14. Weed LL. Medical records that guide and teach, part I. N Engl J Med 1968;278:593−600.
15. Hill JR. The problem-oriented approach to physical therapy care. Washington DC: American Physical Therapy Association, 1977:2.
16. Delitto A. Subjective measures and clinical decision making. Phys Ther 1989;69:585−589.
17. Payton OD, Pzer MN, Nelson CE. Patient participation in program planning: A manual for therapists. Philadelphia: FA Davis, 1990:VIII−IX,7,18−19,34.
18. Currier DP. Elements of research in physical therapy. 3rd ed. Baltimore: Williams & Wilkins, 1990:81−82,87−89,117−118.

CHAPTER 7

Operations Management

OVERVIEW

Operations management involves planning, directing, and evaluating the activities of an organization. A planning process known as strategic planning is introduced in a step-by-step manner. Through this process determination of the organization's strengths and weaknesses is made. The more levels of employees involved the more likely it is that a true assessment of the organization can be obtained. The future direction of the organization is charted based on this intense self-scrutinizing process. The results of the strategic planning process are summarized in a document called the strategic plan. The plan gives focused direction to every segment of the organization so the desired goals are likely to be achieved. Organizational bylaws, policies, and procedures are adapted to facilitate the short- and long-term goals set forth in the strategic plan. The plan is also used to inform external parties about the organization. A format for the plan is presented and discussed. Because the strategic plan identifies who is responsible for carrying out each part and what the expected outcomes are, appraisals of performance are possible. Several appraisal methods unique to health care organizations are presented. Quality assurance programs evaluate the quality and appropriateness of client care and efforts to identify and resolve care-related problems. To determine whether quality care is given in a cost-efficient manner,

141

there are utilization review programs. Program evaluation is an ongoing appraisal of the results of care. Guidelines for implementation of all three types of measurement programs are presented. The reader can practice using service evaluation methods in the case study at the end of this chapter.

Introduction

This chapter addresses management activities related to planning, direction, and evaluation of organizational activities. First, the purpose and process of organizational planning activities will be reviewed. A model for organizational planning and an approach to writing operating goals and objectives will be presented. Next, the topic of work design and standardization through the use of bylaws, policies, and procedures will be discussed. The types of policies and procedures common to physical therapy practice will be reviewed. Last, the types and elements of service evaluation will be presented. Service evaluation will be reviewed in the context of quality assurance, utilization review, and outcome evaluation. This chapter is intended to enhance the ability of physical therapy managers to plan for, direct, and evaluate the organizational activities under their control.

Strategic Planning

During the course of our lives most, if not all, of us will spend some time planning for the future. In looking forward, we set goals that we would like to achieve. We also set time frames for achieving our goals. And, if the goals are important, we develop a course of action which we must follow to meet the goals we have set. Some of us even develop alternate or contingency plans, in case our chosen course of action fails to achieve our desired outcome. Organizations go through similar, albeit more formal, planning processes. Strategic planning is the term used to describe this organizational planning process. A strategic plan is the outcome of the planning process which represents a collection of decisions an organization has made about its goals and the course of action (the strategy) it will follow to achieve those goals.

The use of a strategic planning process should help organizations minimize risk. Risk can be defined as exposure to loss or harm. Organizations face risk when they fail to recognize opportunities or threats. They may also be at risk because of an inability to respond to change or to appropriately utilize limited resources. Strategic planning will help minimize risk because the planning process provides the opportunity for the organization to assess its current situation, adopt a vision of its future, and develop a plan to realize that vision.

USES FOR THE STRATEGIC PLAN
Internal Uses

The strategic plan has several important uses to an organization (Table 7.1). A strategic plan causes the organization to perform an honest

Table 7.1.
Use of the Strategic Plan

Internal	External

Encourages Frank Appraisal of Strategic Position
  Identifies strengths and weaknesses
Identifies Organizational Problems
  Implications
  Plans for resolution
	Educate Outside Parties
	
	Support Requests for Funds
	  Finance organizations
	  Shareholders

Clarifies Performance Expectations Productivity standards set	
Objective Basis for Appraisal and Reward	
Coordinates Activities Organization-Wide Encourages strategic thinking	

assessment of its strategic position. It does this by providing the impetus for an organization to assess its internal and external environment. The assessment of internal conditions should lead the organization to an honest understanding of its strengths and weaknesses (1). Organizational strength might come from characteristics such as a loyal staff, previous successful experiences, or a sound financial position. Characteristics which might weaken an organization include an aging physical plant, management/ labor conflicts, an inappropriate management structure, or an inexperienced staff. A single characteristic can be both a strength and weakness for the same organization. Also, a strength for one organization may well be a weakness for another. An organization's external environment can present both opportunities or threats to future success. In health care, opportunities and threats are driven by the same factors that are driving the industry to change, such as social philosophy about health care delivery, government regulation, health care reimbursement, competition for the health care market, new technology, health care financing, and health care manpower.

The strategic plan can be used to identify internal organizational problems. Problems are identified as a natural outcome of analyzing the organization's strengths and weaknesses. The strategic planning process then causes the organization to address the short- and long-term implications of the identified problems. The response to this assessment is the development of a logical action plan to resolve problems so that organizational goals might be achieved.

Expectations for organizational performance and priorities for management action are delineated in the strategic plan. From these expectations will come the direction for all organizational activities and expenditures. The strategic plan will also provide the basis for setting productivity standards (1).

The strategic plan provides an objective basis for appraisal and reward of employee performance. The strategic plan can be used as a basis for the development of management performance expectations. This can be done through the assignment of responsibility for specific parts of the strategic action plan. In this way the success of the employee is tied directly to the success of the organization. Through the use of incentive or bonus reward systems, the success of the organization can be tied to the success of all employees.

Finally, the strategic plan can be used to coordinate the activities of organizational segments into a cohesive whole. The process of strategic planning will encourage strategic thinking on the part of managers. It will also provide a basis for participatory management practices. Both of these outcomes will create a better understanding of the role each person and segment of the organization has to play to achieve common organizational goals (1).

External Uses

The strategic plan has two major uses external to the organization. The first is to provide outside parties with a clear description of the objectives, structure, and performance of the firm. The second is to obtain funds from external sources such as financial institutions or private investors (1).

TIME FRAMES FOR STRATEGIC PLANNING

Strategic plans are generally related to a specific period of time. It is common for an organization to have both short-term and long-term strategic plans. A long-term plan might set future direction for periods of three, five, or more years into the future. A long-term strategic plan is a general plan which sets the organization's direction for the upcoming years. It is a vision of what and where the organization wants to be at the end of that time period. The current trend in health care is toward three-year plans. The use of a shorter planning cycle can be attributed to the rapidly changing conditions affecting the health care industry.

A short-term strategic plan usually covers a one-year period. Short-term plans are generally more detailed. Short-term strategic plans should provide:

1. Goals to be achieved by the organization during the current fiscal year;
2. Specific objectives which need to be accomplished to achieve the organizational goals;
3. A detailed plan of action for achieving each objective;
4. The person(s) responsible for carrying out specific objectives.

An organization's strategic plan should drive all organizational activity. Planning by organization divisions and subdivisions, such as departments, should be guided by and complimentary to the organization's strategic plan. The annual budget and financial projections should follow the direction set by the organization's strategic plan.

STRATEGIC PLANNING PROCESS

Who Should Participate?

During the 1970s, health care organizations commonly used corporate level professional planners to develop strategic plans. If professional planners were not used, planning was most often done by executive management with some input from the board of directors. The 1980s has seen a shift away from the use of professional planners. The current trend is toward greater involvement of middle management (2). This has been done to gain maximum benefit from the manager's knowledge about the organization, its customers, and its competitors. It has also been done to give middle management a greater appreciation of the organization's plans in relationship to day-to-day operations (3).

Strategic planning is not a guarantee for success. "Why this is so is explained not so much by the actual planning process, but by the way the planning is done and by whom—who are the participants in the planning process" (2). No matter how good a strategic plan might be, its effectiveness will be limited by the effectiveness of the people responsible for its implementation. If we refer back to the earlier discussion in Chapter 3 about employee motivation, we are reminded that creativity, commitment, self-direction, and ingenuity are more likely to be the outcomes of full participation. So it would appear that effective implementation of a strategic plan would be the outcome of full participation by all personnel responsible for the implementation of the plan. The trend toward inclusion of middle management in the corporate planning process is encouraging. The next step would be the inclusion of all staff in some phase of the planning process. The challenge is to develop a fully participative planning process which will still "permit rapid decision making in response to sudden market shifts in customers, competitors, and legislation" (3).

Strategic Questions

Kropf and Greenberg (4) suggest that the strategic planning process is driven by a series of questions that organizations should ask and answer in order to make strategic decisions about their future. These questions, asked in sequence, are listed in Table 7.2.

STRATEGIC PLANNING MODEL

There are many acceptable ways to do strategic planning. There is no one "best" way to do strategic planning. In practice, every organization does it just a little bit differently. There are in fact many "best" ways to get the job done. With this in mind, Pegels and Rogers (2) have developed a model planning process. Their model consists of seven sequential steps and six parallel tasks that support the sequential steps.

While useful to conceptualize the planning process, the Pegels and Rogers model stops short of implementation. It does not address the need for outcome evaluation and/or ongoing analysis and evaluation. The strategic planning process should be dynamic. It must take into consideration both outcome and change. Kropf and Greenberg (4) suggest three addi-

Table 7.2.
Questions to Advance the Strategic Planning Process[a]

How do we define ourselves today?
Where are we today?
Where are we going if we continue along our current course?
What do we want to be in the future?
What will we have to do to get there?
What will happen to our plans if the situation changes?
How will the change affect our course of action?
Who will be responsible and what action will they take?
How will we evaluate the effectiveness of our actions?
Does the evaluation indicate a need to change our action plan?

[a]Adapted from: Kropf R, Greenberg JA. Strategic analysis for hospital management. Rockville: Aspen, 1984:8.

tional steps for the planning model to make it a dynamic process. These are the top three steps in Figure 7.1 which is a complete planning model.

These steps address the need for ongoing evaluation and modification of the strategic plan in response to poor outcomes or changing internal and external environments. The first three parallel tasks are directed toward the analysis of the external environment. They concentrate on market analysis. These first three tasks help to identify external opportunities for and threats to future success. The last three parallel tasks are directed inward. They are focused on analysis of the internal environment of the organization. These tasks help management to identify internal strengths and weaknesses.

STRATEGIC PLAN

The strategic plan is the document used to represent the results of the strategic planning process. The plan presents information obtained through analysis and evaluation of the organization and its external environment. It should also present the goals and objectives of the organization that have been adopted as an outcome of the strategic planning process. Crego and associates (1) suggest that the strategic business plan takes the form of strategic action plans for: 1) market strategy; 2) production/service strategy; 3) research and development strategy; 4) organization and management strategy; and 5) financial strategy.

Market Strategy. A marketing strategy serves to define the organization's customers and the products/services that will be sold. It also defines organizational policy related to pricing, advertising, and promotion. Marketing strategy should be based on an analysis of the market to be served. The market analysis should provide information about customer purchasing behavior such as preference, consumption, and purchasing patterns. The marketing strategy should identify the value of the product or service to the customer. Lastly, it should take into consideration the degree and type of competition in the market (1). Marketing for health care organizations is discussed in Chapter 9.

Production/Service Strategy. Production/service strategy addresses planning issues related to how, where, and in what volume the necessary

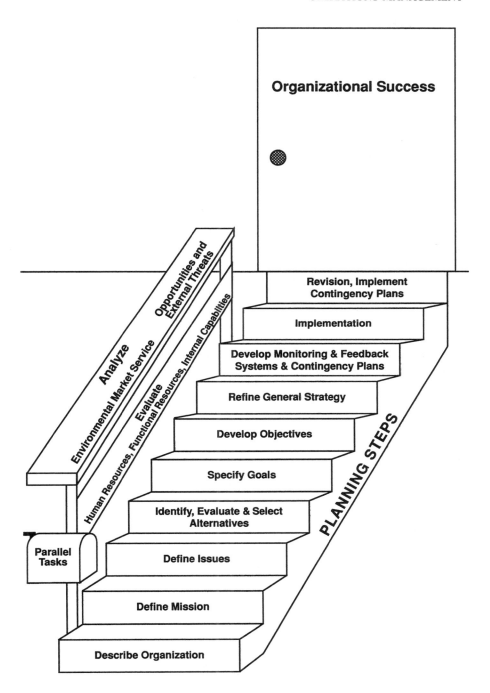

Figure 7.1. A complete strategic planning model. (Adapted from: Pegels CC, Rodgers KA. Strategic management of hospitals and health care facilities. Rockville, MD: Aspen, 1988:XIV,24–25; Kropf R, Greenberg JA. Strategic analysis for hospital management. Rockville, MD: Aspen, 1984:7–9.)

work will be accomplished. It asks and answers questions about technology to be used. It identifies material, equipment, and facilities required to achieve the organization's strategy goals. Production/service strategy also establishes a production schedule which will allow goal achievement within the desired time frames. Completion of the production/service strategy requires analysis of operating costs, availability of resources, productivity, and quality (1).

Research and Development Strategy.   The need for research and development strategy is largely dependent on the nature of the organization and the strategy it adopts. If long-term plans are dependent on product/service innovation or differentiation then research and development activity will be necessary (1).

Organization and Management Strategy.   This part of the strategic business plan will address issues related to what must be done, assignment of management accountability, organizational structure to support the strategic plan, and human resource needs. It will also address issues related to work standardization, control, and employee motivation. Organization and management strategy is dependent on a comprehensive assessment of the organization's mission, strengths, and weaknesses.

Financial Strategy.   The strategic financial plan will answer three basic but critical questions. 1) How will the organization be managed to remain financially viable? 2) How will profits be spent or losses covered? 3) How will the organization pay for planned investments? To answer these questions the organization must have firm control of expenses. It must also have accurate projections of revenues. Only then can it determine the extent to which alternative funding sources will be required to meet future financial requirements (1).

STRATEGIC PLAN FORMAT

A plan can represent an entire strategic plan or a segment of the plan. A segment of the plan might reflect the planning for a new service or it could relate to an existing department, product, or service. There are many ways to format a strategic plan. The method used varies between organizations. Example 7.1 is a format for a strategic plan.

WRITING STRATEGIC GOALS AND OBJECTIVES

In practice, organizations use the words goal and objective in varying ways. Some organizations use the words interchangeably. Some organizations use the terms together to describe one statement.

The authors believe there is a definite difference between a goal and an objective and offer the following definitions. A goal is a statement of what is to be accomplished. For example, "To increase the number of physical therapy referrals by 5% during the next fiscal year." An objective is a statement that compliments the goal by stating how the goal is to be achieved. Objectives which compliment the goal in our example would say, "To enter into two additional managed care contracts for the provision of physical therapy services to their membership" or "To market physical therapy services directly to the client through sports physical therapy

EXAMPLE 7.1
Outline for Preparing a Strategic Plan

I. Organization/Organizational Segment
  A. Mission statement
  B. Describe the organization
    1. Size
    2. Location
    3. Ownership
  C. Department/Program/Service/Product/
    Project (if the strategic plan relates only
    to a specific part of the organization)
    1. Descriptive overview
      a. Relationship to the organization's
       mission
II. Market
  A. Market analysis
    1. Customers
    2. Volume projections
    3. Competition
III. Organization and Management
  A. Staff requirements
    1. Productivity standards
    2. Staff by position type
    3. Cost (salary, benefits, and FICA)
    4. Position descriptions
  B. Organizational chart

IV. Production/Service Strategy
  A. Facilities requirements
    1. Square footage projections
    2. Floor plan
    3. Cost estimates
  B. Capital equipment
    1. Equipment list
    2. Equipment cost projections
  C. Small tools requirements
    1. Small tools list
    2. Small tools cost projections
V. Financial Cost/Benefit Analysis
  A. Direct expenses
  B. Indirect expense allocations
  C. Revenue projections
    1. Fee/price schedule
    2. Sales projections
    3. Gross revenue projections
  D. Projected financial statements
    1. Income statement
    2. Cash flow statements
    3. Breakeven analysis

seminars at local health clubs and amateur sporting events." These objectives are statements of specific actions which will be taken to realize the goal of increased referrals. Under these guidelines, the physical therapy manager can utilize goals (what) and objectives (how) to create performance expectations for the organization and for individuals who will carry out specific objectives. Performance of employees can be tied to performance of the organization.

Work Design and Standardization: Bylaws, Policies, and Procedures

The process of work design has been discussed previously in Chapter 4. Work design is the process through which an organization standardizes and directs the activities of its employees. It is the process whereby performance expectations are defined. Performance expectations can be communicated to employees through a variety of channels. These channels include the employee's position description, job orders, and written rules. In health care written rules which standardize and direct employee behavior are most generally found in the organization's bylaws, policies, and procedures.

BYLAWS

Legally recognized organizations are governed by a set of bylaws which are set down as part of the organization's articles of incorporation. A bylaw is defined as "a rule governing the internal affairs of an organization" (5). Of the three forms of written rules which define performance

Table 7.3.
Common Administrative and Medical Staff Bylaws

Administrative bylaws deal with:
  Organizational ownership
  Purpose of the organization
  Structure of the governing body
  Composition of the governing body
  Selection and responsibilities of the Chief Executive Officer
  Credentials of medical staff members
  Monitoring of quality

Medical staff bylaws (if present) set down guidelines regarding matters such as:
  Membership requirements
  Credential process
  Membership classes
  Member rights and responsibilities
  Medical staff organization

expectations, bylaws are the broadest in scope of influence. Scope of influence refers to the degree of influence over the activities of the organization and its members. Bylaws set the boundaries for all organizational activity. The activities of the organization and its members must follow from and be consistent with the bylaws. Therefore, organizational policies and procedures must follow from, be consistent with, and comply with the bylaws. Large health care providers, such as hospitals, might have two sets of bylaws. The first set are administrative or governing body bylaws. These guide the activities of the organization. The second set are medical staff bylaws. These guide and regulate the activities of members of the medical staff that provide services within a hospital.

Common administrative bylaws set down guidelines regarding matters such as those listed in Table 7.3.

Medical staff bylaws generally require the approval of both the medical staff and the governing body for adoption and modification. For health care organizations, the content of the governing body and medical staff bylaws are regulated by accrediting organizations such as the Joint Commission of the Accreditation of Health Care Organizations (JCAHO). At present, medical staff bylaws are beginning to have some bearing on physical therapy practice. Based on information obtained from personal experience there does appear to be a trend toward the assignment of medical staff privileges to physical therapists. As more physical therapists are afforded the opportunity to become members of the medical staff, medical staff bylaws will impact on their practice. This topic is discussed more fully in Chapter 12.

POLICIES AND PROCEDURES
Purpose

Taken together policies and procedures should answer the questions of what, why, who, when, where, and how any organizational activity shall be performed. The policy is a statement of what an organization or part of an organization will do in a given situation. The policy will also

Table 7.4.
Purposes of Policies and Procedures

Internal

Communicate performance evaluation
Set standards against which performance can be measured
Manage and control work flow
Educate managers and staff
Limit the liability of the organization
Establish and clarify responsibilities
Standardize output
Protect the rights and well being of the organization's employees and customers

External

Meet the requirements for state licensure
Meet the requirements for state and federal certification
Meet the requirements for accreditation
Limit insurance premiums by limiting the risk of performance errors
Control employee interactions with the community

state why organizational activity will be performed in a certain manner. A procedure is a detailed statement of who, when, where, and how an activity will be performed. Policies and procedures serve a variety of purposes. These purposes are related to both internal operations and external factors.

Table 7.4 lists common purposes for policies and procedures related to internal operations and use by external parties.

General Considerations

Responsibility for the development of policies and procedures generally falls to administrators and managers. Implementation and follow-through generally falls to the nonmanagerial staff. To facilitate effective implementation, all affected employees should have input when policies and procedures are developed or revised.

Policies and procedures should support the structure and activities of the organization. In health care, professional standards of practice, community, and organizational norms should be reflected and referenced whenever possible. A professional standard is an accepted criterion or method of practice. For physical therapy, professional guidelines are provided by the American Physical Therapy Association (APTA), JCAHO, and the Commission on Accreditation of Rehabilitation Facilities (CARF). To accommodate changes in the organization's internal and external environment, policies and procedures should be dynamic. They should be reviewed at least annually and modified whenever necessary.

Scope and Type

The scope of a policy or procedure refers to the number of segments of the organization it regulates. The broadest in scope would be the policies and procedures which affect all segments of the organization. These are often referred to as administrative or organizational. Policies and procedures which affect several, but not all, segments of the organization are

EXAMPLE 7.2
Policies in Harmony

Milwaukee Memorial Hospital has an administrative policy that states that all employees are to receive at least one 15-minute break for every four consecutive hours worked. The hospital's physical therapy department wants to limit the disruptive effect of having its employees schedule breaks during peak hours of operation. Peak hours occur during midmorning and midafternoon. The department may not adopt a policy that states that employees may only take breaks if it is not disruptive to department operations. It can adopt a policy that limits the hours during which breaks may be taken. However, the department manager must be sure that all employees will be able to take a break within the nonrestricted times allowed.

often referred to as interdepartmental. Policies affecting a single segment of the organization are referred to as departmental. Policies of limited scope should be consistent with policies of broader scope. Consider the situation in Example 7.2.

Administrative. A health care organization is likely to have administrative policies and procedures which cover topics such as those listed in Table 7.5. The lists presented in this table are intended to give a broad sample of possible topics for administrative policies and procedures. These lists are not all-inclusive. The actual topics addressed in administrative policies will differ between organizations. Some guidance for the topics and content of administrative policy for health care organizations is provided by accrediting organizations such as the JCAHO.

Table 7.5.
Topics Covered by Administrative Policies and Procedures

Administrative Topics	Client Care Topics
Administrative policy review	Admission criteria
Agreements and contracts	Client bill of rights
Charity care	Consents for testing and treatment
Disaster planning	Deaths
Dress code	Discharge criteria and procedures
Employee health	Do not resuscitate
Employee right to know	Documentation
Employee termination	Infection control
Equal opportunity employment	Medical emergency
Evacuations	Medical records
Forms control	Provision of life sustaining treatment
Hazardous waste management	Record retention
Incident reporting	Release of medical information
Media relations	Requests for anatomical gifts
Organizational committee structure	Research
Petty cash	Restrictive procedures
Safety	Safekeeping and release of clients' valuables
Sexual harassment	
Smoking regulation	
Solicitation and petitioning	
Travel	
Visitor restrictions	
Volunteer services	
Work-related injury	

Table 7.6.
Departments that Issue Interdepartmental Policies

Materials Management (Purchasing)
Central Service
Communications
General Stores
Medical Records
Transcription
Human Resources
Payroll
Public Relations
Education
Cafeteria
Maintenance

Interdepartmental. Interdepartmental policies and procedures are written to serve two purposes. First, they clarify how the services of a support department can be accessed by user departments. Table 7.6 presents a listing of departments in a health care organization that might issue interdepartmental policies and procedures for the purpose of clarifying how support services might be accessed.

The second purpose of an interdepartmental policy and procedure is to clarify how segments of an organization must function to compliment the efforts of each other. This type of policy and procedure might be seen in relationship to a department such as admissions. When a client is admitted to the service of a health care organization it may require coordination from a variety of departments such as the admissions department, business office, housekeeping, dietary, nursing, and so on. Another situation which often prompts the development of interdepartmental policies is an interdisciplinary program. A rehabilitation program which requires input from several disciplines is a good example of this situation. An interdisciplinary rehabilitation program may issue policies to direct the actions of 1) nurses, 2) occupational therapists, 3) physical therapists, 4) physicians, 5) psychologists, 6) social workers, 7) speech pathologists, and other members of the rehabilitation team. The goal is to coordinate the activities of different organizational segments into a cohesive service program for the benefit of the customer.

Departmental. Departmental policies relate the the activities of a single organizational segment. Departmental policies have the most limited scope. They are also the most specific and detailed. Departmental policies and procedures cover a variety of topic areas. They provide further definition to administrative and interdisciplinary policies and procedures. They guide activities that are specific to the department for which they are written. Table 7.7 is the table of contents from a departmental manual for a typical physical therapy department which is part of a larger organization. Note that a select number of administrative and interdepartmental policies which will be needed by staff to guide daily activities have been included. The departmental policies and procedures are those required to standardize service delivery within the department.

Table 7.7.
Policies and Procedures for a Physical Therapy Department

Milwaukee Memorial Hospital
Physical Therapy Department
Policy and Procedure Manual
Table of Contents

Section I: Hospital Organization
A. Administrative policy review
B. Organizational chart
C. Mission statement
D. Client bill of rights

Section II: General Departmental
A. Departmental organizational chart
B. Physical therapy department management
C. Objective for physical therapy
D. Referral for physical therapy services
E. Verbal orders
F. Verification of professional credentials
G. Physical therapy quality assurance plan

Section III: Human Resource Policies
A. Hospital human resource policies and procedures
B. Staff assignment
C. Weekend coverage
D. Time off for personal, vacation, and education time
E. Coffee and lunch breaks
F. Time card and payroll processing
G. Interdepartmental communication
H. Telephone usage
I. Position descriptions
   1. PT manager
   2. PT education coordinator
   3. PT clinical supervisor
   4. PT senior
   5. PT staff
   6. PT assistant
   7. PT aide
   8. PT volunteer
J. Orientation of staff and students
K. Employee performance appraisal
L. Dress code

Section IV. Staff Development and Training
A. Staff development policy
B. Presentation of inservices following attendance at outside continuing education event
C. Use of inservice attendance recording form
D. Travel expense reimbursement
E. Mileage reimbursement/petty cash
F. Application for continuing education attendance
G. Evaluation of inservice programs
H. Peer review

Section V: Operational Policies and Procedures
A. Treatment scheduling
B. Outpatient cancellation policy
C. Physical therapy documentation
D. Medical record dictation
E. Medical record abbreviations
F. Physical therapy forms
G. Team conference reporting
H. Client education documentation
I. Client billing
J. Equipment inventory and maintena
K. Chart review
L. Client transportation
M. Client/family involvement in treatm planning

Section VI: Treatment Policies and Procedures
A. Home visits
B. Family conferences
C. Prosthetic and orthotic services
D. Vital signs monitoring
E. Fabrication of a removable rigid dressing
F. Tilt table
G. Client equipment: wheelchair assessment
H. Client equipment: prescription
I. Client equipment: ordering and bill
J. Serial casting
K. Inhibitory casting
L. Adaptive seating

Section VII: Physical Agents
A. Cold packs
B. Hot packs
C. Diathermy
D. Infra Red
E. Ice massage
F. Jobst pressure treatment
G. Interferential current
H. Paraffin
I. Paraffin home program
J. TENS
K. Traction
L. Ultrasound

continues

Table 7.7.   *Continued*

Section VIII: Hydrotherapy
A. General procedures
B. Whirlpool: low boy
C. Hubbard tank
D. Walking tank
E. Cleaning and disinfecting of
   hydrotherapy equipment
F. Sterilization and isolation procedures
   for hydrotherapy
	Section X: Interdepartmental
	A. Consent to photograph
	B. Housekeeping services
	C. Pharmacy services and supplies
	D. Maintenance services
	E. Xeroxing and printing requests
	F. Stores requisitions
	G. Purchase requests
	H. Volunteer coordination
	I. Employee discounts

Section IX: Mobility Training A. Transfer training B. Gait training C. Three point strapping D. Advanced gait training E. Exercise class F. Wheelchair mobility	Section XI: Safety and Infection Control A. Infection control B. Handwashing procedures C. Incident reports D. Safety E. Equipment maintenance F. Hospital safety program G. Evacuation policy H. Hazardous materials and infectious waste handling

Format and Components

Health care organizations use a variety of formats for policies and procedures. Although there is no right or wrong format, an organization should adopt a standardized format to use throughout its structure. A standardized format will increase consistency of content and ease interdepartmental utilization.

Components which are common to health care policies and procedures are listed in the left column of Example 7.3.

Service Evaluation

One of the outcomes of the recent changes affecting the health care industry is an increased demand for accountability. Health care providers are being called upon to demonstrate that they provide quality services, use resources wisely, and produce reasonable and predictable outcomes. The pressure for increased accountability comes from a variety of sources. Consumers, payers, accrediting agencies, and even other providers are asking for "proof" of performance. They want this proof in the form of objective information which demonstrates that an individual health care provider is able to and does produce reliable, high quality service. Consumers want to be sure they will have the best possible outcome with the lowest amount of risk from the least amount of service. Payers are concerned about the same things as consumers. Their reasons may be different. For payers, a poor outcome, complications, or extended service all raise the current and possibly the future cost of caring for the consumer. Providers affiliated with other providers are concerned because their practice and reputation will be influenced by the practices of the other. This is true for a physical therapist employed by a hospital. The practices of

EXAMPLE 7.3
Physical Therapy Policy and Procedure

Milwaukee Memorial Hospital
Clinical Department: Physical Therapy

TYPE	
TOPIC	Subject: Verbal Orders For Physical Therapy Service
DATE OF ADOPTION	Date Effective: July, 1998
DATE OF REVIEW	Date Reviewed: July, 1998, June 1999
DATE OF REVISION	Date Revised:
SCOPE	Distribution: Physical Therapy Department
PURPOSE STATEMENT	Purpose: To establish guidelines for the use and limitations of verbal orders for physical therapy services.
POLICY STATEMENT	Policy: A physical therapist may accept a verbal order for physical therapy services from members of the hospital medical staff. Verbal orders for physical therapy services must be received by the physical therapist directly. Verbal orders must be followed by a written order within twenty-four hours for inpatients or four days for outpatients or service will be discontinued.
PROCEDURE STATEMENT	Procedure: Upon receipt of a verbal order, the physical therapist shall document the order on the Physical Therapy Referral Form (PT-256). Upon receipt of the written order for physical therapy services, the written order shall be attached to the already completed Physical Therapy Referral Form and forwarded to the Medical Records Department for filing. In the event that the referring physician fails to provide a written order for physical therapy services within the allowed time frames, physical therapy services shall be discontinued. The physical therapist shall inform the physician that services have been discontinued pending receipt of the written order. Exceptions to this procedure may be made with the prior approval of the Manager and Medical Director of the Department of Physical Therapy.
SIGNATURE AND TITLE OF AUTHORIZED PERSON(S)	

_____   _____
Manager of Physical Therapy   Date

_____   _____
Medical Director   Date

the hospital will influence the practice of the physical therapist and vice versa. Peer providers, those who are unaffiliated with a particular organization but provide similar services, also can be affected by the reputation or image of similar providers.

Individual health care providers are responsible for providing evidence which demonstrates that they are able to and consistently do provide high quality, efficient, and effective services. Their efforts are guided by standards and criteria established by several types of organizations. Organizations responsible for setting standards for health care providers include governmental agencies, professional associations, accrediting agencies, payers, and consumer groups. Governmental regulation comes from federal, state, and local levels. Professional associations such as the American Medical Association (AMA), APTA, and the American Nursing Association (ANA) set standards for professional conduct and practice. Independent accrediting agencies like the JCAHO and CARF set standards for the practice of health care organizations. These accrediting agencies

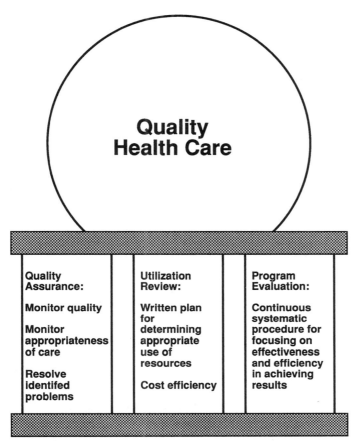

Quality Health Care

Quality Assurance:	Utilization Review:	Program Evaluation:
Monitor quality	Written plan for determining appropriate use of resources	Continuous systematic procedure for focusing on effectiveness and efficiency in achieving results
Monitor appropriateness of care		
Resolve identifed problems	Cost efficiency	

Figure 7.2.   Three measures of quality of health care services.

also provide guidelines for the methods a health care organization might use to analyze the quality, efficiency, and effectiveness of the services that they provide. There are three types of activities that health care providers undertake to demonstrate accountability. These are quality assurance, utilization review, and program/service evaluation activities (Fig. 7.2).

Quality assurance (QA) is defined by JCAHO as a "process designed to objectively and systematically monitor and evaluate the quality and appropriateness of patient care, pursue opportunities to improve patient care, and resolve identified problems" (6).

Utilization review (UR) is defined as a "written program that endeavors to assure appropriate allocation of the hospital's resources by striving to provide quality patient care in the most cost efficient manner" (6).

Program evaluation (PE) is defined by CARF as "a systematic procedure for determining the effectiveness and efficiency with which results are achieved by persons served. These results are collected on a regular or continuous basis rather than by a periodic sampling" (7). Outcome

Table 7.8.
JCAHO Ten-Step Monitoring Process

Assign responsibilities
Identification of activities
Selection of important aspects of activity
Establish quality indicators
Set percent of occurrence thresholds which trigger action
Implement monitoring process
Identify and analyze problems
Resolve problems
Assess outcomes
Communicate with related parties

research is believed to provide the best approach to determine which medical practices are appropriate for which clients and which practices will produce higher quality care (8).

QUALITY ASSURANCE

JCAHO has developed specific guidelines for health care providers to follow in establishing a quality monitoring and evaluation process. This monitoring and evaluation process was "designed to help health care organizations effectively use their quality assurance resources by focusing on high priority quality-of-care issues" (6). To accomplish this, the process involves:

1. Identification of important aspects of client care provided by the organization;
2. Systematic monitoring of the important aspects of care through the use of measurable indicators;
3. Use of thresholds in the monitoring process which trigger further evaluation to identify problems and opportunities to improve client care;
4. Implementation of actions to improve client care and followed by an evaluation of the effectiveness of those actions.

This type of monitoring and evaluation system can be useful in the identification of trends of patterns of care because it relies on the collection and aggregation of data about a series of events. This is in contrast to a collection process that focuses on single events where trends could be easily missed. The goal of the JCAHO quality monitoring system is to pinpoint areas of organizational activity which when monitored will yield the greatest opportunity to improve quality of client care. To assist the health care provider in the implementation of this type of monitoring system, JCAHO has broken the process into the incremental steps listed in Table 7.8.

An additional discussion of the 10 steps listed in Table 7.8 is presented to further an understanding of the monitoring process.

Step One: Responsibility Assignment. Responsibility for the design, implementation, and ongoing management of a quality assurance monitoring system is assigned to member(s) of the organization.

Step Two: Identification of the Activities. The activities of the organization or segment of the organization are delineated.

Step Three: Selection of Important Aspects of Activity. Once the activities of the organization or segment of the organization are delineated, the important aspects of the activities are selected. Important aspects to consider are those that are high volume or have high risk potential.

Step Four: Establish Quality Indicators. Quality indicators are objective measurable criteria which will allow the organization to monitor the selected aspects of care.

Step Five: Set Thresholds. Thresholds can be viewed as tolerance levels. Thresholds are frequently expressed in terms of a percentage of occurrence which will trigger action. For example, a monitor which reflects performance of an important aspect of the organization's activity may be assigned a threshold of 5%. If 5% or less of the monitored occurrences or behaviors fail to meet quality expectations, the organization will consider the performance to fall within acceptable ranges and no action will be taken. If more than 5% of the monitored occurrences or behaviors fail to meet expectations, the organization will initiate a problem-solving process.

Step Six: Implement the Monitoring Process. Once indicators have been selected and performance thresholds set the organization must begin to monitor the organization's performance. It does this through the collection and analysis of data for each indicator.

Step Seven: Problem Identification and Analysis. When data analysis indicates that performance thresholds have been exceeded, investigation for the purpose of problem identification occurs.

Step Eight: Problem Resolution. Once the problem has been identified, the organization takes action intended to resolve problems and improve patient care.

Step Nine: Outcome Assessment. The organization shall assess the outcome and effectiveness of the action taken. This includes the documentation of improvements in client care which have resulted from action taken.

Step Ten: Communication. The results of the quality assurance monitoring process must be reported to all relevant parties. This should include appropriate staff, management, medical staff, and the governing body of the organization.

Under the current JCAHO guidelines it is the health care provider's responsibility to select the most important aspects of their activities, identify the quality indicators by which they will monitor their performance, and set tolerance thresholds which will trigger action. The current efforts of JCAHO are directed toward standardization of critical aspects, indicators, and thresholds. Providers would report negative deviations from established thresholds, the organization's response, and outcomes to JCAHO as they occur. Thus, it is thought that the quality of health care will become increasingly standardized regardless of the provider. The efforts toward the development of national quality standards are in progress as of this writing. The implementation of a standardized quality assurance process by JCAHO is targeted to occur by the middle of this decade.

Quality Assurance for Physical Therapy Practice

Physical therapists in private or institutional practice are often involved in the development of a QA plan. Regardless of the setting, the process should be similar. Example 7.4 presents a QA plan developed for a fictitious private practice, Independent Physical Therapists, Inc. (IPT, Inc.) IPT Inc.'s QA plan follows the 10 steps noted in Table 7.7. This example would be as applicable to a hospital-based practice as it is to a private practice.

EXAMPLE 7.4
IPT, Inc. Quality Assurance Plan

Step One: Responsibility Assignment

Responsibility for quality assurance falls ultimately to IPT, Inc. Board of Directors and Chief Executive Officer. This responsibility has been delegated by the Board of Directors to the Assistant Director of Physical Therapy. The Assistant Director of Physical Therapy shall report the findings of the quality assurance process to all staff and the Director of Physical Therapy. The Director of Physical Therapy shall relay the findings of the quality assurance plan to the Board of Directors.

Step Two: Identification of Activities

For IPT, Inc., the scope of care provided is defined by the organization's mission statement. (See Chapter 2 if you need to review a mission statement.) In a larger organization there should be a specific scope of practice statement for the physical therapy department. Some of the specific activities identified for the physical therapy department are:

Client scheduling	Communication
Client evaluation	Organizational planning
Treatment planning	New service development
Client treatment	Billing
Client/family education and training	Staff orientation and training
Documentation	Student education

Step Three: Selection of Important Aspects of Organizational Activities

IPT, Inc. identified the following as the most important aspects of their activities.

I. Convenient access to physical therapy services
II. Timely scheduling of client care services
III. Appropriateness of service
IV. Consistency of service quality
V. Client and physician satisfaction

Steps Four and Five:

IPT, Inc. then identified clinical indicators of these key aspects and set thresholds which would indicate a need for further evaluation.

Aspect	Indicator	Threshold
I. Convenient access		
	A. Complaints about parking.	2% of visits
	B. Complaints about locating clinic.	2% of visits
	C. Scheduling problems due to operating hours.	2% of visits
II. Timely service		
	A. Average number of work days between referral receipt and start of care	4 days
III. Appropriateness of service		
	A. Presence of appropriate diagnosis and deficits per referral and evaluation	0%
	B. Plan of care appropriate for deficits per medical record	0%
	C. Treatment consistent with plan of care per peer review and written references	0%
IV. Consistency of service quality		
	A. Compliance with treatment protocol policies and procedures per peer review	0%
	B. Development and implementation of treatment protocols, policies, and procedures for major diagnoses, modalities, etc.	15% of treatments
V. Client and physician satisfaction		
	A. Satisfaction of client and physician with facilities, reception, treatment, and outcomes as indicated by results of an ongoing satisfaction survey	5%

continues

EXAMPLE 7.4   *Continued*

Step Six: Implement the Monitoring Process
IPT, Inc. has determined that indicators will be reviewed using the following methods and schedule:
I. Convenient access
   All indicators of convenience of access to IPT, Inc. physical therapy services will be monitored through the use of a survey to be given to all clients at the time of discharge. Survey results will be analyzed and reported upon a monthly basis.
II. Timely service
   Physical therapy receptionist shall keep a log of client admissions which shall include the date of referral, the date of the initial visit, and the number of weekdays in between. This information shall be analyzed and reported upon quarterly.
III. Appropriateness of services
   Chart review and peer review activities shall be ongoing. Twenty percent of all records shall be reviewed. Staff will participate in peer review activities twice per year. Results of peer review and chart review shall be reported upon quarterly.
IV. Consistency of service quality
   Compliance with treatment protocols, policies and procedures shall be reviewed as part of the ongoing chart and peer review process. Treatment protocols, policies and procedures shall be reviewed annually for availability and content.
V. Client and physician satisfaction
   Client satisfaction shall be monitored via a survey to be given to all clients at the time of discharge. Physician satisfaction shall be monitored annually through a survey. Client satisfaction shall be reported upon on a monthly basis. Physician satisfaction shall be reported upon annually.

Step Seven: Problem Identification
When the monitoring process indicates that performance thresholds are exceeded, problems will be identified and analyzed by appropriate parties.

Step Eight: Problem Resolution
Once a problem has been identified, action will be taken to bring performance in line with established thresholds.

Step Nine: Outcome Assessment
All outcomes of actions shall be evaluated and the results documented.

Step Ten:
IPT, Inc. will report the outcomes of the QA process to the board and all staff on a bimonthly basis.

Costs of Quality

At first the costs associated with the development, implementation, and ongoing management of a QA program may seem extensive in comparison to the rewards. The initial thought might be to find the easiest rather than the most meaningful way to get the job done. What is important to realize is that the cost of a QA program must be weighed against the cost of poor quality. Werner (9) assigns the costs of quality to three categories. These are the appraisal costs, prevention costs, and failure costs. Appraisal costs are those that relate directly to the costs of monitoring the quality of the services provided. Prevention costs are associated with proactive problem identification and resolution. Failure costs are associated with responding to problems after the fact, after there has been a situation which has lead to client dissatisfaction or worse. The cost associated with fixing the problem after the fact can far outweigh the costs of appraisal and prevention (9).

UTILIZATION REVIEW

UR is the process whereby a health care provider sets guidelines for and demonstrates appropriate allocation of its resources through the use

Table 7.9.
Topics That a Utilization Review Plan Would Consider

1. Responsibilities and authority of organizational and medical staff members for the UR process	5. Provisions for discharge planning should concurrent review indicate that a client can no longer benefit from the organization's services
2. Meeting frequency and quorum for those organizational and medical staff members assigned to perform the UR activities of the organization	6. Confidentiality policy to insure the privacy of clients whose services are reviewed
3. Procedures for concurrent review	7. Description of methods to be used to evaluate utilization of resources
4. Conflict of interest policies	

of an effective review process. The goal is to ensure appropriate allocation through the provision of cost effective quality patient care (6). UR plans are generally written to monitor activity throughout the organization. In a large organization, the physical therapy manager's role may be limited. In a physical therapy organization, the physical therapist's role would be much greater.

A UR plan has several common characteristics (6). First, it is a mechanism to address overutilization, underutilization, and inefficiencies in the utilization of resources. This translates to a process that is able to determine if a client received too much care, too little care, and/or the right kind of care. Second, the UR plan is written. Third, the organization's UR plan is approved by the medical staff, the administration, and the governing body. Fourth, the UR plan should have a defined process for the identification of resource utilization problems. It should be focused on the organization's identified or suspected utilization problems. Lastly, an organization's UR plan should be reviewed and revised annually.

To be in compliance with 1990 JCAHO guidelines (6), an organization's written UR plan should encompass items presented in Table 7.9.

PROGRAM EVALUATION

PE is a process whereby the outcomes of human services are evaluated. Posavac and Carey (10) provide a list of reasons for conducting PE.

1. Accreditation requirements;
2. Accounting for funds;
3. Responding to requests for information;
4. Internal decision making;
5. Support for program development efforts;
6. Awareness of the effects, intended and unintended, of the program.

A PE system should enable the organization to identify the results of services and the effects of the program on persons served. PE information should be integrated into the organization's decision making at all levels (7). Figure 7.3 identifies four common types of PE (11).

Evaluation of need looks at the target market for human services and attempts to determine their greatest needs. Assessment of need is the

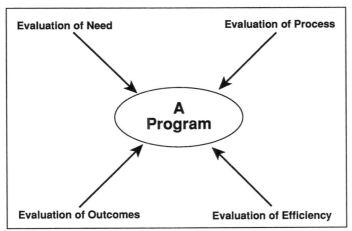

Evaluation of Need   **Evaluation of Process**

**A
Program**

Evaluation of Outcomes   **Evaluation of Efficiency**

Figure 7.3. Types of evaluations made to assess a program.

foundation of planning for human service development. Evaluation of process looks at an existing program in an attempt to determine if it is serving its intended population as it was designed to do. Evaluation of outcome examines the effectiveness of the program in achieving the expected or predicted outcomes. An issue with evaluation of outcomes has to do with the length of time an outcome should be maintained after it is achieved. Outcome evaluation is often done at the end of service and at a follow-up point in the future. Evaluation of efficiency attempts to compare the value of the outcome in human terms to the cost of that outcome in terms of dollars spent. Is the outcome achieved at a reasonable cost? The quantification of human benefit for purposes of objective evaluation is an obviously difficult task.

   PE Process.   To begin the PE process, the organization must define for itself the type of evaluation it will perform. While all four types of PE are used in the evaluation of health care services the most commonly used are the evaluation of outcomes and the evaluation of efficiency.

   Evaluation of outcomes begins with a definition of the objectives the program is intended to produce. What does the organization expect to achieve as a result of the service it offers? Health care program/service objectives can be defined many ways including: length of treatment, amount of treatment, change in function, cost of services, discharge outcome, discharge destination, and status at follow-up.

   Evaluation of efficiency begins with a definition of outcome of the program/service objectives. It proceeds from there to evaluate that outcome in terms of resource utilization. Comparison of outcome to resource utilization results in efficiency measures for the services provided. Efficiency can be expressed in terms of cost per unit of outcome, cost per treatment period, treatment length per unit of outcome, units of service per unit of gain or any other combination of resource used to outcome achieved. Efficiency evaluations are most often used to compare similar human services programs. They allow the selection of a program based on both efficiency and effectiveness. To make these comparisons, the same eval-

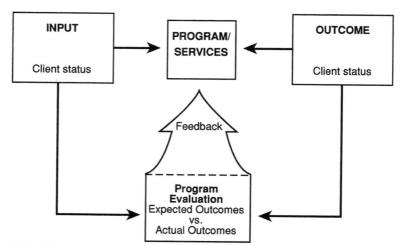

Figure 7.4. The program evaluation process in health care.

uation system must be utilized. The PE process in health care is depicted in Figure 7.4.

Evaluation of Outcomes: How to Begin.   Evaluation of program outcomes begins with the definition of program objectives. Performance expectations must be established for each of the program/service expectations. Performance expectations are often set for subgroupings of clients based on diagnosis. A performance expectation can be expressed as an average expected outcome for the objective, a range of acceptable outcome, or both. Example 7.5 below presents the performance expectations from physical therapy treatment of a client following an uncomplicated total knee replacement.

Discrepancies between actual and expected outcomes should be evaluated. Programs/services are modified based on the outcome of the evaluation. Evaluation may indicate that expectations are unrealistic and need modification. When possible, performance expectations should be based on data obtained from outside sources as well as internal sources.

To assess client outcome, a reliable evaluation tool must be used (11). In Example 7.5, the client outcome was related to range of motion (ROM) and independent function. The measurement of ROM can be standardized and a reliability coefficient determined (12). There is less agreement regarding the measurement of function, in part because of difficulty

EXAMPLE 7.5
Physical Therapy Program Outcome Exceptions

Total Knee Replacement (Uncomplicated)	

Length of treatment
  10 inpatient treatments
  18 outpatient treatments
	Sitting knee AROM:
	  − 5 to 0° terminal extension
	  90 to 100° flexion

Expected outcome:
  Independent mobility—community
  Independent home exercise program
	Cost of services:
	  $2500 to $3000

Figure 7.5.   Common data elements for service evaluation.

defining function (13). An organization could select one of the published reliable and validated methods to define levels of mobility. Alternately, it can design its own system. However, the difficulty of establishing the validity of functional measurement instruments is outside of the interest and capabilities of most facilities. Currently, the trend is toward selecting nationally recognized measurement instruments and methods because of the future potential to compare program/service specific outcome data to a national data base (14).

SERVICE EVALUATION COMMON DATA ELEMENTS

There are a number of similarities and crossover points between QA, UR, and PE. "All reporting for UR, QA, and PE has one essential theme: documentation of patient potential, status, progress and outcome. There is considerable overlap in the design of the elements and the data resources required to report activities" (15). The focus for each is different, but much of the data used to make the assessments is common to all three processes.

There are several benefits of using a common data base which supports all three of the service evaluation processes. The first benefit is cost. By utilizing a common data base for all three functions the organization can save the time and the cost of duplicating the collection of common data elements. The second benefit is the speed with which the data can be translated into usable reports. This last benefit assumes that the data elements are maintained on a computer.

According to Sulton et al. (15), the common data elements include client information, such as admitting diagnosis, status upon admission, program under which treatment was received, actual amount and type of services provided, length of service, status at the time of discharge, and status at follow-up. In addition, demographic and financial data are required to evaluate service needs and program/service efficiency. Figure 7.5 illustrates the concept of the shared data base.

SUMMARY

This chapter has provided physical therapy managers with a background in management activities related to planning, direction, and evaluation of the activities for which they are responsi-

ble. This information should provide the physical therapy manager with a starting point, the basic understanding of how management in health care functions. Each management situation will present variations on the information provided here. The principles and the purposes of the activities should, however, remain the same.

CASE STUDY 7.1
Quality Monitoring in Physical Therapy Practice

Independent Physical Therapists, Incorporated

Independent Physical Therapists, Inc. (IPT, Inc.) has just completed an annual review of its QA plan. A decision has been made to add two new performance indicators to the monitoring process. The first indicator will monitor the consistency of client and/or family involvement in goal setting. The other will monitor the quality of services provided to IPT, Inc. clients by outside agents. Outside agents include equipment suppliers, prosthetists, and orthotists. You have been assigned the responsibility of updating the QA plan. The activities of treatment planning and client referral for outside services are the selected activities. You must now define the important aspects of these chosen activities, establish quality indicators and tolerance thresholds, and determine how these activities can be monitored. The method of monitoring should be as efficient as possible.

Appendix 7.1 may be reviewed after you have worked out your QA plan.

References

1. Crego ET, Deaton B, Schiffrin PD. How to write a business plan. 2nd Ed. American Management Association, undated:1–22.
2. Pegels CC, Rodgers KA. Strategic management of hospitals and health care facilities. Rockville, MD: Aspen, 1988:XIV,24–25.
3. Harrel GD, Fors MF. Planning evolution in hospital management. Health Care Manage Rev 1987;12(1):9–22.
4. Kropf R, Greenberg JA. Strategic analysis for hospital management. Rockville, MD: Aspen, 1984:7–9.
5. Webster's II New Riverside University Dictionary. Boston: Riverside Publishing, 1984:214.
6. The Joint Commission on Accreditation of Healthcare Organizations. Accreditation manual for hospitals. Chicago: Joint Commission on Accreditation of Healthcare Organizations, 1990.
7. Commission on the Accreditation of Rehabilitation Facilities. Standards manual for organizations serving people with disabilities. Tucson: Commission on Accreditation of Rehabilitation Facilities, 1990.
8. McEachern S. All eyes on medical outcomes. Healthweek Feb 1990;26:28,33.
9. Werner JP. The cost of quality. Healthcare Productivity Rep 1989;14(12):7–12.
10. Posavac EJ, Carey RG. Program evaluation: methods and case studies. Englewood Cliffs, NJ: Prentice-Hall, 1985:1–29.
11. Rothstein J. On defining subjective and objective measurements. Phys Ther 1989;69:577–579.
12. Rothstein JM, Miller PJ, Roettger RF. Goniometric reliability in a clinical setting: elbow and knee measurements. Phys Ther 1983;63:1611–1615.
13. Jette AM. State of the art in functional status assessment. In: Rothstein JM. Measurement in physical therapy. New York: Churchill-Livingstone, 1985:137–143.
14. Morton T. Uniform data system for rehab begins: first tool measures dependence level. Prog Rep 1986;15(9):1,4.
15. Sulton LD, Hardisty B, Bisterfeldt J, Harvey RF. Computerized data bases: an integrated approach to monitoring quality patient care. Arch Phys Med Rehabil 1987;68:850–853.

CHAPTER **8**

Facilities Planning

OVERVIEW

*Facility planning refers to a process of planning for a physical
structure which will house an organization. The terms "physical
plant" or "structure" refer to the building, its internal layout, and
the external environment, including grounds, parking area, lighting, driveways, and landscaping. Logically, a major consideration
in facility planning is that the physical plant be designed to accommodate the market(s) and product(s) identified in the mission
statement. Other factors that need to be considered include federal, state, and local building codes, staff needs, service functions,
and equipment. An architectural consultant should be consulted
regarding codes and building matters. Physical therapists, however, must provide the initial input to the consultant on the physical therapy service-related factors.*

*Facility planning for a physical therapy organization is the fo-
cus of this chapter. A planning process will be presented using the
development of a freestanding, outpatient facility for physical therapy service as a model. The role of the physical therapist owner/
manager in the facility planning process will be emphasized.*

Introduction

The formulation of philosophical and mission statements precede
and drive facility and equipment planning as they do all other types of
strategic plans. Once this conceptual guidance is formulated, planning
can proceed. As early as possible in the planning process, those who will
use the space should be involved in identifying how the space will be
used (1, 2). Users include staff and clients (3, 4). Staff will be interested

167

in what fixed equipment will be required and other therapy-related matters. Clients' concerns might include access, convenience, and privacy. The input of those who will use the space is necessary to formulate a general facilities plan. The general plan is used as a starting point by the architect (1). An architect uses these preliminary plans to develop an understanding of the needs and desires of the client. From this understanding comes appropriate recommendations for the building technology, the possibilities the building site offers, and a detailed blueprint of the design of the physical plant (3). The early, or preliminary, plan includes identification of needs, schematic sketches, and indications of the anticipated flows of traffic (1–3, 5). The preceding planning process is presented diagrammatically in Figure 8.1.

The process outlined in Figure 8.1 identifies the earliest components of a facilities planning process. This is where most physical therapists will be called upon for their input. The succeeding stages which eventually result in the actual construction of a physical plant are: design refinement, preparation of construction materials and specification documents, securing bids for material and construction, issuance of the building contracts, and construction contract management (3).

PLANNING MODEL

In the past, facilities planning for physical therapists has been often based on a hospital physical therapy department model (1, 2, 6). In Chapter 12 it will become clear that a different model is needed for the 1990s. The following synopsis of anticipated changes in health care delivery systems includes several considerations for facility planners. The physical plant model for physical therapy services in the future is one which will serve outpatients (2, 3). The facility will likely be freestanding (3) (i.e., an entity separate from a hospital). Preventative services will be provided (4) in addition to treatment of pathological conditions. More clients over 65 years of age will be available for services than ever before (4).

In consideration of the trends noted above, a freestanding outpatient physical therapy facility which offers health promotion and restorative products will be used as the basic model. Facilities planning for this environment will be organized around four steps that a physical therapist can follow to prepare an initial plan for a facility.

Four-Step Facilities Planning Process

The steps involved in the facility planning process are activity description, activity grouping, activity flow, and room design (3).

Step One: Activity Description

The design process begins with a complete identification and description of the activities that are expected to occur in the facility (1–5). The philosophical statement and mission statement of the health care organization should provide the foundation for this step of the process. For example, a value of meeting the needs of the local community and a

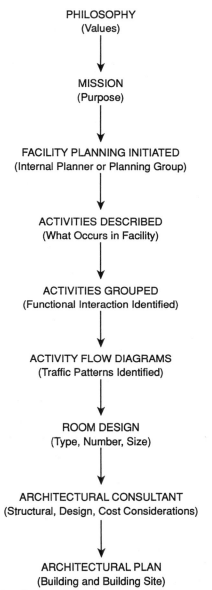

PHILOSOPHY
(Values)

MISSION
(Purpose)

FACILITY PLANNING INITIATED
(Internal Planner or Planning Group)

ACTIVITIES DESCRIBED
(What Occurs in Facility)

ACTIVITIES GROUPED
(Functional Interaction Identified)

ACTIVITY FLOW DIAGRAMS
(Traffic Patterns Identified)

ROOM DESIGN
(Type, Number, Size)

ARCHITECTURAL CONSULTANT
(Structural, Design, Cost Considerations)

ARCHITECTURAL PLAN
(Building and Building Site)

Figure 8.1. Major steps in a facility planning process.

mission to care for clients who have office work-related injuries and disabilities assist the decision-making process in many ways. The location of the facility should be in proximity to a large concentration of office workers. Sufficient convenient parking would encourage patronage. Being open for extended hours would make it convenient to attend therapy without missing work, but may raise concerns about client and staff security.

A broader, more diverse target market will require a more general, less specific approach to facilities planning and equipment selection. The size of the various pieces of equipment, the amount of different exercise devices, the projected frequency of usage, the volume of sound associated with the equipment, and the need for privacy during use all impact on the size of the area dedicated to a particular piece of equipment (3, 5). The sum of these various areas make up the total space required for equipment and utilization.

Activity areas common to a physical therapy practice include reception, waiting, rest rooms, treatment space, offices, conference rooms, storage, employee lounge, and shower/locker rooms.

Step Two: Activity Grouping

Once anticipated activities have been identified and defined, they can be grouped together based on their functional relationships (1–3, 5). Therapeutic relationships such as physical agents followed by mobilization and strengthening activities may be used to identify functional groupings of activities that need to be adjacent to one another in the facility.

A second way to group activities is by work flow. If an aide, an assistant, and a therapist all carry out a portion of the care, then a functional grouping is needed that will allow all three individuals to be near one another. This will allow them to continue to provide services to other clients without neglecting any one client.

Shared functions is a third grouping alternative. Office space, storage, and rest rooms which are used jointly by individuals performing their primary work in different areas of the facility are examples of shared activity areas. Secretarial, reception, and waiting areas are also commonly shared services and spaces.

For discussion purposes, a scenario based on Independent Physical Therapists, Inc. (IPT, Inc.) will be used. IPT, Inc. is planning a new, privately owned facility which will serve a professional office worker market. The specifically designated segments of this market are female secretaries, computer terminal operators, and other office workers who do repetitive tasks while seated. The activities that are anticipated to occur in this new location are shown grouped by functional relationships in Figure 8.2.

Step Three: Activity Flow

The movement of people from activity area to activity area is called the activity flow (3). Activity flow is created by staff, client, and visitor traffic within and between activity groupings. Activity flow can be described in a narrative discussion (1–5), presented in a schematic diagram (1–3, 5), or by a combination of narration and diagrams (1–3, 5). The more complicated the activity flow patterns, the more beneficial diagrams become when communicating with architectural consultants. Facility diagrams at this point in the planning process are very general (i.e., without dimensions or specific shape) (1–3, 5). However, the size of the various activity areas may be represented in proportion to one another. The purpose of activity flow diagrams is to depict the volume of traffic between

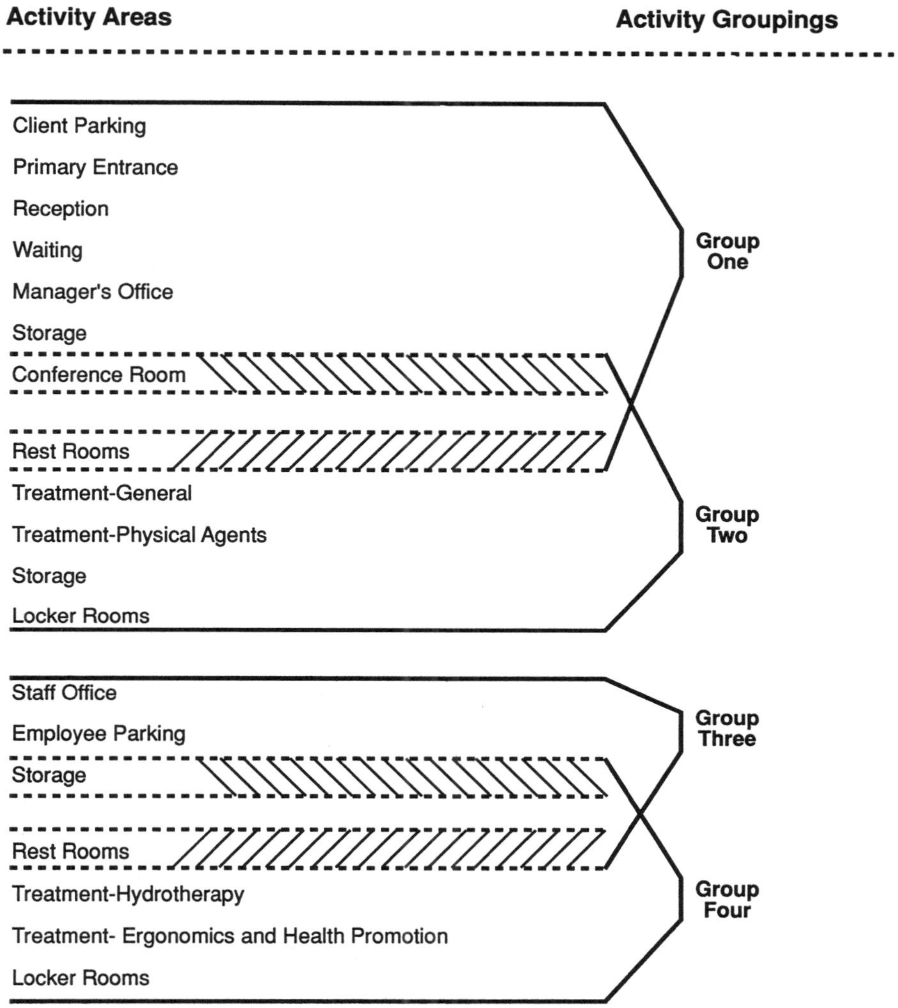

Activity Areas   **Activity Groupings**

- -

Client Parking

Primary Entrance

Reception

Waiting   **Group
                                                            One**

Manager's Office

Storage

Conference Room

Rest Rooms

Treatment-General

Treatment-Physical Agents   **Group
                                                            Two**

Storage

Locker Rooms

Staff Office

Employee Parking   **Group
                                                            Three**

Storage

Rest Rooms

Treatment-Hydrotherapy   **Group
                                                            Four**

Treatment- Ergonomics and Health Promotion

Locker Rooms

Figure 8.2. Activity groupings for IPT, Inc. *Striped areas* represent shared utilization.

activity areas. This gives an early perspective of the overall pattern and volume of traffic for the entire facility. By trial and error, a physical therapist can diagram a facility plan that is very useful to an architect. Figure 8.3 is an activity flow diagram for IPT, Inc.

Estimating Flow Volume. Traffic patterns can be determined by several methods. If a similar type of practice is in operation, observations can be made and tallied for different time periods (1, 2). Past records can be reviewed to determine the number of units of service provided in each treatment area (1, 2). In the absence of physical volume data, it is necessary to use some method of estimating traffic volume. Accreditation agencies and professional associations can provide useful estimates of space, volume, and staff relationships (3, 4, 6). The important factors to consider in estimating space utilization and flow patterns are similar to those used in calculating a fee for services. These factors are (3):

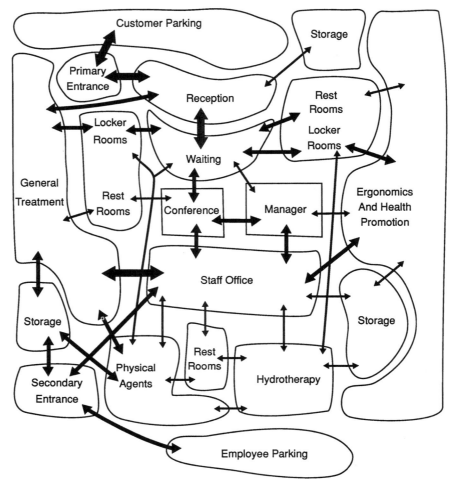

Figure 8.3. Activity flow diagram of IPT, Inc. Width of the *arrows* indicates relative volume of the flow of people.

1. Client visits per year/days open;
2. Type of service(s) provided as percent of total visits;
3. Average length of each type of service provided;
4. Hours of operation;
5. Special equipment needed and how many of each piece of equipment.

A less complicated, but less precise, volume and flow estimate method is to use average values obtained from studies of similar facilities which offer physical therapy services (3), professional association recommendations (3, 4), and personal experience (1, 2, 5). Table 8.1 lists selected physical therapy space recommendations from several sources (1–5).

While the above space recommendations are helpful when no other data is available, following them does not guarantee a suitable physical therapy facility. There are too many variables. For example, treatment durations vary because of individual client needs and therapist skill and treatment preferences. Exercise equipment comes in a variety of sizes and

Table 8.1.
Size Recommendations for Planning Selected Health Care Spaces

Space	Size[a]	Volume Comment	Setting	Ref.
Parking	12 ft wide	1 car with door fully opened plus space between cars	All types	4
	16 ft wide	1 van with wheelchair lift		
Reception	50	Per person	Outpatient	3
Waiting room	15	Per person. Expect escorts.	All types	3
		Total allocation is 1.5 × maximal number of clients waiting		4
Rest room	30	For nonhandicapped user	All types	3
	42–46	For handicapped/wheelchair user		1
Locker	3–7	Sizes vary	All types	3
	10	Per client		1
Shower	20	Per stall, non-handicapped		3
Dressing cubicle	15		Outpatient	3
Exam room	100		Inpatient	2
Treatment cubicle	80	2–3 per 10–20 clients	All types	1
Gym		Used by 66% of clients	Inpatient	2
Exercise equipment	140–160	Each major item	Outpatient	3
Manager office	100–150	1 person, depending on whether there are files to house	Outpatient	3
Staff office	80–120	1 person, depending on whether there are files to house	Outpatient	3
Dictation cubicle	20	1 person and chair	Outpatient	3
Storage		10% of treatment space	Rehab	2

[a]Except for parking, all figures relate to square footage.

shapes and technological advancements are frequent. Computer terminals are being used where handwritten documents were formally constructed. Such variables make space and flow estimates based on general guidelines alone inadequate. These estimates need modification based on personal insights supported by experience working in or planning for like facilities.

Step Four: Room Design

There are three important considerations in designing a room: type, size, and quantity (3). The room type is dependent on the purpose the room is intended to serve. Functional designations for room types are activity, support, and administration (3). For example, in Figure 8.3, there are four treatment rooms used for direct care activities, 10 support areas (parking, entrances, storage, bath, and locker rooms) and five administrative rooms (reception, waiting, conference, and offices). The quantity of rooms that are needed is determined by analyzing several factors. These factors are the projected volumes of activity, the number of staff needed to meet the projected volume, and the reasonableness of combining activities in a single room type (3). The anticipated volume of services estimated by IPT, Inc.'s management is reflected in the relative amount of space allocated to each of the service areas in Figure 8.3.

Design Considerations. Factors to consider throughout the room design phase are visibility, accessibility, safety, versatility, and image (3).

1. Visibility of the client: Can the area activity be seen by the staff when necessary without undue inconvenience or wasted effort?
2. Accessibility to the area: Can the work area be accessed easily by clients and staff?
3. Safety of people and property: Have all reasonable steps been taken to ensure the physical safety of clients, staff, visitors, and their personal property as well as the physical plant and equipment?
4. Versatility of the area: Is the current layout and design reasonably flexible so future needs for expansion or for other configurations can be met?
5. Image presented: Are the philosophy and mission of the organization reflected in the appearance of the environment?

Facilities planning is important to the entire service delivery process. An inefficient, inadequate facility can jeopardize safety, create frustration for clients and staff, and result in financial loss from underutilization and possible legal actions.

Renovation Versus New Facility Construction

Renovation of an existing facility may offer an alternative to new facility construction. The cost of renovation of an existing facility is usually less expensive than new construction (1, 2). A second reason to consider remodeling is to acquire an ideal location to carry out the mission of the organization. More space may be acquired at a lower cost by remodeling an existing structure. Potential limitations of existing structures include structural defects and outdated, inadequate electrical, heating, cooling, and plumbing systems. Replacement of these basic systems may bring renovation costs close to the cost of new construction. An architect may provide comparative costs for remodeling and new construction based on the activity descriptions, activity groupings, and activity flow diagrams provided by the client. The cost of removing an existing structure or acquiring land will have to be added to the construction costs. While large initial cost differences between remodeling and new construction are typical, in the long run, the most energy efficient structure may save some money. It is difficult to bring older structures up to the energy saving standards of newer facilities.

SUMMARY

Planning a facility for providing physical therapy services can be guided by a four-step process. The philosophy and mission of an organization describe, in general terms, the physical environment necessary to provide the services to a targeted market segment. From these general guidelines a list can be made which specifies the direct care service areas that will be needed as well as complementary support and administrative areas that will be needed. A free-hand diagram of various locations of the service, support, and administrative areas can then be drawn. The anticipated traffic flow between naturally related areas is drawn on the dia-

gram. *By trial and error, the various traffic flow relationships be-*
tween functionally related areas can be worked out by a physical
therapist to produce an efficient activity flow pattern. Flow dia-
grams are then submitted to an architectural consultant for dis-
cussion. Once the consultant understands the needs and desires
of the client, he or she will then add detail and building-related
specificity to the facility plan so costs can be identified. Alterna-
tive physical plant designs can also be prepared as revisions of
needs and resources become evident.

CASE STUDY 8.1
Improved Facility Plan

Independent Physical Therapists, Inc. (IPT, Inc.)

IPT, Inc. has been used as an example throughout this chapter. You should review
the activity grouping and activity flow sections of this chapter to reorient yourself to this
corporation. The current operation has been very successful. Plans are being initiated
to build a similar facility in a different part of the same city. One problem you have noted
in the original facility is as follows.

Clients often enter the staff entrance and walk through the entire facility to get to the
reception desk. This increases traffic between the locker rooms, waiting, and physical
agents areas. In bad weather, this outside traffic brings in dirt and snow. Some clients
walk into the staff office area to talk with therapists before or after their treatment time.
This interferes with the therapists' ability to be on time for other appointments.

Locking the secondary entrance or installing an electronic pass card entry system
could rectify the situation at the existing facility. What internal and/or external change(s)
would you suggest in the facility plan depicted in Figure 8.3 for the new setting which
would reduce or eliminate this problem? To depict your suggestions, use Figure 8.3.
Add your suggested changes and rename the various areas in accord with your ideas
for improvements.

Consult Appendix 8.1 for one solution.

References

1. Magistro CM. Department planning, design, and construction. In Hickok RJ, ed. Physical
   therapy administration and management. Baltimore: Williams & Wilkins, 1974:143–183.
2. Magistro CM. Department planning, design, and construction. In Hickok RJ, ed. Physical
   therapy administration and management. 2nd ed. Baltimore: Williams & Wilkins, 1982:59–
   98.
3. Rostenberg B. Design planning for freestanding ambulatory care facilities. Chicago: American Hospital Publishing, 1986:5,18,45–46,79–80,88–89,92,108,115–117.
4. Reizenstein Carpman J, Grant MA, Simmons DA. Design that cares: planning health
   facilities for patients and visitors. Chicago: American Hospital Publishing, 1986:29,106,271.
5. Lord PJ, Johnston BE. Your private practice: planning and organization. Lake City: Peter
   J. Lord, 1982:27–28,129,131–132,136,140.
6. Quinn P. APTA resource guide. Design and planning of physical therapy and rehabilitation departments. Alexandria: American Physical Therapy Association, undated and
   unpaginated.

Health Care Marketing

OVERVIEW

This chapter defines and discusses marketing in the context of health care organizations with a specific emphasis on physical therapy. Health care involves the exchange of a service or product for money. The seller is the care provider and the buyer is the customer. Marketing is an attempt by either seller or buyer to influence the decision of the other party involved in the exchange. Marketing is more than selling. It also entails advertising, market research, new product development, customer service, distribution of service, and anything else that will potentially increase customer satisfaction. Because of this expanded concept of marketing everyone who has contact with customers is involved in some aspect of marketing. A market-oriented organization is one which chooses to focus its activities on meeting customer needs. The organization adjusts its structure to facilitate bringing about customer satisfaction. The utilization of a strategic marketing process is discussed as a complementary and parallel function to the overall strategic business plan. Market analysis and market strategy, the major component parts of a strategic marketing process, are presented in detail. Eight conditions under which marketing strategies can have a specific impact on physical therapy services are discussed. Future trends in health care marketing are highlighted to give the reader additional insights into the ways mar-

*keting can affect the delivery of physical therapy services. The
case study at the end of this chapter appropriately focuses on
marketing physical therapy services.*

Introduction

Marketing is a relatively recent phenomenon in the health care industry. Little over a decade ago, marketing by health care providers was
rarely, if ever, seen (1). Hospitals and physicians were the primary providers of health care services. There was little competition for clients.
Hospitals were generally full and physicians were busy. Health care was
definitely a high growth rate industry. The prosperity of the health care
industry became even greater in 1965 with the advent of Medicare. With
the government as a major purchaser of health care, the demand for these
services increased dramatically.

During the 1980s major changes in the health care industry occurred.
Declining inpatient census and the entry of new alternative providers into
the health care market both led to increased competition for consumers.
Health care providers have responded to these changes with an increased
interest and investment in marketing activities. The first attempts at marketing health care services came from hospitals. These early marketing
efforts were designed simply to reach large numbers of people. They were
often expensive and their effectiveness was hard to measure. Today's
health care marketing is more sophisticated. Marketing efforts are much
more likely to be directed at specific audiences via inexpensive means
(1).

Marketing is more than selling. It is a process that integrates the
functions of selling, advertising, market research, new product development, customer service, and distribution which impinge on customer needs
and satisfaction (2). The goal of marketing should be to maximize consumer satisfaction. To achieve this goal an organization must define, price,
and distribute products and services in a manner that meets customers'
needs. Furthermore, it must accomplish these tasks in a economically
sound and competitively viable manner.

Marketing activities focus on the use of the exchange process to
satisfy human needs and wants. A product or service is exchanged for
money. An organization's market comprises all of the actual and potential
buyers of its product or service. Marketing occurs when either party interested in the exchange of a product or service attempts to influence the
responses of the other party (2).

Health care organizations are involved in many types of exchange
processes. Take for example a private physical therapy practice. The manager of a private physical therapy practice will deal with the labor market
in the search for employees. The manager will deal with the equipment
market when purchasing supplies and equipment. If the practice requires
outside funding the manager may be called upon to deal with lenders.
And, the physical therapy manager will attempt to influence responses
in the customer market. In dealing with the labor, equipment vendors,
and lenders, the physical therapy manager is the consumer. In the cus-

tomer market the physical therapy manager is on the opposite side of the product or service exchange transaction.

Traditionally, responsibility for health care marketing has fallen to a few select individuals identified by such titles as marketing manager, sales manager, customer service representative, or public relations manager. The job of the person responsible for marketing was to stimulate demand for the organization's products or services (2). Today many organizations have a more dispersive view of marketing responsibility. Inside and outside of the health care industries, there is a trend toward global organizational commitment to the marketing effort. Marketing is becoming the responsibility of every member of an organization.

The trend toward an increased customer orientation switches the organization's focus from itself to its environment. Organizations with a customer orientation are referred to as "market oriented" (3). Market oriented means that customer needs, not the demands of competition, determine the organization's marketing strategies (4). It follows that all strategic decisions reflect consideration of the customers' needs and desires. While attention to customer needs is the starting point, an analysis of the organization's freedom to respond to those needs is essential. This analysis must be accompanied by a genuine commitment and willingness to change internally to meet customer needs.

The organization's freedom to respond to identified customer needs can be limited by both internal and external factors. Internal constraints may come from lack of resources, lack of skill, or lack of desire. External constraints come from both competitors and the "interested public" (2). The interested public includes groups that have an interest in and can constrain an organization's ability to respond to the needs of its customers. Health care has many interested and actively involved publics.

The government, the community, the media, financial institutions, professional organizations, such as the American Physical Therapy Association, and independent regulatory agencies all place constraints on the way a health care organization conducts its business.

Strategic Marketing Process
PHILOSOPHY

There are a number of different marketing philosophies which can guide the management of marketing efforts. The more recent of these is the marketing concept (2). The marketing concept focuses on the needs of the buyer, not the seller. The market-oriented concept of marketing is based on three underlying assumptions. These are:

1. That the total market of potential buyers can be segmented based on their divergent needs and wants;
2. That potential buyers will respond favorably to the product or service that comes closest to meeting those specific needs and wants;
3. That analysis and selection of target markets and the adoption of an effective marketing strategy will allow the organization to attract and hold customers.

Figure 9.1. The component parts of a strategic marketing process.

PROCESS

The strategic marketing process starts with an analysis of all potential markets. From this analysis flows the selection of those markets to be targeted. A marketing strategy for each target market is selected. From this strategy, a specific marketing plan can be developed, implemented, and monitored. Figure 9.1 depicts a basic version of the strategic marketing process.

FOUNDATION

The foundation of the strategic marketing process is the organization's strategic business plan. The strategic business plan describes the organization and defines its mission (see Chapter 7 for a review). Through an identification of internal and external issues, the strategic business plan sets goals and objectives for the future. It then seeks to define the competitive strategy which will achieve the desired outcomes. The strategic marketing process is an integral part of the overall strategic planning effort. It complements each step of the strategic planning process. The interdependence of these processes is depicted in Figure 9.2. The processes of strategic planning and strategic marketing are intertwined from start through implementation.

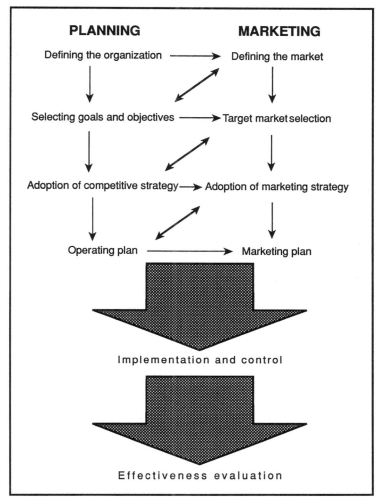

PLANNING   **MARKETING**

Defining the organization ⟶ Defining the market

Selecting goals and objectives ⟶ Target market selection

Adoption of competitive strategy ⟶ Adoption of marketing strategy

Operating plan ⟶ Marketing plan

Implementation and control

Effectiveness evaluation

Figure 9.2.   Strategic marketing as a part of the strategic planning process.

Market Analysis

Market analysis can be broken down into four categories. These are analyses of the environment, market characteristics and customer behavior, market segmentation, and demand measurement and forecasting (2).

ENVIRONMENTAL ANALYSIS

Environmental analysis looks at external factors which may impact on the future success of the organization. For example, what are the trends, opportunities, and threats that face the organization now and in the future? Environmental analysis should investigate factors affecting demographics, economics, the natural environment, technology, the legislative environment, and the cultural environment (2). The outcome of environmental analysis is an enhanced ability to respond to environmental changes. This outcome occurs because the organization will be more aware of environmental changes and will incorporate the effects of a changing environment into its strategic plan.

MARKET CHARACTERISTIC ANALYSIS

Market analysis looks at the customer side of the product and service exchange process. This part of the analysis should provide a solid understanding of the organization's market. There are six questions which will provide insight into the market (2). They are:

1. Who are the current and potential buyers of the organization's products and/or services?
2. What products and/or services do they buy?
3. Under what circumstances do they buy?
4. Who is involved in the exchange transaction? What are their roles?
5. What motivates the market to buy the products and/or services they actually do buy? What do they hope to achieve?
6. Where, when, and how does the exchange actually take place?

The answers to these questions can be complex. This is usually the case for health care situations in which there may be several persons involved in a single transaction. Take for example the purchase of physical therapy treatment for a child with delayed motor development. The physician may initiate the transaction by recommending the purchase of physical therapy services to the child's parent. The parent will ultimately decide from whom to purchase the service. The decision may be influenced by family, friends, the physician, an employer, or other influential parties. The family's health insurance carrier may actually buy the physical therapy service. The child will use the service. For this one transaction, there are five or more parties involved. Furthermore, these parties may be looking for different things. The insurance carrier may be looking for cost-effective services. The parent may be looking for convenience and a better future for the child. The physician may be looking for happy parents, control over all aspects of care, or good communication about treatment plans and outcomes.

MARKET SEGMENTATION

Market segmentation serves to focus an organization's marketing efforts. A single organization cannot be all things to all people. To be effective and efficient, an organization must concentrate its marketing efforts on strategically selected markets which it can serve well (1). Markets may be segregated on the basis of size, location, wants and needs, buying habits, or other differentiating characteristics (2). Health care organizations might focus on physicians, potential clients, third party payers, employers, other health care providers, attorneys, volunteers, or the government as specific market segments. Each of these market segments can then be further subdivided based on their differentiating characteristics. For example, the geriatric market is a subset of the whole consumer market. The physician looking for convenience and communication may be more likely to refer to a therapy practice located in his or her office building. Marketing strategy can be based on any of the preceding differentiating characteristics or combinations of these characteristics.

DEMAND MEASUREMENT AND FORECASTING

Demand measurement and forecasting activities seek to quantify current and potential demand. They also seek to link specific demand forecasts to analysis of environmental factors, market characteristics, and market segments.

Listed below are five bases upon which demand can be measured or forecasted.

1. Organizations can analyze their own past experience. In this way actual cycles, trends, and buyer characteristics and preferences can be identified.
2. Current and potential customers can be asked for their opinions. This can be done through surveys, pilot programs, and individual and/or group discussions.
3. Industry experts can be asked for their opinions.
4. Demographic information available from a variety of public and private organizations can be used to predict demand for specific services.
5. Information about environmental trends can be developed internally or purchased from research firms.

Marketing Strategy

Marketing strategy refers to the methods chosen to meet the needs and wants of the specific market segments that have been targeted for attention. Organizations often look at marketing strategy as a method of establishing an edge over the competition. A gain in market share is often at the expense of a competitor. Beating the competition becomes the goal of marketing strategy. Beating the competition is important for the survival and growth of an organization, but it should not be the first consideration in the design of marketing strategy. In selecting marketing strategy, the focal point is on meeting the real needs of the customer. This priority puts matching services and customers foremost. This is something the organization can control. This focus is considered more appropriate than being driven by what the competition is or may do. What the competition does is not under the organization's control.

MARKETING TASKS

Kotler (2) defines eight different states of demand in which marketing strategy can be used. The marketing task to be performed is determined by the current perceived state of demand for the organization's products or services.

Negative Demand.   When negative demand exists the potential market has an aversion to the product or service. For example, a fitness program for older, obese employees may not be well-received by this group of employees. This is negative demand. Here, the task of marketing strategy is to create a state of positive demand (2).

Lack of Demand. A state of no demand can occur because the product has no known value, no value to a particular group of buyers, or the product is unfamiliar to a group of buyers. For example, sports physical therapy may have no perceived value to the non-athlete. The task of marketing strategy is to create demand (2).

Latent Demand. Latent demand is a situation where there is a strong need for a product or service that is not currently available. Geographical areas that lack sufficient access to physical therapy services may present opportunities due to latent demand. The marketing task would be to develop an active demand for newly available services. This would be a process of drawing a connection between the latent demand and the newly available therapy services (2).

Faltering Demand. This is the state when demand for an existing product or service is on the decline. This will occur when the market has more attractive alternatives to an existing product or service. Hospital-based physical therapy departments might experience a faltering market due to competition from a more convenient, less expensive, or specialized outpatient clinic. Existing physical therapy providers might experience a decline in demand if a key physician begins to provide physical therapy services in his office. The marketing task here is to revitalize the faltering market (2).

Irregular Demand. In the case of irregular demand the cyclical nature of the demand may make economical production difficult. Irregular demand creates a special task for marketing. Here the organization is forced to provide the capacity to meet peaks in demand while that capacity may be underutilized much of the time. This increases the costs of producing the organization's products and services. Physical therapy practices often experience peak demands for specific times of the day, days of the week, and seasons. The marketing task is used to even out the demand and supply cycles. This is often accomplished through use of special incentives for customers who purchase products or services when demand is low (2).

Full Demand. Another state that can benefit from marketing is full demand. Here the task is to maintain the level of demand that currently exists (2). Full utilization of human and environmental resources is an ideal situation for any physical therapy practice.

Overfull Demand. This occurs when demand for a product or service exceeds the organization's ability or desire to supply it. Long waiting periods to start outpatient physical therapy is an example of overfull demand. The marketing task is to decrease this demand. This can be done through the promotion of alternatives to meet customers' needs or adding disincentives to the purchase process (2).

Unwholesome Demand. Here the demand is at a level which is thought to be without benefit to the organization or detrimental to the customer. Excessive demand for physical therapy services which result in not producing a beneficial outcome would be an example of unwholesome demand. In the case of unwholesome demand, the task of marketing is to stop the demand (2). Figure 9.3 reviews the demand states before and after appropriate marketing efforts.

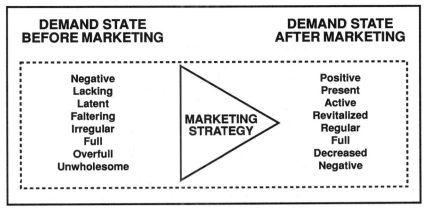

Figure 9.3. The states of marketing demand and desired effects of specific marketing strategies.

MARKETING MIX

One of the key concepts of modern marketing theory is the concept of marketing mix (2). A popular method of classifying marketing mix variables is through the four P classification system (5) presented in Figure 9.4.

The total marketing budget of an organization will be divided between these four marketing variables.

Product

Product deals with all of the features of the product. For physical therapy services this would include such things as general and specialized services, skill of staff, availability of service, physical environment, technology, and level of customer service. A genuine market orientation review suggests that a product should be designed to meet customer and not organizational needs.

Place

Place refers to the method of product or service distribution. Physical therapy services can be delivered in a variety of locations, including the customer's home, schools, physical therapy clinics, or athletic facilities. The choice of place may increase the organization's attractiveness to target markets. Location can also affect the cost of the product or service.

Price

Pricing decisions about basic fee schedules, discounts, payment periods, and credit terms will influence the marketability of the organization's product and services. These decisions also relate directly to the profitability of the organization. Refer to Chapter 5 for a review of the topic of price setting for physical therapy.

Promotion

Promotional activities, also referred to as marketing communications, can fall into one of four categories. These are advertising, personal

Figure 9.4. The four P's to consider in developing a marketing mix strategy.

selling, sales promotion, and publicity. Promotional activities are used to target selected markets and to communicate information about product, place, and price (6).

MARKETING COMMUNICATIONS
Advertising

The use of advertising by health care organizations has grown to nearly a billion dollar investment (7). Advertising comes in many forms, including the use of brochures, directories, displays, flyers, mail, media, and novelties. In addition to conveying information about product, place, and price, promotional advertising is intended to influence the response of the target market. "It is intended to create, reinforce, or change what is in an audience's mind" (6).

Planning for the use of advertising should start with the desired marketing goal, an identification of behaviors required to achieve the goals, the state of mind needed to support the desired behaviors, and the resources required to cause the desired state of mind.

Setting Marketing Goals. Goals can be expressed in terms of financial outcomes or mission outcomes. A financial outcome could be expressed in terms of volumes, revenues, or profits. A mission outcome

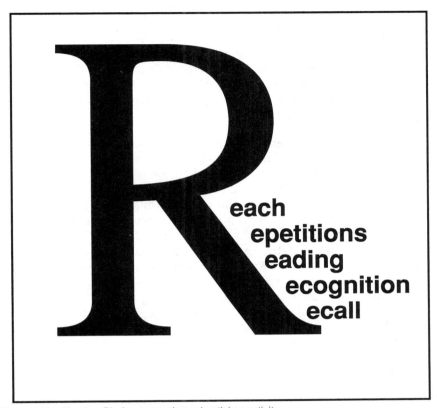

Figure 9.5. The five R's for measuring advertising activity.

might be earlier initiation of physical therapy services for a specific client population such as those with industrial injuries.

Identifying Behaviors. After the marketing goals have been identified, the next step is determine the desired response to advertising. These are behavior effects (6). Behaviors leading to desired financial and mission outcomes might include increased and/or more timely referral practices by physicians. An increased incidence of parents of developmentally delayed children or high school athletes requesting referrals to physical therapy would also lead to the desired outcome.

Required State of Mind. The relationship between state of mind and behavior moves along a continuum from awareness to preference. Preference is closely tied with the intention to act. The goal of advertising then is to move the potential buyer from a state of simple awareness to one of preference and action (6).

Resources. State of mind is affected by the activity level of the advertising effort. The five R words in Figure 9.5 are common ways in which advertising activity is measured.

Reach measures the number of people exposed to the marketing message. Repetition measures the number of times they are exposed to the message. Reading measures the number of people exposed to the message who read or pay attention to the content. Recognition refers to the number of people who can remember having been exposed to the advertising message. Recall measures the number of people who can remember the message content. These measures of advertising activity relate directly to the effectiveness of the advertising campaign. They are influenced by the types and frequency of the advertising selected. Type and frequency relate directly to the cost of the advertising effort (6).

Personal Sales

Personal selling can be performed by a variety of organizational members. Direct sales can be performed by sales representatives hired explicitly for that purpose. This is a well established approach to pharmaceutical sales. Direct sales activities can be one of the responsibilities of management. A service line manager or the president may be involved in sales to major clients or for specific products and services. Specifically designated employees such as sales clerks and receptionists will routinely engage in direct sales. With the trend toward the use of good customer service to increase customer satisfaction and sales, all employees are becoming more active in direct marketing.

Personal sales have three major advantages over advertising. First, personal sales is an active process between two people, which allows an immediate and personalized response to the needs of the customer. Second, personal sales allows for the development of a closer relationship between the sales representative and the customer. Third, personal sales is thought to increase the customer's obligation to buy (2).

Sales Promotion

In the field of marketing anything that does not fit well into the categories of advertising, direct sales, or publicity is called sales promotion. Things such as special events, giveaways, discounts, special purchase plans, and incentive programs are promotion. In physical therapy, offering a free assessment as an inducement to purchase future services would be a sales promotion.

Current Trends in Health Care Marketing
LESSONS LEARNED

During the past decade, health care providers, primarily hospitals, have learned much about the art and science of marketing. Coile (8) summarizes the lessons that have been learned from tactics to budgets. These hard-learned lessons form a good starting point for a discussion of marketing trends for the 1990s.

1. The focus of marketing should be the needs and desires of the customer.
2. The strategic marketing plan should flow from and be consistent with the values, mission, and product/services of the organization.
3. Effective approaches to marketing communications include personal sales to physicians, the adoption of a "consistent look" (8) to enhance customer recognition, and the use of periodic media exposure to develop lasting consumer recognition.
4. Organizational expenditures related to marketing represent a lasting commitment of 1–2% of the organization's budget. These expenditures should be "planned, measured and monitored for return on investment" (8).

TRENDS
Market Segmentation

The first notable trend in health care marketing is an increased emphasis on market segmentation. In contrast to early health care marketing efforts, health care providers are "more likely to target their marketing efforts" (1). Major market segments attracting attention include consumers, physicians, and payers. Segmentation of the consumer market is facilitated by an increased emphasis on product line management. Product line management allows the organization to focus on special services for special market segments. (See Chapter 2 for additional information on product line management.)

Market Research

A second trend in health care marketing is an increased use of market research. This research is directed at analyzing such things as the demographics, differentiating characteristics, needs and wants, and buying habits of the target markets (8). Market research is also used to obtain information about competitors. Market research provides a basis for demand measurement and forecasting. Through the use of market research activities, the organization can determine the marketing tasks to be accomplished and make sound decisions about the marketing strategy (9).

Innovative Marketing Communications

More varied and innovative approaches to marketing communications is another notable trend. Advertising will remain central to health care providers' efforts to reach consumers, but health care providers are no longer limiting themselves to traditional media advertising. This is evidenced by an increased use of personal sales and promotional activities. The use of personal sales activities to market to physician and payer markets is on the rise. Health care organizations are using promotional sales techniques, such as coupons, to differentiate their products/services from those offered by the competition. What will tie diverse marketing communications together will be their common image. A common image or "brand name" will generalize the consumer's knowledge of a specific product line to all of the organization's product lines (8).

Quality And Customer Service

Finally, quality and customer service will become major components of the marketing strategy directed at consumer markets. Consumer research indicates that health care providers will face increased demands from an informed public. Recent analysis of consumer data compiled over a five-year period revealed several preferences of today's consumers. Consumers will: (a) wish to be active participants in selecting a hospital; (b) question recommendations; (c) notice health care advertising; and (d) differentiate between hospital and health care services (10). With the consumer increasingly in control when it comes to selecting a health care provider it is imperative for marketing strategy to address the need for quality and service.

The concepts of quality and service are often inseparable in the mind of the consumer. Health care providers need to create the desired image of quality. Health care consumers judge quality by what they are told about the service, the learned or experienced outcomes from the service, and their satisfaction with the service. These variables challenge health care providers in several ways. First, health care providers must begin to define and quantify the quality of their health care services. The ability to define quality will be extremely important as the information needs and expectations of consumers continue to grow. Second, they must provide consumers with information about the quality of their products/ services. Third, they must meet the consumer expectations they create. Lastly, they must provide health care services in a way that results in an adequate level of customer satisfaction.

The relationship between customer satisfaction and organizational success has long been acknowledged in consumer goods and services industries. Consumers evaluate their experiences with an organization based on more than the product or service purchased. All aspects of the exchange are important. Factors such as long waiting times may deter repeat business from an otherwise satisfied customer. A recent study of client satisfaction with outpatient services indicated that dissatisfaction was caused by factors such as waiting, perceived lack of caring, discourteous staff, and a perception of poor quality (11). This study points out that consumer satisfaction is tied to the attitudes and actions of all of the provider's employees with whom they interact. For this reason, health care providers are implementing organization wide training programs to increase the "customer orientation" of their work force (12).

SUMMARY

In this chapter it has been indicated that health care marketing efforts are becoming more pervasive and more sophisticated. The organization that markets its products and services effectively will be one that has made the effort to understand its markets, design its products and services around that knowledge, select a marketing strategy that is consistent with its mission and products, and set in place a system for monitoring its effectiveness in the marketplace. This series of actions may make an extraordinary demand on the resources of small organizations. Success for both small and large organizations will, however, be dependent on their ability to target marketing efforts at only those markets that can be served well. The cost and effectiveness of marketing efforts can then reach maximum levels of efficiency and effectiveness. Actual selection of marketing communications techniques will flow from the marketing goals, the market definition, and the resources of the organization.

CASE STUDY 9.1
Marketing to the Health Care Consumer

Independent Physical Therapists, Inc.

Independent Physical Therapists, Inc. (IPT, Inc.) relies on physician and payer referrals for all of its new business. IPT, Inc.'s management believes that some of their outpatient orthopedic physical therapy services could be marketed directly to potential clients. IPT, Inc's management would like to coordinate the beginning of their advertising effort with the signing of the state's new direct access legislation. A local media advertising firm has projected that a general consumer advertising campaign using radio and newspapers would cost a minimum of $50,000 annually. IPT, Inc.'s Board of Directors would like some assurances that the advertising expenditure will result in client self-referrals. This is particularly true because some members of the board believe that a direct advertising campaign will be viewed as a negative competitive action by physicians who account for 30% of current referrals. The Chairman of the Board has instructed IPT, Inc. management to further evaluate the concept. To start the evaluation process, list the steps that IPT, Inc. management should take to determine the potential return on investment for the proposed marketing communications activities.

Refer to Appendix 9.1 to check your answers.

References

1. Weiss R. Hitting the target. Health Prog 1990;March:18–20.
2. Kotler P. Marketing management: analysis, planning, and control. 4th ed. Englewood Cliffs, NJ: Prentice-Hall, 1980:16.
3. Shapiro BP. What the hell is "market oriented"? Harv Bus Rev 1988;Nov–Dec:119–125.
4. Ohmae K. Getting back to strategy. Harv Bus Rev 1988;Nov–Dec:149–156.
5. McCarthy JE. Basic marketing: a managerial approach. 6th ed. Homewood: Richard D. Irwin, 1978:39.
6. MacStravic RS. Evaluating health care marketing. Health Care Manage Rev 1988;13(3):45–57.
7. Anonymous. Hospitals advertising budgets grow by 45%. Hospitals 1988;20(Mar):38.
8. Coile RC, Jr. Strategic marketing: 10 approaches that will work in the 1990s. Hospital Strategy Rep 1989;1(Oct):1–4.
9. Louden TL. Successful marketing plans for new products more important than ever. Mod Health Care 1989;17(Nov):68.
10. Christensen M, Inguanzo JM. Smart consumers present a marketing challenge. Hospitals 1989;20(Aug):42–44,46–48.
11. Christensen M, Inguanzo JM. Patient satisfaction levels decline slightly in 1989. Hospitals 1989;20(Aug):43.
12. Goldsmith M, Leebov, W. Strengthening the hospital's marketing position through training. Health Care Manage Rev 1986;11(2):83–93.

Law and Legal Concepts

OVERVIEW

This chapter deals with selected legal considerations for students, recent graduates, practicing therapists, and newly appointed therapist managers. The topics in this chapter were selected on the basis of their importance to all licensed health care professionals, managers, organization officers, and members of boards of directors.

The early part of this chapter presents an overview of legal concepts followed by a brief summary of federal laws with which the manager should become familiar. The discussion continues by clarifying what legal liability is and how it relates to professional negligence. Attention is drawn to similarities and differences between liability attached to being an employed licensed professional, an independent entrepreneur, a manager, an owner, and an organization.

Insurance against liability claims for professional negligence is analyzed from the perspectives of an individual professional employee, an employer, and an entrepreneurial practitioner. Distinctions between personal professional liability insurance, institutional liability insurance, and commercial insurance are made.

Documentation and access to medical records are discussed because they have legal implications. One implication is that note documents are often the only information available to counter claims of professional negligence. A second implication is that ac-

cess to medical information is regulated by state and federal legislation.

The final section of this chapter compares and contrasts legal and ethical obligations. This focus on the interrelationships between law and ethics sets the background for Chapter 11 which deals with values and ethics.

Introduction

The health care industry is highly regulated by state and federal laws. Licensure to practice, business laws, and fair labor practice laws are examples of legal regulation. As licensed health care professionals, physical therapist managers are under legal obligations in several different ways. For example, therapist managers are legally responsible whether treating clients themselves or delegating and supervising employees. They are also legally responsible when they deal with personnel matters such as employment, promotion, and dismissal. In order to function effectively and legally, managers require a background in management concepts and organizational behavior and an understanding of legal principles (1). Familiarity with legal principles associated with licensure, business, and employment are areas of particular interest to all health care managers. Risk of litigation can be minimized through regular and systematic consideration of the legal implications of managerial decisions (1). Conversely, the failure to recognize the legal implications of managerial decisions can lead to expensive and lengthy litigation (1).

Therapists who are members of a professional association are under the additional, and often more stringent, obligation to perform their duties in accordance with a code of ethics. Laws and ethics impose distinct obligations on health care professionals and their employers. Table 10.1 presents a parallel comparison of the major features of law and professional ethics.

Law

Law can be divided into two major categories, private law and public law (2), as shown in Figure 10.1.

PRIVATE LAW

Private law deals with the rights and obligations in activities involving other people. Private law is also called civil law (2). Civil law defines a person's legal rights and obligations, and they are stated in the statutes of the level of government which formulated them. Civil laws, which protect the rights of all citizens, are: freedom from bodily harm, defamation of character, and invasion of privacy and the right to enjoy property and to work. A violation of any of these rights may be a civil wrong, a tort, or a crime depending on the statutory laws in a jurisdiction and the severity of the infringement (3). Torts are a denial of any of the

Table 10.1.
Major Comparative Features of Law and Professional Ethics[a]

Features	Law	Professional Ethics
Formed by:	Elected governmental officials	Elected volunteers
Scope:	All members of society in a jurisdiction; mandatory rules	All members of an association; voluntary rules
Purposes:	Protect society, define societal and private wrongs; related to conduct; identify punishments, provide compensation	Protect society, define professional behavior, benefit profession; related to motives, attitudes, as well as conduct; identify punishments
Basis:	Statutory law, common law, administrative law	Philosophical principles
Formal documents:	Statutes, court decisions, executive and administrative orders, ordinances, bylaws	Code of ethics, guide for conduct, association policies, judicial committee opinions and statements
Enforcement:	Law officers and courts	Peer affiliates and association judicial committee
Penalty options:	For crimes—intent is to punish guilty party by fines, suspended sentence, an alternative to incarceration, or incarceration; For torts—intent is to compensate injured party with money or specified actions of the defendant	Intended to maintain membership standards by responding to actions which are professionally embarrassing with a reprimand, censure, suspension, or dismissal from the association.

[a]Based on the 1987 Code of Ethics of the American Physical Therapy Association.

primary rights which cause injury to another person. Negligence, malpractice, slander, and libel are covered under tort law. Other subdivisions of private law that would have applicability to health care managers are contract and commercial law, corporation law, and property law. Contractual agreements are considered secondary rights because they are voluntarily entered into and they involve only the parties identified in the contract.

Private law is largely judge-made law (4). Judges make rulings which are based on standards and customs in their jurisdiction as well as on previous court decisions. Common law is the aggregate of case law decisions (5). Common law is the result of court decisions taken when there was no statutory law related to a case (1). It is important for health care professionals to understand that adherence to prior decisions gives a judge legal backing for his or her decision. If there is no prior court decision to call upon, then a precedent-setting decision has to be made. This decision in turn becomes a new guide for other judges to weigh (1). If the precedent is useful to others, it becomes incorporated into the body of common law. Medical malpractice is one of the areas that is heavily dependent on precedent cases.

Divisions of Law

Private Law (Civil Law)	Public Law (Criminal Law)
Contract & Commercial	Administrative
Corporation	Constitutional
Family	Criminal
Property	International
Inheritance	
Tort (includes Malpractice Law)	

Figure 10.1. General branches of law. (Modified from Schwartz B. Law. In: World Book Encyclopedia. Chicago: World Book, 1985;12:117.)

PUBLIC LAW

Public law defines a person's rights and obligations in relation to society and the various levels of government (1). In addition to criminal law, other divisions of public law that have particular importance to health care managers are administrative law and constitutional law. Administrative law includes acts regulating workers' wages and hours. Constitutional law includes civil rights acts which pertain to hiring and other work-related activities (6). These latter two areas are more likely to have clearer application to the daily affairs of health care managers than does criminal law. Table 10.2 summarizes public laws with which a health care manager should become familiar.

HYBRID LAW

Private or public legislated laws are also called statutory laws. Statutory laws are defined in the statutes of the level of government that created them. Once law, a statute has to be tested in a court and a judge must interpret the law in a specific case. The result is a judge-made decision. This interpretation of the applicability of a statutory law has been called hybrid law (4).

Because of the recentness of physical therapy-related direct access legislation, continual advances in technology and basic knowledge, and the extremely dynamic nature of the health care industry, many legal questions affecting physical therapy will be answered through hybrid law. The constant interpretation and reinterpretation of court decisions make the legal process dynamic. Small differences between cases are the bases for determining whether or not a precedent case is applicable (7).

Legal Diversity

States have the right to make their own individual laws as long as they do not conflict with federal laws. What is legal in one state may not be legal in another state because of different interpretations of common law principles (4). Licensure laws reflect this diversity. Examples of these

Table 10.2.
Summary of Federal Laws Important to Management[a]

Law	Key Features
Age Discrimination in Employment Act of 1967, amended 1974 to include governmental employees, amended 1978 to raise the upper limit to 70 years	Prohibits employers of 20 or more employees from discriminating against individuals 40–65 years of age; and from depriving an individual of employment opportunities or adversely affecting status on the basis of age
Americans with Disabilities Act of 1990	Prohibits discrimination in employment on the basis of mental or physical disability
Civil Right Act of 1871, amended 1964 by Equal Employment Opportunity Act of 1972, amended 1978, Uniform Guidelines on Employee Selection Procedures	Prohibits employers of 15 or more employees from not hiring, discharging, or otherwise discriminating on the basis of color, national origin, pregnancy, age, religion, sex; and from depriving an individual of employment opportunities or adversely affect status on the bases noted above
Fair Labor Standards Act of 1938, amended in 1963 to include Equal Pay, amended in 1967 to include hospitals and in 1972 to include administrative, executive, and professional personnel[a]	Requires keeping certain work-related records, defines work week, overtime pay rate requirements, sets meal and rest break guides, sets minimum wage rate, and regulates other workplace-related activities
Federal Privacy Act of 1974	Limits the acquisition of information on U.S. citizens by federal agencies to safeguard the information; a citizen can gain access to information contained in federal agency records regarding themselves and correct or amend such records
National Health Planning and Resources Act of 1946, Hill-Burton program for funding hospital construction, amended in 1974 and 1979, encouraged comprehensive regional health care coordination in planning and services and stimulated competition between health care organizations to meet consumer needs.	The receipt of Hill-Burton funds requires the provision of below cost or free care to those unable to pay; the extent of this obligation is the lesser amount calculated as 10% of the construction loan or 3% of the operating budget
National Labor Relations Act of 1935, Taft-Hartley amendment 1947, Labor Management and Disclosure Act of 1959, amended 1974 to include health care institutions	Protects employees from retribution for organizing labor unions and supervises votes by workers on whether or not to form a union; defines unfair labor practices, collective bargaining items, contract-related guidelines, and other bargaining-related activities
Occupational Safety and Health Act of 1970	Protects the safety and health of employees by establishing industry-wide standards, conducting inspections, and investigating complaints

continues

Table 10.2. (*Continued*)

Law	Key Features
Rehabilitation Act of 1973	Requires government contractors to prepare an affirmative action plan applicable to handicapped employees. Prohibits any organization which receives federal assistance to discriminate solely on the basis of a handicap.
Robinson-Patman Act of 1936	Refined the prohibition of price discrimination between customers; differences in prices must be based on actual differences in the costs associated with the provision of services
Social Security Act of 1935, amended 1939 to include wives and dependents of retired workers and wives and dependents of deceased workers, amended 1950 to include nonprofessional self-employed workers and other workers; amended 1956 to include professional workers	Three general parts: old-age survivors, disability, and health insurance; unemployment insurance; and workers' compensation. Workers' compensation laws define employer's responsibility in the case of injury or disease occurring from activity related to an employees work. Workers' compensation component is largely administered by individual states

^aTrainees such as affiliating students are generally exempt (8).

differences are in the minimal acceptable score on the licensure examination and the opportunities for clients to have direct access to physical therapists. Because each state has its own history of interpretation of common law principles as well as its own statutes (2), it is difficult to be very specific in discussing legal matters in a multiple topic textbook such as this one. Because of the individuality of each state's statutes and court interpretations, the following discussion deals with legal principles rather than individual state laws. The absence of a large body of case law involving physical therapists (8) requires using legal analogies from the relatively large number of cases involving physicians and nurses.

Legal Concepts
Liability

Liability is defined as a duty that must be performed. There can be a duty to carry out an act or a duty to refrain from doing something. To be legally liable means that a person can be held accountable for harm caused another person (1). The harm may be a result of doing something or commission of a libelous act. Harm may also result from the failure to do something or an omission. A claim of liability is the basis of most private lawsuits in the health care field.

Negligence and Malpractice

Every citizen is liable for his or her own actions. If harm is inflicted on another person, the injured party may file suit for regress or compensation for the injury. The terms "ordinary negligence" are used to describe such cases. When an injury is alleged in a suit against a professional the term "malpractice" is used (5). Malpractice is professional negligence. Health care professionals may be specifically named as defendants in a malpractice suit because of alleged professional negligence.

When a claim of professional negligence is made, the following five factors are considered in determining whether there is liability on the part of a health care professional (9).

1. A duty was owed to the client;
2. There was a violation or breach of the duty;
3. Harm resulted from the act or omission;
4. The act or omission was the cause of harm;
5. The harm was foreseeable.

To be held legally liable for medical malpractice requires that the professional be accountable for acts of negligence he or she personally committed (10). While the thought of being sued is unnerving, some comfort can be gained from the following findings. Over 75% of medical malpractice suits are resolved in favor of the defendant (the health care professional accused of causing harm). Less than half of the suits won by the injured plaintiff resulted in any type of compensation (10). Finally, the majority of malpractice suits are settled out of court. They never go to trial (10, 11). These general findings, however, are not limited to cases in which physical therapists were the defendants.

The physical therapy malpractice situation reflects recent trends in increasing numbers of malpractice suits involving other health care professionals. A review of legal cases found that of 19 recorded suits against physical therapists, 13 (68%) of these suits occurred after 1975 (12).

The experience of one insurance carrier of malpractice insurance who covers members of the American Physical Therapy Association indicates that physical therapists have a higher number of claims and settlement costs than other non-dentist and non-physician health-related professionals they insure (13). This carrier also found that over 70% of claims filed against physical therapists from 1981 through September, 1986 involved self-employed physical therapists (11). Another carrier reported an incidence rate of 0.42 per 100 treatment exposures for all physical therapists they insured between 1983 and 1987 (12). Information from an American Physical Therapy Association staff member has identified a 13% per year increase in claims over the past several years (personal interview of Marcia Horting by Ronald J. Scott, June, 1990) (12). In general, the view of malpractice insurance carriers is that they are experiencing increasing numbers of claims filed against physical therapists and the settlements are for higher dollar amounts compared to several years ago (11, 13).

Information on the incidence of suits against physical therapists since direct access legislation has come into existence is limited. At least five years of data is preferred to establish trends in malpractice suits. Based on two carriers' findings, similar conclusions can be made. At this time, no increase in malpractice suits can be attributed solely to the availability of direct client access to physical therapists (13, 14).

Relationship between Malpractice and Licensure Laws

A state's licensure statutes related to physical therapy define the profession and the scope of activities for those practicing in the state. While the definition and the scope of practice differs by state, the purpose of the statutes is the same. Licensure is intended to protect the public and the profession from unauthorized practice and it limits practice to those who meet specific qualifications (8). By limiting licenses to those who meet stipulated criteria, the public is protected from exposure to those without sufficient preparation to safely and appropriately meet their physical therapy needs. Secondarily, the integrity of the profession is maintained by issuing licenses only to those who meet requirements. As a result of these requirements, licensure statutes can limit the number of people who can practice (8).

The common contents of licensure laws include (7):

1. Definition of the profession and scope of practice;
2. Requirements for licensure;
3. Grounds for suspension or revocation;
4. Criteria for reciprocity;
5. Penalties for practicing without a license.

The statutory scope of practice of a profession and the standard of practice are important elements considered in a malpractice suit. Licensure grants permission to engage in a given profession within the bounds of the statutory definition. The expectation is that the safety and welfare of clients will be maintained because of appropriate educational and practical experiences.

Standard of Practice

A license to practice carries the legal obligation or duty to practice as a hypothetical, competent physical therapist would practice. The duty is to do what a prudent physical therapist would have done under similar circumstances (15). Prudent is a key word. To be prudent is to use good judgment or common sense in handling one's duties. In other words, a prudent professional is careful about his or her professional conduct (16). This abstract standard of care also encourages a licensed professional to adhere to current standards of practice (10).

Acceptable standards of practice have been based on national practice rather than local practice norms in many jurisdictions (5, 15, 17). The decision to apply national norms is intended to encourage the use of the best treatment procedures that are currently available (5).

Standards of practice are determined by examining various sources of information. Standards may be determined from sources within a defendant's workplace such as job descriptions, policies and procedures, and procedure manuals. External sources of standards include professional organizations, specialty groups, governmental guidelines, manufacturer's instructions, and expert witnesses (2).

Although unlicensed, students are not exempted from the responsibility of providing the same level of care as a licensed physical therapist. Students in clinical settings are held to the standard of practice of their profession (1).

In cases alleging lack of professional skill, expert witnesses are used by both sides in the case (2). Since jury members are not likely to have the expertise to understand the intricacies of health care matters, expert witnesses are called upon to explain how the defendant did or did not act with due professional skill and care (17). With the recent developments in physical therapy fostering the growth of board certified specialists, the standard of practice can reasonably be expected to be higher in these areas of specialization as the number of specialists increases. Those who practice exclusively in an area where specialist certification exists may be held to that higher standard in court.

Statute of Limitations

There are many situations that can result in allegations of professional carelessness, for example, practicing beyond the defined scope of practice, attempting to apply a treatment without sufficient skillfulness or knowledge, or not providing due protection to a vulnerable client (17). When a client is injured under these kinds of circumstances, the injured party has a time period within which they may make a claim of medical malpractice. This legal time limit is known as the statute of limitations. Since the passage of time makes the gathering of information difficult, statutory limits are short for malpractice claims as compared to contracts. For malpractice claims the statue of limitation time range is from one to four years. The time is generally considered to begin from the time the damage occurred (17).

Criminal Malpractice

Another type of malpractice is possible in the physical therapy environment. That is criminal malpractice. Two examples of criminal malpractice are assault (threat of bodily harm) and battery (inflicting bodily harm) (7). An example of assault would be to rebuke clients by telling them that if they do not stop causing disruption in the gym you will give them more trouble than they can imagine, and they believe you. To actually physically abuse the client would be to commit battery. Battery also relates to unpermitted contact with one's body or clothing (18). There is a clear implication for physical therapists here. Consent to touch in order to treat should be requested and granted to avoid a claim of battery. Without such consent, a client might consider the contact insulting and offensive enough to make a claim.

Assault and battery are considered intentional acts that are crimes. Medical malpractice is considered an unintentional act. This difference in intent is reflected in differences in severity of penalties between crimes and torts (see Table 10.1).

LEVELS OF LIABILITY

Each professional is liable for his or her own acts. However, there are circumstances in which others may also be liable for an act of negligence. A manager may be named in a suit as a defendant along with a staff therapist. The employing organization may also be a defendant. The physician responsible for a client may be named as a defendant. Each of these situations calls upon a different set of legal principles.

Vicarious Liability

Under the common law principle of respondent superior, an employee of a health care organization is considered to be in a master-servant relationship (8). The principle perceives the employer as the master and the employee as the servant. As an agent of the master, the acts of the servant reflect upon the master who is responsible. Even though the employer did not commit the negligent act, and may even have tried to prevent it, the employer can be found liable for the acts of the negligent employee (17). The logic is, since employers receive financial benefit from the work of employees they must also share the burden of negligent employee acts (2). For liability to be extended to the employer, the negligent act must have been performed as part of the job description. The potential for vicarious liability encourages employers to maintain employee competence. Also, the provision of competent legal assistance for an employee can benefit the organization. If the employee is found not liable, the employer is also not liable under the master-servant doctrine (19).

A second form of vicarious liability is based on the doctrine of the borrowed servant. An example of this doctrine is when an employee performs professional duties negligently while under the direction of a physician who is not an employee of the same organization (2). The borrowed employee is considered to be under the control of the staff physician rather than the employing organization. Under this form of vicarious liability, the physician is equated with the captain of a ship. The captain is assumed to be in control of the crew when he is present (17). This extends the liability of the employee to the physician.

Joint Liability

The current trend is for shared liability. Employers and physicians are more likely to have higher limits of insurance coverage than does an individual therapist. The concept of shared liability means that there is potential for more compensation to injured plaintiffs proving professional negligence. One example of joint liability is where an employee is considered to have a dual servant status. The employer and the physician "borrowing" the physical therapist may be identified in the liability claim (2). Understandably, neither the employer nor the physician wishes to be found liable. Others named in a claim besides the primary defendant will make every effort to show that they were not liable. As will be discussed later, this is a very strong point to consider when making a decision whether or not to purchase personal malpractice insurance.

Managers, because of the responsibilities they have for the work of others, can be liable for the acts of staff members under certain conditions

(19). The following scenarios identify several potential areas where a manager may be considered liable.

---

1. Delegation of duties that are beyond the training or skill of a staff member;
2. Failure to observe the actions of employees and to intervene appropriately when potential harm is evident;
3. Not supervising an employee adequately;
4. Inadequate enforcement of policies and procedures which relate to client and employee safety.

These examples all relate to the responsibilities of the individual manager. As long as a therapist manager is also an employee, he/she is not held liable for the atrocious acts or omissions committed by employees whose work is under his/her control (1). The employer, however, under the doctrine of respondent superior, remains liable for damages to injured plaintiffs resulting from the acts and omissions of all employees.

Because of the extended opportunities for a manager to have an indirect connection with a negligence claim, the manager may have a greater need for personal liability protection than do staff therapists and assistants.

Corporate Liability

For many years health care organizations were granted charitable immunity from negligence cases involving their employees. However, in 1965, a hospital was found negligent for not meeting the standard of care that was owed to a client. Failure to provide the services of a medical specialist and the failure of the nursing staff to recognize a critical situation resulted in an amputation. The hospital was found liable for not providing competent medical and nursing staff (1). As a result of this precedent case, health care organizations can be found liable if they do not provide competent staff and a safe environment for clients. This concept is called corporate liability. Corporate liability applied to a health care organization means that the organization has a duty to its clients which is separate from its duty to its employees: to provide competent care in a safe environment (19). Areas identified in corporate liability cases include providing sufficient numbers of staff, adequate equipment and space, and security, and the responsibility to maintain competent physicians on staff (19).

Two means of protection from liability claims available to health care organizations are risk management programs and institutional liability insurance. The purposes of risk management programs are twofold. One purpose is to identify and remedy potential situations that may lead to harm to employees, clients, or visitors. The second purpose is to minimize the risk of civil suits and the amount of awards when claims of liability are made against the organization (20). An integrated risk management program brings together quality assurance, security, human resources managers, and other care and safety-related departments to carry out its purposes. Institutional liability insurance policies are purchased to cover acts and omissions of employees. More will be said about institutional liability policies later in this chapter.

Another potential source of liability for employees is their employer. If an employer is found liable for the acts or omissions of the employee, the employer may seek reimbursement for the damages paid to the injured plaintiff (7). The legal term for this reimbursement is indemnification. An employer may legally seek indeminification for all damages paid by the institutional insurance carrier (7) or for the amount of compensation paid out which exceeded the limits of the policy (21). While this has rarely occurred in the 1980s (21), there is no guarantee that the same pattern will be followed in the 1990s. If the size of compensation awards continues to increase, insurance rates will also increase appreciably because of larger claims.

Protection from Malpractice Claims

In the law column of Table 10.1 the penalty for torturous behavior is listed as financial compensation to the victim. Malpractice is also covered under tort laws. If a plaintiff proves that financial, emotional, or physical injury was suffered, some form of relief is awarded for these damages (2). Compensatory damages include losses to the plaintiff for medical costs, missed wages, impairment of future gains, and past and future pain and suffering (1). The potential total amount awarded through court settlements or by a jury for claims against physical therapists can be sizable. However, the average claim costs noted by one carrier in 1986 was less than $2000 for employed therapists and over $7000 for self-employed therapists (11).

LIABILITY INSURANCE
Personal Liability Insurance

Protection against professional liability suits is available to physical therapists through two forms of liability insurance. These insurance policies are called claims made policies and occurrence policies. These policies are issued in the name of the professional. The essential features of each type of policy are compared in Table 10.3.

Determination of the need for and type of liability insurance requires each professional to assess the potential for malpractice claims associated with each individual professional situation. Direct care as well as management responsibilities carry the possibility of libelous actions. In the area of direct care, students and new graduates may be at risk for negligent acts and omissions due to inexperience. Experienced practitioners could be at risk for utilizing techniques that may not meet current standards of practice or of practicing beyond the statutory scope of practice. Managers often have the dual obligations of direct care and supervision of the work of others through delegation of responsibilities, implementation of policies, and staff education. For the manager, these multiple responsibilities present many possibilities for liability.

While cost is often an important consideration in purchasing malpractice insurance, many lawyers recommend purchasing the more ex-

Table 10.3.
Key Differences between Professional Liability Insurance Policies

Factors	Claims Made	Occurrence
Relative cost:	Least	Most; extended liability period increases cost
Maximal limits:	Same options available in both policy types	
Exclusions:	The same exclusions apply to both types of policies. These include criminal acts, coverage of activities outside the setting, coverage for acts beyond the scope of practice as defined by licensure statute, punitive damages may or may not be covered.	
Insurance period:	As long as the policy is in effect the insured party is protected against claims.	The insured party is covered against claims arising when the policy was in effect at any time in the future.
Options:	An additional policy called a tail policy can be purchased for future protection against acts or omissions that were not reported when the claims made policy was in effect. A second option is to purchase a prior acts endorsement. This provides coverage for acts and omissions that were never reported but occurred before the effective date of a new claims made policy.	Coverage for private practitioners which includes protection against negligent acts of employees is available at a higher cost than employee's pay. Employees may also obtain coverage against liability claims for profesional acts or omissions occurring during the provision of professional services outside of their regular work setting.

pensive occurrence form policy (2, 19, 21, 22). The alternative to having a personal professional liability insurance policy is to pay damages from personal resources. This means that personal savings, investments, property, future wages, and inheritances must be used to pay compensatory damages (21).

Institutional Liability Insurance

It is not unusual for employees to believe that they are covered for their acts and omissions through their employer's institutional liability insurance at no cost to themselves. While this may be true, there are some pitfalls of which to be aware. The purpose of the institutional policy is to protect the institution. Without a certificate of insurance issued in the name of the individual by the institution's insurance carrier there is no proof that a specific individual is insured. A careful reading of the insuring agreement section of an institution's liability policy to see who is defined as the insured may provide satisfactory evidence of coverage for a particular professional employee (21). However, the likelihood of an employee being given access to the policy is not great.

Even if covered, and defended by the institution's insurance carrier, the limit of the coverage may be inadequate in today's courtroom. Most institutional policies carry a low maximal dollar compensation limit for most employees (2). This means the institution and possibly the individual professional are personally obligated to pay compensation beyond the institutional policy limit. A second concern is associated with the quality of legal counsel given to the employee (2). The adequacy of legal counsel can only be answered definitively when a claim is made, and not before.

There are two defenses available to an institution named in a suit involving an employee. One is to show that the injury was not the result of an action related to an employee's position description. The other is to prove that the act did not take place in a work-related activity (2). An activity such as volunteering to provide services at a high school athletic event on a weekend may fall into the latter category. Most institutional liability policies do not provide payment for expenses involved with gathering information or for wages lost from time away from work related to defense in the claim (2, 21). Finally, if an institution chooses to seek indemnification from the professional employee, the employee may be without coverage. Institutional liability policies typically will not pay for representation of the employee (2). A carrier's lawyers are only obligated to defend their clients. In this case, the institution, not the employee, is the insured party. To defend both would be a conflict of interest for the carrier.

Commercial Liability Insurance

A professional operating his or her own business is an entrepreneur. An entrepreneur has a need for considering other insurances besides their own professional liability insurance. Commercial liability insurance offers additional protection from claims. Commercial liability insurance can cover everyone associated with the business entity. This includes agents, members of the board of directors, officers, and professional and other employees (21). The need for insurance against malpractice is self-evident because, as the employer, the entrepreneur is vicariously liable for the acts of his or her employees. Under the concept of corporate liability, the entrepreneur is as duty-bound to provide a safe environment and the same quality care as is any equivalent health care provider.

Owner Liability in Different Types of Business Arrangements. Entrepreneurial practitioners may be legally organized in any one of several types of business entities. Each form of business, however, carries a different set of obligations associated with liability. These differences in the liability attached to ownership need to be understood for appropriate insurance protection to be selected.

Health professions typically form the following types of business entities: corporations, general or limited partnerships, sole proprietorships, and professional service corporations (21, 23). Besides differences in how these businesses are taxed, there are differences with regard to personal liability.

Some forms of corporations limit personal liability because the corporation is recognized as a separate legal entity from the owners (23). The personal resources of the owner and shareholders (23) are not considered part of the business and therefore do not have to be used to pay debts of the corporation. The limited personal liability of health care organization owners and shareholders is less limited today than in the past.

For a general partnership to be formed there must be at least two owners. Each partner is personally liable for the obligations of the business as well as the acts and omissions of the other partner(s). In a limited partnership there is a difference in the amount of involvement in the management of the business between the partners. The limited partner has a limited liability which is determined by the extent of his/her ownership and he/she is not personally liable for the obligations of the partnership (23).

One person is the owner of a sole proprietorship. In this single-owner business entity the owner is directly responsible for all liabilities and obligations arising from the business (23).

In most states, licensed professionals can form professional, personal, or service corporations (23). These are business entities formed by members of a single profession who provide professional services to the public. The limitation of membership to like professionals and the provision of professional services as opposed to selling goods distinguishes the purpose of these types of corporations from regular corporations. Liability differences also exist. While there is limited personal liability in a regular corporation, this is not so in a professional, personal, or service corporation. In this form of business, each corporation member retains full personal liability for their own negligent acts or omissions as well as for the acts or omissions of those whose work they control while rendering professional services (23).

In addition to personal and commercial liability insurance, an entrepreneur may have other insurance needs such as bonding employees, protection against theft, or damage to equipment and premises. Decisions regarding the need for additional insurances are best determined in consultation with several commercial insurance agents.

Liability and Documentation
Note Documents in Malpractice Litigation

Principles of writing note documents were previously presented in Chapter 6. The intent of this discussion is to bring attention to clinical notes as legal documents and, to a lesser degree, the legal obligations associated with handling, access to, and storage of medical records.

There are five legal situations which commonly make use of note documents. These situations are: disability claims, insurance cases, personal injury claims, workmen's compensation cases, and professional malpractice claims (19). While the professional caregiver usually writes a note for medical purposes, in legal proceedings the legal implications of the contents of a note document take precedence (19). The legal considerations that follow are related to malpractice litigation, but these same considerations are applicable to the other four legal uses of note documents.

Liability claims for malpractice inevitably require scrutiny of clinical note documents written by the health care professionals providing the care. It is possible that the written note documents are the only evidence to show that the standard of practice was as it should have been (24). This is particularly true when claims are filed years after the occurrence of a negligent act or omission.

In legal proceedings, the written record outweighs verbal renditions of "how things were" at the time of the alleged negligent act or omission (7).

Standards

There are no legal standards regarding note document format but there are indications that the format should facilitate completeness. The problem-oriented format has been singled out as meeting this purpose (5, 19). There is also no legal standard for the content of a note document (19). Standards as defined by a profession, accreditation agency, or third parties rather than a court are currently used (24). Together with the seven guidelines listed below, the format and content suggestions made in Chapter 6 are likely to satisfy legal scrutiny of note documents.

1. The date, and in some cases, the time of an observation, treatment, or other action will pinpoint the time frame (24).
2. The statements should be true (24).
3. The note document should be as complete as is reasonably possible (24). Statements related to client responses, complaints, performance, signs of fatigue, therapist actions related to the safety of the client, identification of any untoward events, and actions taken are all substantively relevant to the care and welfare of the client. In deciding what to enter into the record, ask "Is it significant to the care of the client." If the answer is yes, enter the information (19).
4. Valid, objective measurements and objective terms should be used (2). Comparisons should be made in the same measurement terms used previously in order to gauge changes in responses and performance. Detailed, but concise, professional observations directly related to the care of the client and the client's reactions to treatment are components of the expected standard of practice.
5. Note documents are permanent records. They should be legible to everyone (24). Since records are often reproduced, the use of black ink may enhance readability and reduce the need for ad lib interpretations.
6. The complete signature and official title of the document writer should appear at the end of the document so no additional entries can be made before it (2).
7. Corrections should be made by a single line through the incorrect entry so it remains legible. The word "error" should be placed near the lined entry along with the date and name of the person making the correction (2). Records should not be corrected after notification of a claim against anyone related to the care of the plaintiff (19). Changes for any reason may be mistaken for an attempt to falsify the note document.

MEDICAL RECORDS
Ownership and Access

All evaluation forms, radiographs, slides, photographs, and note documents completed by those caring for a client are part of the client's official medical record. The medical record is owned by the health care provider (25). The use of the information contained in the record, however, is subject to the client's consent (25). This distinction between who is responsible for the physical keeping of a medical record and who has access to the information contained in the record merits further discussion.

Who can have access to a medical record is summarized in the following statement. In most states, "The medical record is a confidential document, access to which should be restricted to the patient, to the patient's authorized representative(s), and to the attending physician and hospital staff members who have a legitimate need for such access" (25). This means, in most circumstances, that the client or their representative has the legal right to inspect and copy the medical record (25). A client requesting access to their medical record while they are hospitalized has that right in some states. Other states leave it to the discretion of the health care institution. The final word on such accessibility may ultimately come from the attending physician. His or her decision will be based on the value or harm such access would bring to the client (25).

Familiarity with situations that pose potential legal risks in the area of disclosing medical information may deter health care professionals, students, and educators from making costly legal errors. The common situations associated with the disclosure of medical information which have resulted in litigation include the following (1):

---

1. Providing information to individuals who were not authorized in writing by the client;
2. Permitting an unauthorized person access to a medical record;
3. Discussing client-related information in public;
4. Taking pictures of clients without their consent;
5. Publishing a client's picture without his/her consent;
6. Using information for a purpose substantially different from the purpose for which the client originally granted consent;
7. Failing to provide anonymity in a case presentation given in public.

The reader should also be aware that the medical records of AIDS, alcohol and drug abusing clients, and minors are subject to special regulations to protect the confidentiality of the information (25).

Medical Record Protection

A health care organization has the legal responsibility to safeguard its medical records as well as the information contained in them (25). In hospitals, the responsibility rests with the medical records department. In a small practice, it is the owner's responsibility. Not all medical information requires client consent. No consent is necessary for quality assurance, financial audits, research where anonymity is preserved, transfer of records to another health care institution, or when a health care facility closes (25). Release of any portion of a medical record to a law enforcement official requires client authorization or a court order called a subpoena. Under this latter circumstance, consultation with a lawyer is advised.

Suggestions regarding the length of time medical records should be kept varies according to the situation and state statutes. Generally, medical records are kept for a minimum of five years. This length of time is beyond

Figure 10.2. Possible outcomes of a managerial decision. (Modified from Henderson VE. The ethical side of enterprise. Sloan Manage Rev 1982;23(3):37–47.)

the statute of limitations for filing a claim for malpractice. The records of minors should be kept until the minor reaches the age of majority plus the number of years allowed by the statute of limitations (7). This precaution is necessary because a minor may make a claim upon reaching the age of 18 or 21 years. Also, there may be intermittent involvement with these individuals over time. Records of research subjects should be kept until the subject expires. This practice encourages access to data that is valuable in determining long-term effects of experiments. It also retains the original information in case of a future claim.

While the preceding information was presented using the hospital as the model, the implications are similar for all health care providers. An entrepreneur physical therapist is under the same obligations for safekeeping note documents and their contents as is any other health care provider.

Law and Ethics

As a transition between this chapter on law and the next chapter on ethics, the relationship between these topics and the implications for the health care manager will be discussed.

Law reflects the ethics of society through democratic processes (26) which result in the election of legislators by the majority of the voters. The expectation is that through democratic processes laws will be made and modified so they are considered just by the majority of society.

Justice is an ethical as well as a legal concept. While law and ethics are distinct fields, they are interrelated. Neither law nor ethics provides absolute answers to every question (26). Arriving at a legal and ethical decision requires thoughtful interpretation of the circumstance and applicable precedents and principles. Even after deliberation, a legal decision may be reached which presents an ethical problem (26).

Health care professional managers are often required to make decisions that have both legal and ethical implications. Figure 10.2 diagrams the possible outcomes of a decision that has such dual implications.

In order to manage in a manner which is legal and ethical the manager needs information on both topics. The emphasis here has been on selected legal aspects of health care management. The following chapter will meet the second informational need as it is dedicated to the ethical perspective.

SUMMARY

A health care professional in a managerial position has a duty to meet direct care, supervisory, and professional responsibilities in a legal and ethical manner. Law and ethics were briefly discussed because laws reflect societal values and values determine ethically preferred behaviors. An introduction to the legal side of this dual responsibility has been presented in this chapter. Emphasis was placed on explaining key legal terms associated with liability and relating these terms to physical therapy practice settings. Three levels of liability were identified. These were the employee, the manager, and the organization or owner. This was done to make clear that liability can be distributed among parties. Liability arising from one's own actions or omissions or from those of subordinates and failure to protect medical information were the three major topics discussed. Malpractice insurance was suggested as a protection against a claim of professional negligence. The general types of liability insurance available to protect the personal resources of individuals, employers, and organizations were compared to make potential purchasers aware of differences between the various types of policies.

CASE STUDY 10.1
Client Falls for Student

Background

Stan Upnshout is unusually upbeat about his upcoming graduation from Upstate U. He will finally realize his long-term wish of becoming a physical therapist. He has completed his first two clinical affiliations with few problems. The current affiliation, his third, is different from his prior experiences in that there are a large number of amputee clients. In the mid-affiliation evaluation Stan was complimented for being conscientious and hard working and for making satisfactory progress toward entry level competence in dealing with clients with lower limb amputations.

Incident

Stan applied a pylon to a new client. The pylon was not adequately fitted. While walking in the parallel bars the client fell, injuring her stump and wrist. The client sued the hospital for damages claiming the organization was negligent for letting an unlicensed and inexperienced person apply the pylon.

Questions to answer:
What legal principle would be involved here?
Was the basis for liability appropriate?
If you think there is another legal basis, what is it?
Do you think the hospital was found negligent?

Compare your answers to those presented in Appendix 10.1.

CASE STUDY 10.2
An Expensive Lunch Break

Background

Anna Roll has several years of experience treating adults with head trauma. She is a staff physical therapist employed by a hospital. Anna has been suggesting to her manager that she consider allowing opportunities for some head trauma clients to interact with the local community under supervision. Anna provided articles explaining the values of these kinds of opportunities and some models to follow.

In the month since Anna presented her suggestion, nothing has happened. Her manager has said that she brought the idea to the attention of her superior but has not heard anything further.

Situation

A head trauma client of Anna's requested that he be allowed to accompany her on a visit to a nearby bowling alley where he previously worked. Anna, an avid bowler, often rolled a few games there at lunch time. She agreed to let the client accompany her.

The client was so excited to be visiting friends that he rushed forward as he neared the bowling alley door, pulled it open, and was struck in the face by the door. He was stunned by the blow, fell, and suffered a concussion. The client's parents filed suit against the hospital for damages.

Questions to answer:

Was the hospital negligent?
Was Anna negligent?
Was Anna's manager negligent?

What do you consider to be the key elements in this situation which identified who was liable?

Compare your answers to those presented in Appendix 10.2.

CASE STUDY 10.3
When Is an Aide Not an Aid?

Background

Patham and Bakeum are two physical therapists who own an outpatient physical therapy clinic. One aide is on vacation. The other aide was unable to make it to work today because her child is ill. The business is open 12 hours a day. Patham works 7:00 AM to 3:00 PM. Bakeum works 12:00 to 8:00 PM. To meet the midmorning needs, Patham asked the receptionist to help out whenever she had time. She has helped in the clinic on rare occasions in the past.

Situation

Patham asked the receptionist to watch her put together a hot pack and then requested her to put together another hot pack for the next client. The receptionist did this. The next client was waiting for the pack. From behind a curtain Patham told the receptionist-aide to place the hot pack on the left shoulder of the waiting client. She complied. The phone rang and she left the clinic for the office to answer it. By now several clients had arrived and needed attention. When Patham got to the client with the hot pack on his shoulder, it was too late. A burn had occurred because the hot pack was prepared inadequately to keep the hot pack itself off the client's skin. The client sued.

Under each of the following conditions determine who was liable for damages:

General partnership
Limited partnership (therapist present is the manager)
Professional corporation

Check Appendix 10.3 for answers.

References

1. Cournoyer CP. The nurse manager and the law. Rockville: Aspen, 1989:6,8,17–18,21,130–132,137,143,146,212.
2. Guido GW. Legal issues in nursing, a source book practice. Norwalk: Appleton and Lange, 1988:8–9,24,40,88,100–101,110–113,162,164–165.
3. Creighton H. Law for physical therapists. Phys Ther Rev 1958;38:22–25.
4. Stiller JA. A practical guide to legal consideration in ethical issues. In: Anderson GR, Glesnes-Anderson VA. Health care ethics. Rockville: Aspen, 1987:12–13.
5. Creighton H. Law every nurse should know. 4th Ed. Philadelphia: WB Saunders, 1981:1,182–183,326–327.
6. Kelly ME. Introduction to federal and state systems of government. In: Northrop CE, Kelly ME. Legal issues in nursing. St. Louis: CV Mosby, 1987:15–18.
7. Helmet MD, Mackert ME. Dynamics of law in nursing and health care. 2nd Ed. Reston, VA: Reston, 1982:3,12,25–26,78,173,181,183.
8. Horsh DJ. Medico-legal aspects of physical therapy. In: Hickok RJ, ed. Physical therapy administration and management. 2nd Ed. Baltimore: Williams & Wilkins, 1982:180,184.
9. Cushing M. Nursing jurisprudence. Norwalk: Appleton and Lange, 1988:26.
10. Feutz SA. Nursing and the law. 3rd Ed. Eau Claire: Professional Education Systems, 1989:7,15,21.
11. Scanlon J. Malpractice. Today's Student PT 1987;(Spring):15–19.
12. Scott RW. Instruction on health care malpractice issues in entry-level physical therapy curricula. Allied Health 1990;19(3):211–217.
13. Burch E, Jr. Direct access. In: Mathews J. Practice issues in physical therapy. Thorofare, NJ: Slack, 1989:30–31.
14. Anonymous. Direct access findings. Prog Rep 1990;19(2):9.
15. Griffith CC, Griffith C. Law for the physical therapist. Part I. Clin Manage 1981;1(4):22–24.
16. Webster's II new Riverside university dictionary. Boston: Houghton Mifflin, 1984:948.
17. Kelly ME. Professional negligence overview. In: Northrop CE, Kelly ME. Legal issues in nursing. St. Louis: CV Mosby, 1987:39–41,45,47–48,52.
18. Kelly ME. Intentional and quasi-intentional torts and civil rights. In: Northrop CE, Kelly ME. Legal issues in nursing. St. Louis: CV Mosby, 1987:58.
19. Fiesta J. The law and liability, a guide for nurses. 2nd Ed. New York: Wiley, 1988:16,24–25,174,191–192,211.
20. Bowyer EA. Risk management. In: Northrop CE, Kelly ME. Legal issues in nursing. St. Louis: CV Mosby, 1987:427.
21. Feutz SA. Professional liability insurance. In: Northrop CE, Kelly ME. Legal issues in nursing. St. Louis: CV Mosby, 1987:441–444,446.
22. Griffith CC, Griffith C. Law for the physical therapist. Part II. Clin Manage 1982;2(1):9–10,12.
23. Kelly ME, Northrop CE. The nurse entrepreneur. In: Northrop CE, Kelly ME. Legal issues in nursing. St. Louis: CV Mosby, 1987:537–539.
24. Mech AB. Quality assurance and documentation. In: Northrop CE, Kelly ME. Legal issues in nursing. St. Louis: CV Mosby, 1987:459–460,462.
25. Roach WH, Jr, Chernoff SN. Confidentiality of patient record information. In: Anderson GR, Glesnes-Anderson VA. Health care ethics. Rockville: Aspen, 1987:215,218,223–224.
26. Darr K. Ethics in health services management. New York: Praeger, 1987:xxii–xxiii.

CHAPTER 11

Values and Ethics

OVERVIEW

Values are enduring but dynamic beliefs held by a person or members of an organization about the worth of something. Values motivate behavior. Judgments about right and wrong or good and bad are moral judgments based on values. In the course of human interactions there are many situations in which it is difficult to make a decision because values come into conflict. Conflict between moral values results in an ethical problem. Major influences on moral decision making in the health care environment are personal, professional, and organizational values. An analysis of each of these influences is presented. Values, whether personal or organizational, are hierarchical. That is, there is a rank order of values for a particular situation. Values must be clarified if moral decisions are to be reached.

Clarification comes from serious, thoughtful consideration of the effect decisions have on others. An individual or an organization must engage in values clarification to develop a personal decision-making process that fosters ethical behavior. For an organization this personal ethic is expressed in the form of a value or philosophical statement. When personal or organizational values come into conflict ethical decision-making processes can be employed to resolve problems. The analysis process differs from most decision-making processes only in its focus which is on making a moral decision rather than a fiscally related decision. An ethical decision is selected from among morally acceptable courses of action. An analysis of each option is conducted using four ethical principles as criteria. These principles are:

1. *Do no harm (nonmaleficence);*
2. *Do what is best for others (beneficence);*
3. *Respect others by allowing them self-determination (autonomy);*
4. *Be fair to all concerned (justice).*

Several models for applying these principles to guide ethical problem solving are introduced using physical therapy management situations. Examples of ethical problems associated with each of the ethical principles are presented as they relate to clinical practice, to management, and to an organization. A case study dealing with recruitment matters is provided to allow practice in applying the ethical problem-solving models.

Introduction

An exposure to and application of ethical reasoning processes to deal with ethical problems can lead to actions considered by ethicists to be morally correct. The development, presentation, and implementation of ethical reasoning processes applicable to health care organizations in general and physical therapy managers in particular is the focus of this chapter.

PHILOSOPHY

The terms moral and ethical are often used interchangeably by most health care industry workers. Both terms will be used in this chapter as equivalents unless there is a need for a distinction to be made.

Decisions that deal with morality are decisions that have significant social importance in terms of the way they affect the welfare of others (1). Moral decisions are those which are correct according to philosophical principles. An individual or organization committed to pursuing moral courses of action needs a means of identifying correct options. Principles for comparing moral options come from the field of ethics. Ethics is the branch of philosophy focusing on morality. The basis for deciding what is a morally correct choice of action is one's value system (2, 3). One option is considered morally superior to other options because of the order of importance a person or an organization places on each of its values (4).

Introspective consideration of one's value hierarchy leads to a personal ethic (5). Ideally, a person or a group can make morally correct choices by following a decision-making process which involves contemplation and weighing the effects of each choice according to ethical principles (5–7). This process is similar to the strategic planning process presented in Chapter 7. The difference is whether the bottom line relates to moral preference or fiscal implication.

New experiences and reflection can bring about changes in the value hierarchy. This makes the ordering of values somewhat dynamic (2). The values of a person or organization influence its decisions and eventual behavior (3).

Health Care Is a Business

Friedman (8) said a business leader's responsibility was ". . . to conduct the business in accordance with their desires, which generally will be to make as much money as possible, while conforming to the basic rules of the society, both those embodied in law and those embodied in ethical custom." In practice this ideal has not been lived up to (9, 10). Only recently has serious consideration been given to ethical matters as part of the strategic planning process in most business organizations (10). Some writers have indicated that only since the 1970s, after the Watergate scandal, have business ethics become a popular organizational topic of discussion (11, 12).

To the contrary, health care organizations have a tradition of concern about moral issues and the application of ethics to the decision-making process. This tradition is due, in part, to the tenets of the Hippocratic oath, the historical involvement of religious groups in health care, the values of individuals who choose health care careers, and the codes of ethics of the various professional organizations to which health care workers belong. Health care organizations, because they provide a minority of their services gratis, are in the business of health care. The precepts of business can be compatible with the endeavor of health care as well as all other types of business as long as there is responsible leadership.

Value Conflicts

Everyone involved in the delivery of health care is directly or indirectly involved in the business of health care. Customer service, marketing, public relations, and education can be provided by all staff members. Filling out charge slips, keeping departmental service statistics, as well as providing direct care (the product sold) are business aspects of revenue-generating departments. Health care managers have a responsibility to meet needs of clients, staff, and the organization. Because the needs of those served may be in conflict, there is potential for the manager to experience conflicts of values. A conflict occurs whenever the manager can not fulfill equally their duty toward all those to whom they have a responsibility. When values conflict, which choice of action should be taken? Should the manager advocate for the needs of the client? Give priority to the staff members needs? Give up something for the department to help the organization serve clients another way? These are questions with moral implications. Solutions to moral questions require organized introspection (13).

Resources to Aid in Making Ethically Correct Choices

There are several resources to help develop an ethics-based decision-making process for use when values or moral choices are in conflict. The resources listed in Table 11.1 may be used individually or in combinations.

Taking personal initiative in solving a moral problem is the option available to everyone. However, the ability to apply formal ethical principles to moral questions is variable. This may be an unsatisfactory option for physical therapists because so few have had formal ethics courses as

Table 11.1.
Six Ways to Deal with Moral Problems in the Health Care Environment

1. Think about your own values, the situation, and then apply your own values system and ethics.

2. Review the code(s) of ethics of your professional organization(s) to aid your thinking.

3. Consult the organization's philosophy and mission statements for insights and direction.

4. Initiate the ethical problem-solving process by consulting your institutional ethics committee chairperson.

5. Seek the consultation of a clergyman, lawyer, ethicist, or other individual or group trained in ethical reasoning. Look within the organization for assistance.

6. Supplement your personal knowledge of ethics by learning the rudiments of an ethical decision-making process and applying the principles to moral conflict situations. Seek out external resources.

part of their basic academic preparation (14). Without supplemental ethics information, decisions are made on the basis of "what feels right."

Reliance on personal feelings is an example of what is known as ethical relativism. In philosophy, ethical relativism is associated with a rejection of universal ethical standards of right and wrong (9, 15). The contrary position is taken by most philosophies of ethics (9, 15). Personal values are developed and shaped by a variety of life experiences. Every person has values which they use to make choices. Values are dynamic to the extent that influences of the organization, community, professional associations, and past experiences all interact to shape and reshape personal values (6). Experience with ethical problem solving may facilitate the development of a personalized moral decision-making process. However, if an organization relies only on the personal values of its staff members and a variety of individualized decision-making processes, there is little assurance that a consistent moral standard will emerge.

There is some concurrence that neither business codes of ethics (6, 9, 10) nor health care workers' professional codes of ethics (5, 16) have had a significant effect on day to day practices. The concept of self-scrutiny has not worked effectively because of conflicts of interest and imprecise language (16). Professional codes of ethics have limited circulation. Not all individuals in practice are members of the voluntary professional organizations that they are eligible to join. About half the number of licensed physical therapists are members of the American Physical Therapy Association (APTA). Choosing not to join professional organizations such as the APTA or the American College of Healthcare Executives could affect access to Option 2. Nonaffiliates may also lack access to current interpretations of codes or code revisions which are often published in the literature of the professional organization for members and subscribers.

The organization's philosophy statement may not be specific enough to guide the day to day decision-making processes. The use of a combined mission-philosophy statement can lead to this problem. Alternatively, a

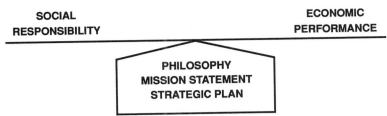

Figure 11.1. The directive influence of the philosophical statement on the operations of an organization.

philosophy statement could be very specific but cover a limited scope of potential circumstances (16). Each of these impacts on the value of Option 3.

Not all health care organizations have ethics committees. In settings without an institutional ethics committee Option 4 is not available. A middle ground approach has been suggested for organizations without the internal resources necessary for an ethics committee. This approach involves several organizations joining together to develop a shared ethics committee (17). Since only about half of the hospitals in this country currently have institutional ethics committees (18) this sharing concept has a large potential audience.

Options 5 and 6 require time expenditure, personal effort to pursue additional information, and the availability of appropriate educational resources such as a specialized library and instructors during non-work hours. Because of these requirements, small organizations and solo or isolated practitioners may find these options to be impractical.

Options 1 and 6 are interrelated. If entry level professional preparation incorporated adequate preparation in ethics, Option 1 would become a more reasonable option to consider. However, since a background in ethics is generally lacking in the education of physical therapists, basic information about the utilization of principles of ethics will receive most attention in the following sections.

MANAGEMENT'S ROLE

Upper Management

Those empowered by the charter of an organization are members of the board of directors or the officers. The board, as the highest level of authority, sets the ideals of the organization through development of the philosophy and mission statements. Through a strategic planning process these ideals are operationalized. The ideals should be evident in the action plans, policies, and procedures formulated by management. Figure 11.1 shows an idealized balancing effect of a humanistic philosophical statement on the overall operation of an organization.

Ethical Guidance for Managers

The Codes of Ethics of the American College of Healthcare Executives and the American Hospital Association identify similar areas of moral concern for health care managers (5). These areas of concern include:

1. Accountability to the organization and the profession;
2. Conflicts of interest;
3. Confidentiality of information;
4. Relationships with similar organizations;
5. Governing body and medical staff relations;
6. Resource allocation;
7. Advertising;
8. Mechanisms for bringing legal and ethical claims forward;
9. Consideration of a plan for adequate health care services for all individuals;
10. A commitment to broaden and advance managerial knowledge;
11. Respect toward those entrusted for care demonstrated by being an advocate for meeting the total needs of each individual.

The preceding topics should be addressed within the fundamental document(s) of the organization. It would be cumbersome to address every morally important issue which a board of directors might wish to include along with the mission statement. Moral values need to be stated with enough specificity to make clear to management, in particular, and all other affiliated persons, what is considered correct behavior. This would include employees, volunteers, affiliated providers, contractors, and so on. Combining the philosophical and mission statements often leads to less specific statements to guide behavior.

In Chapter 2 the organizational philosophy and mission statement was presented within one document. This is a common practice in health care organizations. However, a complete philosophical statement should stand alone (5, 19). A lack of specificity means that little direction is provided. Enforcement of ethical standards and measurement of compliance may not be possible without specificity (5). Adding this amount of information to the mission statement would make a voluminous document.

PHILOSOPHICAL STATEMENT

According to some authors (5), a comprehensive philosophical statement should be developed prior to and separate from the mission statement. There are several reasons for this suggestion. Giving consideration to the moral issues first provides an ethical context for the mission statement (5). By identifying the value hierarchy the board of directors sends a moral mandate throughout the organization. This mandate is interpreted in the mission statement and operationalized through the strategic planning process. These interrelationships are clarified in Figure 11.2.

By developing the philosophical statement first, ethical considerations are not relegated to a secondary status after business matters nor are they noted as afterthoughts (5). Without a clear directive from the board of directors through the statement of philosophy, ethical oversight of the actions chosen through the strategic planning process lack this input. As noted in general business settings, seldom has the strategic planning process included substantial consideration of ethical precepts (10). A way to infuse ethical considerations into the strategic planning process is through

Responsibilities of the BOD

Organizational Philosophy

Focus: Moral Values

Mission Statement

Focus: Purpose
            Goals
            Policies
            Procedures

Responsibilities of Management

Strategic Planning Process

Focus: **Analysis of Internal and External Factors**

Objectives

Strategies

Figure 11.2.   The role of the board of directors (*BOD*) in setting the guiding precepts of an organization for management to enact.

the mission statement, which itself reflects the influence of the philosophical statement. If consistent direction is taken from the philosophical statement, the strategic plan will include ethically correct actions. Example 11.1 traces the influence of a single philosophical statement on the mission statement, strategic planning process, and strategic plan. Managers, because they are responsible for implementing the strategic plan, are closer to day to day activities than is the board. Managers, therefore, are in the position to be the active conscience of the organization (5). Management, through the organizational structure, is directly responsible for the ethical bottom line.

MAJOR ETHICAL PRINCIPLES APPLIED TO MORAL ISSUES IN HEALTH CARE

Personal, professional, and organizational ethics have a common set of principles. However, the hierarchy or ranking of these principles can differ in each situation because of value weighting differences (2). The following discussion will present the principles in a hierarchy that corresponds with the authors' values. The reader should already have a sense

EXAMPLE 11.1
From Philosophical Statement to Strategic Plan

Responsibilities of Governing Body

Example from Philosophical Statement
Value 1: We value most highly those actions which demonstrate an authentic, warm, and caring attitude toward everyone with whom we interact.
   Standard: Consistent demonstration of respect for self-determination, fairness, and the choice of actions which benefit those who are unable to make their own decisions.

Example from Mission Statement: Our purpose is to deliver health care services in a uniquely individualized and participative manner. This entails substantive involvement of clients or their agents in all decisions which affect the client's welfare.

Responsibilities of Management

Example from the strategic planning process

Strengths	Weaknesses	Opportunities	Threats
Unique service orientation. Demonstrated client interest in more involvement in the decision-making process. New medical director supports this change.	Time consuming to implement. Service volume may decline. Difficult to assess if staff will accept this mode of functioning.	Nearest competitor with a reputation for personal care is 150 miles away. They are very labor intensive. We could develop our reputation in a more cost-efficient manner.	Concept requires changes in the way services are delivered. This can cause staff discontent. If we are successful, others will follow suit.

Example from the Strategic Plan

Action 1: Form an interdisciplinary institutional ethics committee to ensure implementation of Value 1.
   The committee will develop procedures for others within the organization to bring ethical concerns forward in a confidential manner. The committee shall be formed within three months and will be in operation within six months. The committee chairperson shall be elected by the committee. The chairperson will report to the board of directors.
1. Membership should include at least one representative from each of the following groups: The board, management, medical staff, nursing, therapies, medical groups, nonprofessional staff, consumer representative, clergy, legal representative, and a consultant as needed.
2. The group shall meet quarterly as well as when circumstances dictate.
3. Liability insurance shall be provided by the organization for each member of the committee and consultants.
4. Compensation time will be awarded for time spent beyond the usual work week.

---

that there are not absolute answers to moral questions. A particular option is determined to be the ethically preferred option under the existing circumstances (4), based on the prevailing hierarchy of values. This is not to say that ethical correctness is a fickle concept. The statement is intended to recognize that introspection leads to new insights and new insights may result in the reordering of the value hierarchy. Values evolve (3, 19).

Four Ethical Principles

Ethical principles are needed so consistency can be maintained in the actions chosen regarding a specific group of related issues (6). Four basic principles for guiding choices in the health care environment are identified and described in Table 11.2.

Table 11.2.
Four Ethical Principles for Identifying Correct Choices

Ethical Terms	Practical Definitions	Examples of Noncompliance
1. Nonmaleficence	Do no harm	Attempting a treatment technique without previous instruction or experience.
2. Justice	Equal treatment	Giving a competent client personal attention and ignoring a confused client.
3. Autonomy	Self-determination	Setting treatment plan and goals for a competent client without consulting the client.
4. Beneficence	Select best treatment	Trying to do range of motion on an agitated child rather than applying a relaxation technique.

Nonmaleficence. The principle of nonmaleficence directs a moral person to do no harm to another. Situations in which short-term discomfort is caused in order to bring about a long-term benefit would be considered under this principle (19). In physical therapy, an example of nonmaleficence would be to choose to do wound debridement on a burned child. Not to do it could lead to infection.

The physical therapy manager shares the moral responsibility of protecting the client from unnecessary harm. Assigning the client to an unskilled therapist or not ensuring that staff were trained in sterile techniques would be ethical problems attributable to the manager according to the principle of nonmaleficence.

A health care organization that does not monitor the occurrence of improper care is not acting morally under the requirements of the nonmaleficence principle. An organization that chooses not to act when evidence of improper care is present likewise is making an unethical choice.

Justice. Fairness is dictated by the principle of justice. Individuals are always to be treated equally. However, merit and individual needs are recognized as acceptable reasons for unequal treatment (5). Consistency in the way that merit or special needs are identified and met can be a problem of justice. A physical therapist who employs significantly different treatment techniques (those requiring one to one attention versus unattended, self-directed, or delegated activities) on two people whose conditions and attributes are very similar may not be acting morally according to the principle of justice. A manager who allocates salary increases arbitrarily is acting unjustly. An organization that discharges clients when their insurance limits are reached is challenged to justify its action under the principle of justice.

Autonomy. The principle of autonomy is considered by some as the principle to be followed if there are no other principles clearly applicable (20). An autonomous person or organization is self-governing. Autonomy requires that competent individuals be encouraged to actively participate in the planning and selection of the activities that affect their well-being (5). Two requirements are associated with making an intelligent, informed choice. First, the information provided must be accurate and truthful. Second, the information must be presented so it is understandable to the person making the choice. Once the information is considered, the choice should be honored. This can present a problem if an individual's decision is to decline treatment or if they select an option not strongly supported by the professional. Even so, these choices must be accepted by the health care professional according to the principle of autonomy.

In a physical therapy context, an example of respect for autonomy would be to give a client the option whether or not to be treated by a student.

This principle also applies to the clinical manager. By adapting a democratic style of leadership at a time when an issue is important to the staff the manager is recognizing the autonomy of staff members.

An organization which develops and adopts a client's bill of rights is reflecting among other things recognition of the right of clients to express self-determination. This right is the essence of the principle of autonomy.

Beneficence.   The statement "Do what enhances the welfare of others" is an expression of beneficence. This ethical principle is enacted by preventing, minimizing, or eliminating actual or potential harm that may come to another person. Beneficence is a fundamental principle of health care organizations (20). Clearly, anything related to safety in the physical therapy environment honors this principle.

The principles of beneficence and autonomy can be antagonistic. This can cause ethical conflict in health care settings. The beneficence principle suggests that the wisdom of the board of directors and the professional staff should be weighted more heavily in the decision-making process than the wishes of those they serve. In contrast, the principle of autonomy unquestionably indicates that the decisions of competent groups and individuals should be followed. An example of conflict in the clinical setting is the decision whether or not to restrain a client. If the client asks not to be restrained but the staff restrains the client for safety reasons, the principle of beneficence overrides autonomy. In the absence of potential harm to a client or others, the principle of autonomy should be applied. The principle of beneficence should be followed when harm to one's self or harm to others is likely.

MAKING ETHICAL DECISIONS

Decision-making processes, whether intended to make business decisions or to identify morally correct options, involve similar steps (5, 19). The major difference is that an analysis of the ethical correctness of various options has seldom become part of traditional decision-making processes (10, 19). One way of arriving at ethical decisions is to subject alternatives to assessment by each of the four philosophical principles presented previously. The prioritizing of the four principles involves introspection which precedes the implementation of a decision-making process.

Three ethical decision-making models will be presented. One is simple and requires little time. A second model is more complex and is set up as a decision tree. The final model is quantitative. It uses ordinal scales to rank options with respect to how well they meet the requirements implied by the four ethical criterion principles.

Model I: Quick Ethics Check

Blanchard and Peale (21) propose three questions to be asked to help clarify an ethical situation. The first question is, "is it legal?" An affirmative response allows the next two questions to be asked. If the answer is no, the self-questioning process may or may not continue. Is there a conflict with organizational policy? Is it possibly illegal? Or is it assuredly illegal? Legal issues are dealt with through organizational or legal channels depending on where the problem lies. When unsure if there is a legal problem, continue questioning.

Question two asks, "Is it balanced?" This question relates to the principle of justice. By choosing a particular option will one party at any time be treated more favorably than another? Will the choice result in a win-lose situation or will it more likely be a win-win situation?

The final question is, "how will it make me feel about myself?" This assumes that an ethically wrong action will engender a tell-tale "uncomfortable feeling." The opposite effect, feeling good about oneself, is evoked by an ethical decision. One's personal ethic, or conscience as Blanchard and Peale call it, is invoked by this question. This last question is very global. It is difficult to relate it to a specific ethical principle. This question assumes that a reasonable, prudent person recognizes right from wrong and will make the morally correct choice.

The ethics check provided by the three questions can be a quick and personal way to screen choices, but it is an example of ethical relativism discussed earlier. More intense analyses are indicated if the four ethical principles are to be applied to several options under consideration.

Model II: An Ethical Decision Tree

Hiller (22) described a qualitative decision-making process for ethical issues. We modified his description and translated it into the decision tree model presented in Figure 11.3. The questions asked are general and generic enough not to limit consideration of any type of ethical issue. Direction is given throughout the decision-making process. It is assumed that the decision maker has a basic understanding of the four philosophical principles discussed earlier.

A decision tree forces a yes or no response. There are no shades of gray. Being forced to make a decision can lead to making something of nothing or dismissing a meager piece of important evidence because of lack of correlating evidence. This decision tree method of ethical analysis is an improvement over the preceding self-questioning method because it requires assessment based on the four ethical principles. However, this decision tree method is not suited to determining which morally acceptable option is the best option to choose when there are several acceptable options.

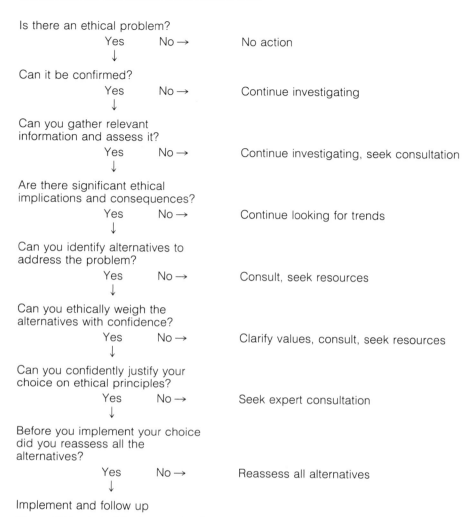

Is there an ethical problem?
                Yes   No →   No action
                 ↓

Can it be confirmed?
                Yes   No →   Continue investigating
                 ↓

Can you gather relevant
information and assess it?
                Yes   No →   Continue investigating, seek consultation
                 ↓

Are there significant ethical
implications and consequences?
                Yes   No →   Continue looking for trends
                 ↓

Can you identify alternatives to
address the problem?
                Yes   No →   Consult, seek resources
                 ↓

Can you ethically weigh the
alternatives with confidence?
                Yes   No →   Clarify values, consult, seek resources
                 ↓

Can you confidently justify your
choice on ethical principles?
                Yes   No →   Seek expert consultation
                 ↓

Before you implement your choice
did you reassess all the
alternatives?
                Yes   No →   Reassess all alternatives
                 ↓

Implement and follow up

Figure 11.3.   A decision tree method for making ethical decisions.

Model III: A Formal Ethical Decision-Making Process

When the information load challenges memory capacity a more formal method of tracking the ethical decision process becomes attractive. This limit can be reached quickly if several alternative choices of action are considered under the four philosophical principles. In practice all implications and consequences must be considered. This means that nonethical matters of importance such as fiscal impact and politics need to be recognized. Nonethical factors, however, have no bearing on identifying whether or not a choice of actions is ethical (21). Table 11.3 presents guidelines for using the proposed formal model for ethical decision making. Table 11.4 is a tally sheet to organize the ranking information for easy calculation.

The quantified ethical decision-making process is the most complicated of the three models proposed. It will, however, allow the assessment

Table 11.3.
A Formal Ethical Problem Analysis Guide

State the ethical problem:

List all ethically justifiable alternatives:

Circle ethical criteria to evaluate alternatives:

Ethical Criteria	Rules	Other Considerations
Nonmaleficence	Truthfulness	Law
Justice	Honesty	Politics
Autonomy	Respect	Economics
Beneficence	Security	Philosophy
Others	Others	Others

Formulate value statements for each criterion circled above:

> Rank each value statement (1 = least important):
>
> Quantify by using Table 11.4 to aid you in carrying out the process described below.
>
> Weight each ethically justifiable alternative according to its promotion of each of the value statements: 0% = no promotion of the value, 100% = greatest promotion of the value.
>
> For each alternative multiply each value statement rank by its promotion percentage:
>
> Sum rank × percentage of promotion products for each alternative:
>
> The alternative with highest sum is the preferred option available to deal with this moral problem.

of multiple options relative to each ethical principle. It assists in organizing a large amount of relevant information as it guides the decision maker through the moral reasoning process. It may appear that assigning numerical values to philosophical construct terms is just a complex example of ethical relativism. This is because subjective judgments are made in assigning values. This argument can be countered by noting that intense mental processing is required to apply this method of decision making. Depth of thought, what we have been calling introspection, involves ana-

Table 11.4.
Tally Sheet for Formal Ethical Decision-Making Model Using All Ethical Principle Categories and Three Ethical Alternatives

Weight each alternative according to its perceived promotion of each of the value statements. A 100% weighting indicates that an alternative fully meets a criterion.

Alternatives	Value Statements and Relative Ratings				Totals
	A (×4)	B (×3)	N (×2)	J (×1)	
1	%	%	%	% =	
2	%	%	%	% =	
3	%	%	%	% =	

The ethical choice is the alternative with the highest total based on the hierarchy used.

lyzing, weighing, justifying, choosing, and evaluating. All of these steps are incorporated in the formal ethical decision-making model.

CASE STUDY 11.1
What to Say at the Recruitment Fair

The Situation

You have been selected by your superior to be the physical therapy representative on your institution's recruitment team at a three-day recruitment fair. This is the largest recruitment fair in the country for health care professionals seeking positions. As in past years, recruitment of additional physical therapists is a priority for your team. Your superior stressed that it was very important that you represent the department and institution positively to prospective employees. She suggested that you emphasize active physician involvement in planning physical therapy programs, the opportunity to treat a great variety of clients, and the availability of the full spectrum of the most current physical agents equipment.

You are aware that there has been a consistently high yearly turnover rate among physical therapists. Exit interviews have identified the main reasons for therapists leaving: lack of control over treatment decisions, the pressures of treating large numbers of clients, and the apparent lack of concern on the part of the manager about the predominance of physical agents as the sole treatment for many clients. These conditions have not posed problems for you so far. Work has kept you extremely busy. In fact, you have not had much time to think about the implications of these conditions. Your superior says you are doing a fine job. She implied that you will be promoted in the near future.

On your way to the fair, you begin to think about what to say to prospective coworkers that would allow you to fulfill your obligation to represent the institution positively yet answer pertinent questions truthfully. Your options are to answer questions positively, negatively, or avoid negative answers by saying you are not sure about the answer.

Your Task

Identify ethically acceptable answers to give to potential position seekers. You recognize your obligation to honor your superior's request as well your personal belief in being truthful with potential coworkers. You can resolve this ethical problem by applying one of the problem-solving models presented in this chapter. Use the applicable parts of Figure 11.3 and Tables 11.3 and 11.4 to assist you in arriving at an ethical decision.

Appendices 11.1 to 11.3 contain example solutions for Models I to III, respectively.

References

1. Beauchamp TL, Walters L. Contemporary issues in bioethics. 3rd Ed. Belmont: Wadsworth, 1989:1–2,29–32,348–349,395,605.
2. Rokeach M. Beliefs, attitudes and values. New York: Jossey-Boss, 1972:3,7–11,121,123–124,159–160,164.
3. Rokeach M. The nature of human values. New York: Free Press, 1973:3–7.
4. Steele SM, Harmon VM. Values clarification in nursing. 2nd Ed. Norwalk: Appleton Century Crofts, 1983:1,4–7,49,55,58.
5. Darr K. Ethics in health services management. New York: Praeger, 1987:xvii–xviii,xxiii,1–85,129,131,147–154.
6. Cavanaugh GF. American business values. 3rd Ed. Englewood Cliffs, NJ: Prentice-Hall, 1990:1–2,63–92,128,156,170.
7. Ackerman TE. The role of an ethicist in health care. In: Anderson GR, Anderson-Glesnes VA. Health care ethics. Rockville: Aspen, 1987:308–311.

8. Friedman M. The social responsibility of business is to increase its profits. New York Times Magazine 1970,Sep.13:32–33,122–126.

9. Hoffman WM, Moore JM. Business ethics readings and cases in corporate morality. 2nd Ed. New York: McGraw-Hill, 1984:7–11.

10. Robin DP, Reidenbach RE. Business ethics where profits meet value systems. Englewood Cliffs, NJ: Prentice-Hall, 1989:21,26–32,135–136.

11. McNeary WJ. Ethics in health care. In: Anderson GR, Anderson-Glesnes VA. Health care ethics. Rockville: Aspen, 1987:4–6,8.

12. Mathews MC. Strategic intervention in organizations. Newbury Park: Sage, 1988:51,133,137.

13. Etzioni A. The moral dimension: toward a new economics. London: Free Press, 1988:166–180.

14. Purtilo RB. Ethics teaching in allied health fields: report of a survey. Hastings Center Rep 1978;8(2):14–16.

15. Barry V. Moral issues in business. 2nd Ed. Belmont: Wadsworth, 1983:2,10–12,58–60.

16. Peterson SR. Professional codes and ethical decision making. In: Anderson GR, Anderson-Glesnes VA. Health care ethics. Rockville: Aspen, 1987:321–326,342–344.

17. Kanoti GA, Vinicky JK. The role and structure of hospital ethics committees. In: Anderson GR, Anderson-Glesnes VA. Health care ethics. Rockville: Aspen, 1987:293–294,299–300,305.

18. Mayer D. Increasing number of hospitals rely on ethics groups. Healthweek Executive Briefing Paper 1990;(Mar 12):31,33.

19. Gregory L. Health care managers, values and decision making. In Anderson GR, Anderson-Glesnes VA. Health care ethics. Rockville: Aspen, 1987: 37,41–45.

20. Wenston SR. Applying philosophy to clinical dilemmas. In: Anderson GR, Anderson-Glesnes VA. Health care ethics. Rockville: Aspen, 1987:25–30.

21. Blanchard K, Peale NV. The power of ethical management. New York: Fawcett Crest, 1988:7–33.

22. Hiller MD. Ethical decision making and the health administrator. In: Anderson GR, Anderson-Glesnes VA. Health care ethics. Rockville: Aspen, 1987:330–349.

CHAPTER 12

American Health Care Environment: Beyond 1990

OVERVIEW

This chapter presents a view of the health care environment through the 1990s. Much attention is directed toward pointing out the influences of possible future changes in this environment on the field of physical therapy. No one can claim to foresee the future. However, there is consensus about likely changes in the nation's economic situation, social philosophy, medical technology, population demographics, health care manpower, payment for services, and other areas that will directly impact in some way on both physical therapy education and practice. Since physical therapy is only a segment of the health care environment, there has been less comprehensive study by governmental and private organizations of the implications of future changes on this profession. The future of the profession of physical therapy as presented by the authors is therefore based on extrapolation, insight, and optimistic thinking. The authors take consensus opinions related to the future changes expected in the health care environment and translate the impact of these changes on the field of physical therapy. The future of physical therapy education and practice through the 1990s is discussed in depth. This discussion raises many issues that future therapists, educators, and practitioners should address for their continued well-being throughout the coming decade.

A conservative view of the future is that prospects are good for physical therapists to advance their stature in the health care marketplace. The major challenges for the profession related to maintaining the viability of the profession will be opportunities to be reimbursed fairly for services and the availability of sufficient numbers of therapists to provide the services.

Introduction

The evolution of the American health care delivery system will continue through the 1990s. Escalating costs, declining reimbursement, and competition all threaten the continued existence of today's health care providers. A changing economy, shifting demographics, the cost of health care services, and declining availability of skilled professionals threaten the access of many Americans to health care services. Limited access will influence social philosophy and public policy. The push for survival will drive health care providers toward change. Together these forces will cause continuing change in the American health care delivery system for years to come. The profession of physical therapy will confront both opportunities and challenges as a result of health care system dynamics. Providing adequate numbers of physical therapists to match the demand for services will be a major issue facing the entire profession.

An Environment for Change
ECONOMY

The economic trends that acted as an impetus for change in the 1980s will continue through the 1990s. America will continue its shift from an industrial to a service-based economy. The ability of organized labor to obtain or sustain health care benefits for workers will continue to decline. The escalating cost of health care will make it increasingly difficult for many small employers to provide coverage for their employees.

Large employers who do provide coverage will continue efforts to shift their financial burden to the employee and the health care provider. This shift will result in an increasing number of Americans who are uninsured or underinsured. Americans who lack health care insurance rely on government programs, charity care from providers, or simply go without health care services. The financial burden on health care providers will increase and be compounded by regional economic trends. This is evidenced by the correlation between regional economic trends and hospital closures (1).

The effect of Medicare in the 1990s is as yet unclear. Certainly, the federal government will continue efforts to control health care expenditures. The severity of future efforts will be determined by the balance achieved between federal health care policy and budget policy (2). Advocates of health care policy would like to see funding margins, the differences between actual costs and funding received, increased up to 5%. Budget policy advocates are pushing for a 7 to 10% decline from current margins. Many forecasters believe that providers will face declining Medicare reimbursements through the first part of the decade. The margins will, however, increase during the second part of the decade due to a backlash against earlier spending cuts. The message here is clear. If Medicare margins continue to fall during the first half of the decade, providers will be forced to shift costs to other reimbursement sources. If cost shifting is not possible, the provider may not survive.

Despite continued efforts at cost containment, total health care expenditures are predicted to grow. A recent forecast predicted that health care expenditures, as a portion of the gross national product, would grow from 11.9% in 1990 to 13.1% in 1995 (3). The forces driving the growth in spending include technological advances, new product and service development, and the increased demand for geriatric services. The major force constraining this rate of growth will be society's ability to pay. It is questionable whether the government or business will be able to control the demand for services.

While total expenditures on health care continue to grow, health care providers themselves will face a rate of inflation higher than the consumer price index (3). As represented by the hospital market basket index, health care providers will face a compound inflation rate of 32% during the first half of the decade. Increases in cost will be related to the cost of technology, new products, and labor. Of these, the most important cost element is salaries.

The effects of economic recession have been present as of early 1991. This will have mixed effects on the health care industry (4). On one hand, a recession would cause business to step up efforts to control health care-related expenditures. Unemployment would increase the number of uninsured and underinsured people in need of health care services. Government programs would be strained to keep up with demand. Providers would be called upon to provide more charity care with less of a base for cost shifting. On the other hand, a recession would be expected to increase the size of the available labor pool, which would relieve salary pressure caused by shortages and slow the inflation of labor costs (3).

CHANGING DEMOGRAPHICS AND DEMAND

The American population is aging. A survey of 1600 health care leaders identified the growth of the elderly population as the health care industry's greatest issue for 1995 (5). The number of people over 65 will increase from 28.5 million in 1985 to 35 million by the year 2000 (6). This represents a 40% increase over a 15-year period. Other significant trends include growth of the Hispanic population and an emphasis on wellness.

Demographic changes will lead to changes in types of services demanded by consumers. Demand for services related to the management of chronic illnesses will increase. The demand for rehabilitation services will also increase. Outpatient care will continue at a growth rate of 7 to 15% over the next few years. An increased demand for inpatient services is predicted for the second half of the decade. The aging of the population will fuel an increased demand for services. But, because the majority of these services will go to Medicare clients, providers will be at greater risk for underfunding (7).

TECHNOLOGY

The 1990s promise to be a period of technological boom. Advances in cardiology, women's health, orthopedics, and neurology are among the most likely areas to benefit from significant technological developments (8). Rehabilitation is a secondary opportunity in most of these product lines. In health care, technological advances can impact cost, length of treatment, the inpatient/outpatient mix, and manpower needs. The availability of new technology generally results in high utilization. Both medical professionals and consumers want access to the newest and the best possible care (9). However, the trend is for physicians to use both old and new technologies rather than discarding older forms of care. This practice more than doubles the cost of diagnosis and treatment.

The cost effects of technology are important to both providers and payers. Providers, forced to invest in expensive technology, want to minimize their investment and ongoing cost. Maximum use of the new technology is in the provider's best interest. Payers see technology as an additional financial risk. They would like to see the use of new technology linked to guidelines for appropriate utilization. In the 1990s we are likely to see more providers joining together to share the financial burden and benefit of new technology (10). It is also likely that there will be an increased demand for proof that newer is better, not just more expensive.

Issues

A survey of national health care leaders indicated that the issues of access, cost, and quality would dominate the health care industry during the 1990s (5). Lack of adequate insurance, manpower shortages, and an uneven distribution of health care resources overtly limit access of portions of American society to adequate health care services. Often, access is limited on the basis of age and income. The problem of access is compounded as the cost of health care continues to escalate. Competition and the demand for accountability have focused on quality as the basis for control of future health care spending and purchase decisions. The resolution of these issues will not be easy. Efforts at finding solutions have already begun. It is anticipated that these efforts will be the focus of public and private debate in the decade to come. The issue of cost has been discussed in detail. The issues of access and quality could benefit from further review.

ACCESS

Higgins (11) summarizes the issues of access to the American health care system well. He points to the increasing problems faced by the uninsured and underinsured which include: a recent court ruling that has declared one state's Medicaid system invalid because it failed to provide reasonable access to care; the 15% plus annual inflation experienced by employers who do provide health care insurance; and proposed cuts of $5.5 billion in the 1991 Medicare budget. All of these issues indicate that many people who cannot afford adequate health care services simply have no alternative but to do without health care. In 1987 it was estimated that 37 million Americans had no health care insurance. An additional 15 to 30 million Americans are underinsured. The American College of Healthcare Executives (12) identified the special groups in need of basic health care services. In order of priority the groups identified were:

1. High-risk infants, children, and youth;
2. Isolated and frail elderly;
3. High-risk obstetric clients;
4. Minorities with language or cultural barriers;
5. Minority AIDS clients.

Health Care Rationing

A number of approaches to the problem of access have been proposed. Among them are the concepts of formal health care rationing and universal insurance coverage plans. To date, proposals which promote health care rationing as a means of controlling costs have been primarily aimed at state and locally subsidized programs which provide coverage to the elderly, poor, and disabled. These plans attempt to eliminate or limit coverage for certain types of procedures which would be covered by other payers (12). Overt attempts at rationing have met with a mixed response. In some states, taxpayers have supported these efforts. Responses from the federal government and the health care industry have been less favorable.

Health Care Reform: Universal Coverage

Ineffectiveness of existing controls to slow health care costs and issues of limited and denied access are the bases for a rising call for sweeping health care system reform (13). Comment and support for health care system reform is coming from business, the medical community, government leaders, and the public. A 1989 public opinion poll indicated that many Americans were dissatisfied with the current American health care delivery system (14). Of those polled, 89% said the system was in need of fundamental change or complete restructuring. At this time, six proposals for national health care reform have been developed. These proposals vary in terms of coverage, benefits, administration, financing, and cost. Four of the six discuss specific methods of measuring quality of care. All address the issue of cost containment. Some build on the existing Medicaid and Medicare system. Some dismantle current systems and start over. The issues for debate are (13):

1. Should all or part of the existing system be salvaged or should we start over?
2. Who should be responsible for health care insurance coverage: employers, the government, or the individual?
3. Who should finance the cost of health care coverage: employers, the government, or individuals? What mechanism should be used?
4. Should all individuals be covered by the same system? Is it acceptable to have different systems to cover the elderly and poor? Should there be coverage differences between states?

Insurance Reform

One alternative to universal coverage, which may either precede reform or circumvent it, is insurance reform. Congress is currently considering proposals which would make it economically feasible for employers of small or high risk employee groups to afford employee health care insurance. This would be accomplished by forcing insurance companies to base premium rates on community experience rather than the limited experience of the small or high-risk employer (15).

QUALITY

There are two perspectives to the issue of health care quality. There is the consumer perspective and there is the industry perspective. Industry leaders agree that by 1995 there will be standard definitions of quality. Providers will be able to measure and compare the quality of their services, and they will routinely report on quality indicators to regulatory bodies (5). Payers will purchase health care on the basis of quality as well as price. The push for quality standards will come from both consumers and providers. Through education, consumers will come to understand quality in industry terms. However, they will continue to define quality in terms of environment, comfort, and customer service as well. To be successful in the 1990s providers will need to meet both industry and consumer quality expectations (16).

Ongoing Evolution of the Health Care Delivery System
INDUSTRY CONSOLIDATION

Although the details differ somewhat, most of the predictions about the future structure of the American health care delivery system share the following points (17–20).

1. The basis of the structure will be a vertically integrated continuum of services.
2. The structure will link local primary care providers with regional secondary and tertiary care providers.
3. Joint ventures, mergers, and acquisitions will unite physicians, ambulatory care centers, hospitals, and long-term care providers together. These relationships will be used to lock in larger volumes of clients.
4. There will be fewer full service providers. Providers will specialize in those services they can provide efficiently and effectively. Duplication of services between providers in the same system will be eliminated.
5. There will be a continued shift of services out of the traditional hospital setting. Hospitals will provide limited specialty care which cannot be delivered in an alternative setting. It is predicted that "within 10 years, 70% of health care services will be delivered outside of the hospital setting" (20).
6. Health care organizations will adopt flatter structures to allow for rapid response to change and competition (21).

Undoubtedly, the consolidation of the health care delivery system will lead to the closure of some existing providers. A total of 65 community and 15 specialty hospitals closed in 1989 (22). By the year 2000 over 2000 more hospitals are expected to close or change their focus (23) as alternative providers fill needs currently met in hospital settings.

Implications for Physical Therapy Education and Practice through the 1990s
PERSPECTIVE

It would be reasonable to predict that the profession of physical therapy will be in a strong position to at least maintain, if not improve, its status in the health care environment during the next decade. This prediction is based on consideration of information from many sources. The preceding information on the future of the health care industry presented the overall provider outlook. To relate this outlook more pointedly to physical therapy an analysis of the physical therapy educational and practice environments is needed.

Table 12.1 presents a summary of many future changes that are likely to occur and have an impact on the field of physical therapy. This table incorporates much of the preceding American health care system information and it presents a summary of the authors' perspectives of the physical therapy educational and practice environments for the next decade. Following Table 12.1 are discussions of selected topics presented in a strategic analysis format. Various futuristic scenarios are presented to stimulate thoughts of possibilities and difficulties physical therapists may encounter over the next 10 years.

OPPORTUNITIES, THREATS, AND SUGGESTIONS FOR EDUCATION
Demographic Changes

For at least a decade, students admitted to physical therapy entry level programs have been among the most academically capable students

Table 12.1.
Important Likely Changes That Will Impact on Physical Therapy in the 1990s

Clients

Fewer people insured
More limited health care coverage (underinsured)
Increased need for charity care
Increased need for governmental aid
Growth of non-Caucasian populations
Increase in the number of Spanish-speaking people
High-risk segments of society will include poor children, frail elderly, pregnant women,
    minorities with AIDS, individuals with cultural and language differences
Increased number of AIDS victims
Increased number of children born to substance-abusing women
Increased proportion of the population classified as elderly
Increased number of older individuals with chronic conditions
Greater interest in prevention than currently exists

Third Party Payers

Increased control of expenditures
Greater control of access to care
Termination of fee-for-service agreements
Increased requirements for justification if services are to be authorized and paid for
Inpatient hospital stays will be challenged
Increased demands for accountability in standardized, objective terms
Standardized definitions of quality care
Increased monitoring of providers
Payments likely to be made only if outcomes are within time and cost norms based on
    local, regional, or national norms
A form of national health care which involves private insurers is likely to come into being
    within the decade

Institutional Providers

Increased competition for clients
Increased competition for staff
Increased vertical integration with emphasis on outpatient services
Greater diversity in where and when services are offered
Rehabilitation, prevention, and health promotion services will increase in prominence
    throughout the decade
Decreases in specialized inservice services will occur
Increased consolidation resulting in fewer but larger megacorporations who will be the sole
    health care providers in some regions
More joint ventures
More and new managed care organization relationships
Nongovernment income principally from some form of capitated health care plan
Partial relief from the burden of some charity care by end of decade
Increased ethical conflicts related to efforts to remain fiscally viable

Medicine and Physicians

There will be an oversupply of physicians by the end of the decade
Physicians are likely to widen the scope of what they do into areas of care previously
    carried out by nonphysicians
Increase in numbers of clients with chronic illnesses
Improved management of cardiac, neurological, and orthopedic problems through technical
    advancements
Greater concentration on medical problems of women and minorities
Increased emphasis on prevention, health promotion
Proliferation of conflict of interest situations are likely to occur as physicians attempt to
    maintain their income levels   *continues*

Table 12.1.   (*Continued*)

Education

Continued but slower growth of the number of entry level programs in the first half of the
  decade

Consolidation, fewer but larger programs later in the decade

Some institutions may specialize in graduate, postdoctoral, and postboard certification
  programs

Some institutions may specialize in formal reentry programs for previously licensed
  therapists, preparation for board certification, and pregraduate program preparation

Continued undersupply of potentially tenurable faculty, continued short-fall in the
  numbers of new graduates which the market demands

Faculty without doctorates or board certification as clinical specialists will be replaced by
  those having one or both of these credentials

Increased competition for faculty, clinical sites, and students

Increased faculty specialization

Some confusion as to what the background of a physical therapist entails will exist as
  practitioners will hold a variety of degrees from bachelor's degrees through clinical and
  academic doctorates

Reconsideration of a clinical doctorate for entry level

Attempts to increase enrollments without increased resources

Increased cooperation between academic and clinical institutions in recruitment, financing
  students, providing clinical experience, continuing education, and other areas

Remuneration of some kind to clinical sites

Practice

Increased percentage of independent entrepreneurial practitioners to the middle of the
  decade

Increased numbers of practitioners becoming members of managed care groups during the
  second half of the decade

Decreased percentage of therapists working in inpatient institutions

Increased diversity in practice locations treating outpatients

Increased numbers of board certified therapists in more areas of specialization

Increased competition by other professions for segments of the physical therapy market not
  being met because of insufficient numbers of available therapists

Direct access legislation could be passed in all states by the end of the decade

Medical staff privileges will likely be commonly granted to physical therapists by
  institutions by the middle of the decade

Increased competition among therapy groups and institutional physical therapy
  departments for clients will not be sufficiently modulated by the professional code of
  ethics to avoid some negative influences on the profession as a whole

Continued concern about physician-owned physical therapy services

at their respective educational institutions. This trend will continue as long as the numbers of qualified applicants remain several times larger than the number that can be accommodated.

A decline in the number of high school graduates began in 1989. This decline is expected to result in a 12% decrease in the number of high school graduates over the next three years (24, 25). Since the onset of the the applicant pool decline there has been increasing extramural competition among educational institutions for qualified new students and intramural competition for the students admitted. In 1990, the APTA responded with a task force to investigate the concept of a centralized student application support service (26). This service, if available, could provide valuable firsthand data on all aspects of the applicant pool. It could also serve an important role in maintaining a sufficiently large applicant pool when the demographic trends are less favorable. With an increasing percentage of minorities in American society it may be possible, through a coordinated effort of a centralized service, to bring about greater minority student representation in all physical therapy educational programs. A centralized applicant support service could give physical therapy educational programs a competitive advantage over other fields which are also seeking to maintain an academically capable student body from among fewer applicants. If this downturn in the number of high school graduates results in a drop in physical therapy enrollments, the predicted manpower shortage will be exacerbated. This will weaken the position of physical therapists in future health care markets (27).

Curricular Content

The development and acceptance of new criteria for accreditation to be enacted in 1992 (28) will give some direction to educational programs for preparing future physical therapists for a changing health care services environment. The desired outcomes of the educational process are identified in broad categories. These categories are client care, physical therapy delivery systems, and the health care system and society. There are specific criteria related to the topic of management. Accredited programs will have presented evidence that their curricula included content on the implications of demographic changes, health care system dynamics, quality assurance, and fiscal requirements for the practice of physical therapy. These and other criteria will require changes in curricular content at some educational institutions.

In the area of management, the criteria and performance measures are specific enough to guide content selection. Since management principles are part of the infrastructure that fosters the delivery of quality care, these principles will need to be presented with more depth than they were in the 1980s. More extensive preparation for dealing with the business aspects of independent entrepreneurial practices and institutional practices will be needed (29) to complement the increased professional autonomy that will be available in the future.

One interpretation of the new accreditation criteria is that an increase in liberal arts content is called for. A biosocial blend of coursework is encouraged rather than an expansion of biological science content (24). A wider liberal arts background has been purported to facilitate flexible thinking, increase adaptability, and support development of unique problem-solving strategies (30). Such skills would be very useful in an unpredictable and dynamic environment like the American health care system. This encouragement could result in non-physical therapist faculty members being employed where there are presently no experts in the psychosocial sciences among the existing faculty members. Also, during the downturn in enrollments, other departments may be willing to tailor-make a course or teach a new block of material specifically to meet the needs of physical therapy students.

There will be continued variability in the content presented among individual educational programs due in part to differences in the makeup of the various faculties (31). Each program will meet the new criteria in unique ways and in varying degrees as they have in the past. There will be a continuing struggle to maintain balance between desires to deepen and expand "hard science," new technology, and skills content and the need to increase the amount of psychosocial, ethics, management, and educational content. Our educational programs will have to develop or revise their philosophy and mission statements to accommodate new criteria and to give direction to faculty, students, and external groups.

Faculty

Faculty Structure.   A tiered faculty, comprising those members with doctorates and those without doctorates, exists already in some physical therapy programs. This tiering may produce philosophical conflicts and limit integration of information between courses. Ph.D. faculty in particular often tend to focus on research, to be protective of their research time, and to stick closely to their areas of expertise. Nondoctoral faculty will likely teach lower level courses, have more diverse and larger teaching loads, be responsible for clinical education, and have more non-teaching responsibilities.

Competition for Faculty.   Competition between educational institutions for limited numbers of faculty with doctoral degrees will continue to increase salaries for this group. Increased financial reward may influence more physical therapists to complete a doctorate. The possibilities of earning a reasonable salary and having improved job security may influence doctoral degree holders from other fields to become physical therapists. Such individuals would add interesting diversity to any physical therapy faculty they might eventually join. Improved salaries may make teaching a more attractive alternative to clinicians, particularly board certified specialists, who desire to refine the theoretical tenets of their practice areas through advanced study and research. Board certification may be an alternative to a doctorate for some of the current academic faculty members with master's degrees (32).

Shortages of faculty will continue throughout the decade (24). Some instructional needs will continue to be met by inventive, but stopgap, measures such as purchasing instruction from local clinical experts, bringing in faculty from other institutions for selected instructional blocks of material, and computer-aided instructional methods.

Interactive computer programs will become a more common supplemental instructional tool. However, it is unlikely that computers will significantly lessen the need for more faculty within the first half of this decade (33). The lack of programming skills, hardware, and time to develop materials and resistance to change are some reasons for this prediction.

Clinical Training Sites

Competition for desirable clinical settings for student experiences has increased over the past 10 years. New educational programs, larger enrollments, and a trend toward interspersing clinical experiences throughout the educational period have, at times, strained relations between academic and clinical groups. The demands and the desire to foster cooperation has resulted in attempts at forming regional consortia to co-ordinate handling requests from academic programs for clinical resources. Such efforts will likely continue with limited success. Changing membership, unpredictable workplace dynamics, conflicts of interest, and varying degrees of commitment to cooperation will hinder these consortia.

The demand for clinical sites will continue throughout the foreseeable future. The numbers of educational programs will continue to increase slowly. The 1992 accreditation criteria (28) may require some educational programs to increase clinical experience opportunities. These increased demands will be made on facilities which, too frequently, will be understaffed and overworked because of continuing staff vacancies.

A foresightful suggestion for dealing with clinical education in the near future was made by Johnson (25). She reasoned that institutions are becoming vertically integrated. Vertical integration brings a variety of care environments under one administration in a single locale. It would be beneficial experientially and economically for students to be exposed to continuity and diversity in one locale. It has also been suggested that students be assigned to clinical sites on the basis of the opportunities that exist for participating in diverse but continuous levels of care (31). There is some agreement that vertically organized organizations should be the preferred clinical sites through the mid 1990s.

A significant advantage for clinical sites is the opportunity to influence affiliating students to join them after graduation (34). However, the pool of students with the freedom to choose their employment during affiliations is diminishing. Financial necessity has influenced some students to accept assistance in exchange for a commitment to a future work obligation. Some clinical sites, particularly those who are short-staffed, have been less willing to accept student affiliates they have no chance of recruiting. If this attitude becomes prevalent, sponsoring organizations who do not as yet participate in clinical education programs will have to get involved. A logical choice would be to become part of the clinical education resource pool of the institutions attended by their aid recipients. There will be continued availability of private scholarships, loans, gifts, and other inducements to students (31). Governmental funding for entry level education for the most part is in the discussion stage (35).

OPPORTUNITIES, THREATS, AND SUGGESTIONS FOR PRACTICE
Manpower Shortage

Failure to increase faculty and the number of graduates in the near future will encourage, and possibly force, institutional employers to seek other means of providing physical therapy services. Potential relief could come from existing professionals such as occupational therapists, athletic trainers, exercise physiologists, behavioral therapists, and some nurses. Physical therapist assistants could have a strong role as substitutes for physical therapists in some settings. A second alternative could be the preparation of new hybrid groups of allied health personnel who could do some aspects of nursing and other activities (36). An extreme option would be to discontinue providing physical therapy services in some settings. In the future, hospitals will be providing primarily services related to saving life and nonroutine surgery. Under extreme financially constrained conditions physical therapy may be perceived as a luxury as it relates to improving the quality of life rather than saving life. In an extreme situation such as a major recession, only life-saving health care services could be afforded by most payers.

Direct Access

Based on 1989 licensure information (37) it is estimated that 49% of licensed physical therapists are licensed in the 25 states which have enacted some form of direct access legislation (37, 38). Direct access has the potential to increase the autonomy of physical therapists. Increased autonomy may lead to more therapists staying in the field and practicing longer and it may attract individuals from other professions to the field of physical therapy. Direct access is very likely to be enacted in more states within the next few years (39).

As long as reimbursement for federally mandated programs requires a physician referral for physical therapy services, direct access will remain more of a philosophical victory than a recognition of the professional status of physical therapists. The challenge of providing satisfactory evidence to demonstrate the cost effectiveness of direct access will be met within the decade. This may bring about changes in payer requirements for physician referral.

Traditional restrictions on institutional physical therapy practice (underutilization, referral requirements, etc.) tend to diminish the expression of professional autonomy (29). However, changes to enhance professional autonomy in institutional settings are inevitable. Recruitment of physical therapists into institutional practice will depend on it.

Medical Staff Appointments

In 1984 the Joint Commission on Accreditation of Hospitals repealed their rule which excluded nonphysicians serving as members of a hospital medical staff (40–42). This accreditation change allowed independent licensed health care professionals, in addition to physicians and dentists, to make application for medical staff membership to a hospital's board of directors. Such appointments to physical therapists who practice outside of the institution will allow clients who have been treated by these therapists to request their services when they are institutionalized. Medical staff appointment is another example of increased autonomy which benefits physical therapists.

Board certified physical therapist specialists in particular will be in an advantageous position for being granted medical staff privileges where no such specialists are present among the institutional physical therapy staff. Physicians may come to recognize the value of a physical therapist specialist and request the services of a specific therapist as they do when they refer to their medical specialist colleagues.

Manpower shortages and alternative practice opportunities are causing a decline in the number of therapists employed by hospitals. Should this trend continue, independent medical staff-appointed therapists may become a major source of inpatient therapy toward the end of the decade.

Board Certified Specialization

The establishment in 1985 of a board certification process for recognizing physical therapists with specialized clinical expertise was a major step toward increasing autonomy for the profession (43). Credentialed expertise has long been recognized in medicine and dentistry. General assumptions associated with clinical specialization are concentration on a defined topic which focuses knowledge and clinical expertise related to that topic. Also, specialized knowledge and expertise will likely result in more appropriate care decisions and the most skillful application of treatment techniques. If these assumptions are accepted by the public, the following scenario could occur. As the number of certified physical therapist specialists increases, a smarter market, including the public and third party payers, will seek out and request services from these specialists (44). Customers will choose to spend their health care dollars on recognized, specialized care as long as fee-for-service arrangements exist. As physicians gain additional experience in working with board certified therapists, they will become more comfortable with referring clients as well as requesting the services of certified physical therapist specialists. The seven current areas of specialization are a beginning. There will be several more specialization areas recognized within the next few years.

Practice Environments

Rehabilitation. Physical therapy, with its emphasis on independent function and the management of long-term disability, is in a strong position to continue to be a high demand service. Increased utilization of physical therapy has continued in an era of cost containment. Of the growing number of elderly people in the United States, it is the oldest segment of the aging population that is increasing at the fastest rate (45). This segment will have the greatest need for function-enhancing services (46).

Geriatrics. The recent addition of geriatrics as a board certified specialty is timely. Expertise in dealing with the special needs of aged individuals will help solidify the place of physical therapists in the care of elderly clients (44) and, possibly, in the prevention of amenable hypokinetic-related problems (47).

An alternative view of the place of physical therapy in the care of geriatric clients is that we may have already lost this market to others (29). For the past 10 years many physical therapists have had an infatuation with orthopedic and sports physical therapy. The momentum is for graduates to pursue employment in the orthopedic and sports areas rather than in geriatric care. In the long run, these trends may have a negative influence on physical therapy being recognized as a profession dedicated to meeting the health care needs of the aging population.

Entrepreneurial Practice. Independent entrepreneurial private practices are often built around orthopedic, sports injury, and industrial injury clients. With a ready supply of motivated new graduates each year, there are sufficient numbers of employees to replace those who go into business for themselves or make other career moves. Most health care organizations also serve these same categories of clients. One wonders if there are too many therapists concentrating their efforts in too small a segment of the health care market. Practitioners and organizations emphasizing care primarily for orthopedic, sports, and industrial injury clients may find themselves in significant financial jeopardy with the growth of managed care and a decline in fee-for-service payers.

Consolidation of the health care industry into vertically integrated systems will threaten the independent practitioner. Survival of independent practitioners will eventually come through membership in some type of group practice arrangement (29, 48, 49) most likely affiliated with a managed care organization (47) or as part of a larger system. Three group practice models that are likely to emerge are dedicated groups, diversified groups, and interdisciplinary groups. A dedicated group would include certified specialists in the same specialty area. A diversified group would consist of certified specialists in different but complementary areas. An interdisciplinary group would include specialist professionals from a variety of fields. Because of the impending dominance of managed health care organizations some forward-looking physical therapists have already formed preferred provider organizations (50). It is likely that many physical therapists will be in group practice, involved in managed care, and be reimbursed on a capitated basis within this decade.

Generalists.   Of course, not all physical therapists will become specialists or entrepreneurial independent practitioners in the next decade. Therapists who are not certified specialists or do not have doctorates will likely work for others. The future role of the physical therapy generalist may be limited by law, by third party payers (44), or by employers.

Institutional Practice.   Greater autonomy may become available to therapists who are employed by institutions that are not able to afford the salaries of those with advanced certification or degrees. Institutional salaries will continue to escalate but they will remain lower than those offered by noninstitutional employers. Hospital physical therapy departments that are cost effective, and able to retain staff with the highest credentials available, will do more than survive. They will become the models of the industry. Those who are not able to do this will be supplanted by qualified, cost effective alternative sources of service.

Prevention: A New Market.   It is predicted that there will be an increased participation by the general public in preventative health practices (25, 29, 48). A possible future scenario identifies health promotion and wellness as the primary emphasis of physical therapists (25, 29, 48). The concept of a "health coach" has been formulated as part of this scenario which foresees most people actively taking charge of their own health care needs (48). Although physical therapists were not specifically identified as the future "health coach," the concept of prevention includes many areas common to the practice of physical therapy. The older population is as interested in maintaining or improving their health as other age groups in order to support an enduring, fulfilling lifestyle. If physical therapists are not increasingly involved with the noninstitutionalized elderly in health promotion and injury prevention programs, they will be missing out on a significant opportunity to deal with 95% of those classified as elderly (45, 46). Orthopedic problems associated with active lifestyles and chronic disabilities will continue to exist within the community-living elderly population. Treatment of these problems, however, will be a secondary market for physical therapy services. The primary services will be in the prevention areas (25, 29).

The vertical integration concept can be applied to marketing services to the elderly population. It would be reasonable to assume that a specialized physical therapy organization could well serve the older population by providing a continuum of services from prevention to hospice care. A healthier older population has been predicted to result in a compressed morbidity (48). This means that many people will enjoy active lifestyles throughout most of their lives. A precipitous decline in health will occur very late in life in a very short time period. The healthy lifestyle can be supported by some form of health coaching and self-selected and administered medical, noetic, and bioelectrical treatments (29, 48). Physical therapists typically have the background to be the "health coach" in all but one of these areas. Utilization of cognitive techniques to influence physiological systems and other supportable holistic health care concepts are areas that have not yet received sufficient attention by physical therapists (50). In the future, meditation, visual imagery, biofeedback, and other noetic techniques are anticipated to be commonly used by the general population as part of a personal health care program (29, 48). Those who master these techniques will teach them. Physical therapists could be the teachers.

ACCOUNTABILITY

A final prediction deals with accountability. In time there will be national data bases which include physical therapy information (33, 48). Reporting will be done on computers in networks. A defined and common language for conditions, treatments rendered, and results will emerge (33, 48). The data will, in a sense, form the fingerprints of the department, group, or individual physical therapist. The outcomes of services will be identified for each practice setting and compared. Local, regional, and national norms will emerge (33). Such information can be rewarding or incriminating. On the positive side, national data bases will be able to identify what and whose treatments result in acceptable outcomes within specified time frames. As an option to going to a book or a journal for current treatment information, inquiries about the preferred treatment for a problem will be available via computer networks. On the negative side, pooled data can lead to undesirable outcomes. Third party subscribers to the data networks (48) are likely to quickly discontinue using the services of those found to produce results that are below the norms. The norms most easily identified are those relating to functional outcome and duration of service. Consumer groups will also purchase access to some aspects of the data bases. They will rate institutions, practice groups, and individual practitioners for subscribers to their services (48). Issues of accountability will be a major concern for physical therapists in all practice settings throughout the 1990s because payment will be tied very closely to outcomes.

Other Considerations

There are other factors that will impact on the practice of physical therapy in the future. Currently, the AIDS epidemic is a great concern. AIDS will be a significant medical but a secondary physical therapy problem throughout the decade. The numbers of children born to substance-abusing mothers will increase during the foreseeable future. Both of these factors will offer significant challenges and unique opportunities for many dedicated physical therapists within and outside hospital environments:

Demographic projections for the 1990s indicate there will be increasing ethnic diversity within American society (51). Caucasians will become a minority in some additional geographical areas of the country. Spanish is the primary language of the fastest growing minority group. This observation suggests that competence in Spanish will be an increasingly desirable asset to physical therapists in some regions. Having familiarity with the values of other cultures and an understanding of racial and gender physiological and behavioral differences will take on increasing importance by the end of the decade. National data bases will provide the information needed to increase individualization of therapeutic activities beyond what is possible today. Even though societal diversity will increase, individual needs will be able to be met more specifically because of sophisticated monitoring of responses and feedback.

SUMMARY

Taken as a whole, the preceding mixture of facts, impressions, interpretations, and extrapolations suggest that the overall demand for physical therapy services will continue to grow through the next decade. The demand for physical therapy in the traditional, nonspecialized, inpatient setting has stabilized and probably will stay stable at least through the middle of the decade. Service areas with the greatest future growth potential are ambulatory care, specialized inpatient programs, prevention programs, and long-term care for the elderly. The aging of the population, the increasing prevalence of chronic illness, advances in life-saving technology, increasing need for functional rehabilitative services, and interest in wellness will all contribute to a growing demand for physical therapy services. Competition to hospital physical therapy departments will come from independent entrepreneurial physical therapy practitioners and groups of physical therapists working together under some form of managed care arrangement or as a part of a larger health care system.

It appears that actions taken by the American Physical Therapy Association in the 1980s have been well-targeted to position the profession to develop further recognition and prosper through the 1990s. This analysis assumes that a significant increase in the

*number of graduates will be forthcoming by the middle of the
decade.*

References

1. Henderson JA. Hospital closings prompt more specialization. Health Industry Today 1989;May:24–25,31.
2. Solovy A. Medicare margins in the 1990s face a policy battle. Hospitals 1989;20(July):37.
3. Solovy A. Health care in the 1990s: forecasts by top analysts. Hospitals 1989;20(July):34–36,38–43,46.
4. Solovy A. Recession prospects mixed bag for health care. Hospitals 1989;20(July):44.
5. Anonymous. The future of healthcare: changes and choices. Chicago: Arthur Anderson and Co., American College of Healthcare Executives, 1987.
6. Anonymous. The trauma of transformation in the 1990s. Minneapolis: Health One Corp., 1989.
7. Coile RC, Jr. Healthcare 1990: top 10 trends for the year ahead. Hospital Strategy Rep 1989;Dec:1–8.
8. Wilkinson R. New technology that will change key services. Hospitals 1988;20(May):56.
9. Los Angeles Times Service. Can US afford medicine's machines? The Milwaukee Journal 1990;March 11:23A.
10. Ward M. Hospitals here also pay more heed to the price of medical technology. The Milwaukee Journal 1990;March 11:23A.
11. Higgins T. Cracks in our health care system are widening. Healthweek 1990;Feb 26:41.
12. Kirshner E. Executives cautious about rationing of health care. Healthweek 1990;March 12:1,53.
13. Kern R, Bresch JE. Systematic healthcare reform: is it time? Health Prog 1990;Jan–Feb:32–44.
14. Blendon RJ, Taylor H. Views on health care: public opinion in three nations. Health Affairs 1989;Spring:149–157.
15. Kimball MC. Congressional mood favors assault on health plans' cost to small biz. Healthweek 1990;Apr 23:15,40.
16. Lawrence S. Hospital success strategies for the 1990s. California Hospitals 1989;Nov–Dec: 21–22.
17. Brown M, McCool BP. Visionary strategies for the 1990s. Health Care Strategic Manage 1989;Oct:12–15.
18. Green J. Health futurists offer glimpse of structure of hospitals in 1990s. AHA News 1989;Sep 18:1,5.
19. Shortell S. Insider interview. Healthweek 1990;Jan 22:18–20,45.
20. McManis GL. Challenges of new decade demand break with tradition. Modern Healthcare 1990;8(Jan):60.
21. McManis GL. Managing tomorrow's healthcare organization. Healthcare Exec 1990;Jan–Feb:15.
22. Anonymous. 65 community hospitals closed, 12 opened in 1989. AHA News 1990;April 9:1.
23. Anonymous. Almost half of all US hospitals expected to close by the year 2000. Phys Ther Bull 1989;4(31):1,36.
24. Anonymous. Higher Education and National Affairs. 1989;37(22):1.
25. Johnson GR. Issues and trends in physical therapy education. In: Mathews JS. Practice issues in physical therapy. Thorofare, NJ: Slack, 1989:1–21,24.
26. American Physical Therapy Association. Letter, Department of Education, April 10, 1990.
27. Mathews JS. Toward a profession of substance. In: Mathews JS. Practice issues in physical therapy. Thorofare, NJ: Slack, 1989:ix–xii.
28. Commission on Accreditation in Physical Therapy Education. American Physical Therapy Association. Evaluative criteria for accreditation of educational programs for the preparation of physical therapists. April, 1990.
29. Mathews JS. The future of physical therapy in hospital settings. In: Mathews JS. Practice issues in physical therapy. Thorofare, NJ: Slack, 1989:159–166.

30. Brand MK, Gurenlian JR. Extending access to care: preparing allied health practitioners for nontraditional settings. J Allied Health 1989:261–269.
31. Mathews JS. Clinical education forces for change. In: Mathews JS. Practice issues in physical therapy. Thorofare, NJ: Slack, 1989:75–88.
32. American Physical Therapy Association, Faculty Activity Survey. June, 1989.
33. Walter J. Information management: the technological revolution. In: Mathews JS. Practice issues in physical therapy. Thorofare, NJ: Slack, 1989:127–144.
34. Yohn J. Study: PT students return to CES site for first position. Prog Rep 1987;18(8):6.
35. Pickard NW. Legislative successes for physical therapists in 1989. Prog Rep 1989;18(10):5,11.
36. Walsh AC. Wave of the future holds threat for physical therapy. Phys Ther Bull 1989;4(36):3,35.
37. Anonymous. Physical therapy licenses reported by state. Prog Rep 1989;18(7):3.
38. Horn J. Texas becomes 25th state to approve direct access. Phys Ther Bull 1991;6(20):1,39.
39. Hunter K. Some 200 bills affecting PT introduced in 41 states. Prog Rep 1990;19(7):10–11.
40. Edelstein K. JCAH eases standards: medical staffs may now include non-MDs. Prog Rep 1984;(March):1–3.
41. Precious T. Professionals battle for privileges. Prog Rep 1984(April):1,12.
42. Anonymous. Q & A: JCAH's new medical staff privileges. Prog Rep 1984(June):6.
43. Kigin C. Specialization in physical therapy. In: Mathews JS. Practice issues in physical therapy. Thorofare, NJ: Slack, 1989:45–61.
44. Mathews J. Physical therapy specialization presents wide-ranging challenges. Prog Rep 1988;17(5):6–7.
45. U.S. Senate Committee on Aging, American Association of Retired Persons, Federal Council on the Aging, U.S. Administration on Aging. Aging America: trends and projections, 1987–88. Washington, D.C.: U.S. Government Printing Office 1987–88:12–16.
46. Spense DL, Brownell WW. Functional assessment of the aged person. In: Granger CV, Gresham GE, eds. Functional assessment in rehabilitation medicine. Baltimore: Williams & Wilkins, 1989:257–258.
47. Lewis CB. Clinical implications of musculoskeletal changes with age. In: Lewis CB. Aging: the health care challenge. Philadelphia: FA Davis, 195:120–121.
48. Bezold C. The future of health care: implications for the allied health professions. J Allied Health 1989:437–457.
49. Weinper M. Alternative delivery systems for physical therapists. In: Mathews JS. Practice issues in physical therapy. Thorofare, NJ: Slack, 1989:109–126.
50. Bisht H. Letter to the editor. Prog Rep 1988;17(9):2,10.
51. Henry WA III. Beyond the melting pot. Time (April) 1990:28–31.

APPENDIX A

Responses to Case Studies

RESPONSE TO CASE STUDY 2.1

The organizational structure suggested for Very Special Medical Center (VSMC) is presented in appendix Figure 2.1. The design is based on the values and mission statement. Considerations in selecting this design are summarized below.

1. Commitment to both education and research is demonstrated by the creation of a nonmanagerial position dedicated solely to those activities. The title of the position takes it out of the hierarchy and allows more relaxed interaction at all levels. The position is also freed from operational priorities. Education and research remain its focus. The position's direct reporting relationship to the Executive Director indicates the position's organizational power and authority over all education and research matters.
2. The structure of the the the divisions of the Physical Therapy Service should reflect that of the organization which it serves. If the organization is programmatic, then the division should be programmatic. There should also be continuity between divisions of the same service. Note that the titles are similar for like positions. This will facilitate interdivision communication and transfers.
3. The titles and structures of the physical therapists responsible for the operation of outpatients clinics reflect the difference in roles, responsibility, and autonomy for decision making. These job features must always be recognized or role confusion could easily occur. The differentiation also facilitates different compensation arrangements based on different job descriptions. The decentralization of management in the outpatient satellites allows more rapid decision making in this more competitive environment.

The mission statement of the VSMC Physical Therapy Service should reflect the activities of all of its divisions. It could read as follows:

VSMC Physical Therapy Service
Mission Statement

The mission of VSMC Physical Therapy Service is fourfold. First and foremost, it is to provide for the general and specialized physical therapy needs of all persons served by member organizations of the VSMC. Second, to contribute to the development of specialized services provided by VSMC member organizations in which the Physical Therapy Service will play a clinical role. Third, to be a regionally recognized center for the training and development of student and graduate physical therapists.

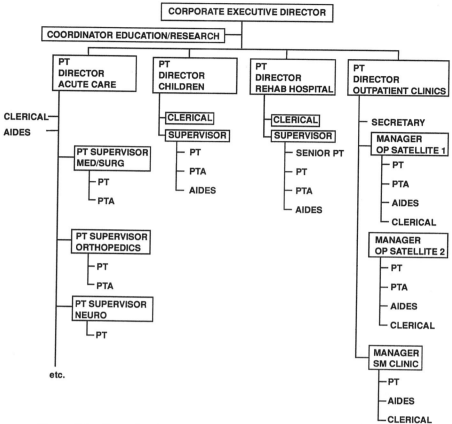

Figure 2.1.   Example of reorganization of VSMC physical therapy services.

Fourth, to contribute to the growth and development of the profession of physical therapy through the performance and publication of clinical research related to the practice of physical therapy. VSMC Physical Therapy Service shall pursue its mission in a manner which remains mindful of the human dignity of all persons, its fiscal responsibility to the community, and the values and ethics of the medical community, medical center, and profession of which it is a part.

RESPONSE TO CASE STUDY 3.1

Under a traditional style of management, Iona would review the problem, identify and evaluate possible solutions, and implement the one she feels is best. She would not believe that staff wants to, is able to, or should have input into the problem-solving process.

Under a participative style of management, Iona would start the problem-solving process by seeking staff input. Staff input would be used to define the problem from both the management and staff perspectives. Iona would involve the staff in the generation and prioritizing of possible alternative solutions. She may allow staff to make the final decision or

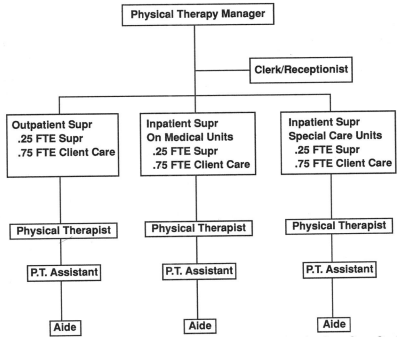

Figure 4.1. Suggested restructuring of OGH physical therapy service from Case Study 4.1.

reserve that authority for herself. Staff would share in the responsibility for solution implementation.

There are several methods Iona could use to obtain staff input. A staff meeting, a survey, or a task force representative of the work group are all possibilities. Most importantly, Iona would let staff know how their input shaped the decision-making process and influenced the chosen solution.

RESPONSE TO CASE STUDY 4.1

Method One

Restructure the department into sections serving different types of client referrals. Department activity could be segmented on the basis of client type, treatment setting, etc. The new organization might look something like Figure 4.1.

Method Two

Create a career ladder based on clinical expertise rather than supervisory responsibility. Each step of the career ladder would have its own set of minimum qualifications. The steps could be identified by advanced titles such as staff, senior, and specialist. A salary increase, more continuing education money, or other benefits could accompany promotion to the next step of the ladder.

Method Three

The department could adopt a policy which encourages each physical therapist to become a specialist in a specific area of clinical practice. The area of specialization would be selected by the physical therapist. The department would provide time off for continuing education, financial support for education, certifications, and memberships in professional associations. The opportunity for physical therapists to become involved in clinical education at local PT schools could be pursued.

Method Four

Create two additional lead positions: one, a Coordinator of Clinical Education who is also responsible for staff and program development and the other, an Assistant Manager. The first position would allow for growth along a clinical track. The second position would allow for growth along a management track. Both positions would have 0.50 FTE client care responsibilities. Together they represent the addition of one supervisory position.

Method Five

Provide staff with financial bonuses for longevity and program development activities. Allow therapists who develop new clinical programs to assume responsibility for ongoing operations of new programs developed.

RESPONSE TO CASE STUDY 4.2

The following performance expectations have been defined in behavioral terms on a five-point scale for the pysical therapy department of Milwaukee Memorial Hospital.

B2: Schedules the work of physical therapist assistants and aides for assigned clients.

Level

5 — Schedules work of physical therapist assistants and aides to maximize staff productivity and efficiency of client care.

4 — Schedules work of physical therapist assistants and aides in a manner which results in efficient and timely client care. Occasional periods of staff underutilization.

3 — Schedules work of physical therapist assistants and aides to maximize the efficiency and timeliness of client care but with minimum amount of staff down time. Requires some assistance from supervisor.

2 — Schedules work of physical therapist assistants and aides inefficiently. Work gets done but clients may have to wait for services. Staff utilization is irregular with low productivity. Constant supervision required.

1 — Makes frequent errors in staff and client scheduling. Errors result in poor staff utilization and client dissatisfaction.

C2: Participates in the development of departmental policies and procedures.

Level

5 — Independently recommends policy and procedure additions and/or modifications. With prior authorization, drafts needed policy and procedure statements and submits same for approval.

4 — Independently recommends policy and procedure additions and/or modification. Requires supervisory assistance to draft needed policy and procedure statements. Uses appropriate channels for authorization and approval.

3 — Willingly participates in the development of policy and procedure additions and/or modifications upon request.

2 — Needs encouragement to participate in the development of department policy and procedures.

1 — Does not participate in the development of department policies and procedures when requested.

D5: Maintain open lines of communication with clients, families, other employees, the medical staff, management, administration, and other community professionals.

Level

5 — Indicates efforts to maintain open communication in all directions at all times. Identifies and resolves communication problems independently.

4 — Initiates efforts to maintain open communication in all directions most of the time. Infrequently seeks assistance with problem identification and resolution.

3 — Initiates efforts to maintain open communication in all directions the majority of the time. Requires occasional intervention from supervisor for problem identification and resolution.

2 — Requires supervisory direction and support to maintain open lines of communication.

1 — Fails to maintain open communication even with supervisory direction and support.

RESPONSE TO CASE STUDY 5.1

At the start of a new program of service, the physical therapy manager must estimate the amount and cost of staff based on both volume projections and productivity expectations. In the case of Good As New Rehabilitation Center, the salary budget will be based on the following assumptions:

1. Only physical therapists will be hired during the first year of operation.
2. A full time equivalent (2080 hours paid) will work an average of 1872 man-hours annually. The difference between hours worked and paid represents time off for illness, vacation, education, and holidays.
3. A physical therapist is expected to produce twenty-four 15-minute units of client care per eight hours worked. This is a productivity rate of 75% of man-hours worked (MHW) or 67.5% of man-hours paid (MHP). At this productivity rate, a FTE physical therapist can produce 1404 hours of client care annually.

Client Care Hours

Period	Referrals	×	Care Hours/Referral	=	Care Hours/Period
Q1	25	×	20	=	500
Q2	50	×	20	=	1000
Q3	75	×	20	=	1500
Q4	100	×	20	=	2000
Annually	250	×	20	=	5000

Staff Requirements

Period	Hours Client Care/Period	Hours Care/FTE	Average FTE/Period
Q1	500	351 (1404/4)	1.40
Q2	1000	351 (1404/4)	2.85
Q3	1500	351 (1404/4)	4.27
Q4	2000	351 (1404/4)	5.70
Annually	5000	1404	Avg. 3.60

Assuming a smooth growth pattern throughout the first year of operation, staff should be added on an incremental basis throughout the year. This will minimize over- and understaffing. Practically speaking, staff must often be added in increments of one FTE. In that case, it is probably better to bear the financial burden of overstaffing than to find the program in a position of being unable to meet the demand for this new service.

FTE Budget

Budget One would be used if the addition of part-time increments of staff is feasible. Budget Two would apply if staff could only be added in one FTE increments.

RESPONSE TO CASE STUDY 5.2

It is obvious from the results of the time study that a more effective and efficient skill mix could be used in Middlesize Memorial's (MM) physical therapy department. Determination of a more appropriate skill mix may be achieved using the following calculations.

Productivity

Following a redistribution of activities, the productivity of staff as a percentage of direct billable services to total man-hours worked (MHW) would be at the following rates:

Position	Rate	Hours of Billable Service
Physical therapist	65%	1217 (2080 × 0.9 × 0.65)
PT assistant	72%	1348 (2080 × 0.9 × 0.72)
Aide (nonbillable)	90%	1685 (2080 × 0.9 × 0.90)
Aide (billable)	80%	1498 (2080 × 0.9 × 0.80)
Clerical	90%	1685 (2080 × 0.9 × 0.90)

Current Physical Therapist MHW

Current total MHW can be calculated by multiplying the current number of FTEs (30) by 2080 hours per FTE. This will give the total number of man-hours paid (MHP). Ninety percent of MHP are worked. Total MHW equals:

$$30 \text{ FTE} \times 2080 \text{ Hours/FTE} = 62{,}400 \text{ MHP}$$
$$62{,}400 \text{ MHP} \times 0.9 = 56{,}160 \text{ MHW}$$

Current MHW per Activity Category

Of current physical therapist MHW, time is distributed between the activities as follows:

Activity	MHW
Direct care	30,888
Indirect professional activities	14,040
Prep and clean up	5,616
Clerical tasks	5,616
Total MHW	56,160

Possible Skill Mix Based on Volume of Activity by Category

A. Clerical Tasks
   At a rate of 1685 productive hours per clerical FTE, the department has enough volume to support 3.33 FTE (5616 MHW/1685 productive hours/FTE).
B. Prep and Clean Up
   At a rate of 1685 productive hours per aide FTE involved solely in prep and clean up tasks, the department has enough volume to support 3.33 FTE (5616 MHW/1685 Productive Hours/FTE).
C. Direct Client Care by Skill Required
   Direct client care consumes 30,888 MHW annually. The skill levels required to provide current services is:

6,178 hours	Aide, PT assistant, or PT
9,266 hours	PT assistant or PT
15,444 hours	PT only

Based on skills required for current client care services, the department could utilize the following numbers of physical therapists, physical therapist assistants, and aides for client care. Note the FTEs are presented as ranges. This is because the department could always substitute a higher skilled FTE for a lower skilled FTE as it does now.

Position	FTE Range
Aide	0 – 4.12
PT assistant	0 –11.50
PT	12.70–25.38

The recommended skill mix would take advantage of all three skill levels but leave a little cushion in favor of the higher skill levels. This is done to cover for unexpected situations such as vacancies in the higher skilled positions or temporary shifts in the type of care required in favor of higher skilled services. Recommended skill mix for MM physical therapy department would be:

Position	FTE	Care Hour	Expense
Clerical	3.3	0	51,480
Aide	6.33	4,494	78,998
PT assistant	10.00	13,489	187,200
PT	10.60	12,914	330,720
Total	30.23	30,888	$648,398

Cost Comparison

The salary expense for the current department would be $936,000 (30 FTE × 2080 hours/FTE × $15/hour). Salary expense using the recommended skill mix would be $648,398. A change in skill mix will save the department $287,602 annually. Thus, the financial implications of skill mix become clear.

RESPONSE TO CASE STUDY 6.1

Initial Evaluation
Client: Nancy Nice
May 15, 1997
Diagnosis: Unspecific shoulder pain
Referral: Evaluate and treat

History: Client reports the recent onset of right shoulder pain and decreased mobility. Onset was two weeks ago. Client reports moving heavy furniture prior to onset. No other specific incident leading the client's condition can be identified.

Subjective Data: Severity of shoulder pain is reported to be at a level 8 on a scale of 10 at all times. Client reports that shoulder pain causes her to have difficulty dressing, showering, combing her hair, and doing regular household duties. She also has difficulty sleeping.

Physical Examination: Palpation reveals tenderness at the apex of the shoulder. Tenderness and muscle spasms present in the rhomboids, traps and cervical spine muscles. No signs of external trauma noted.

Joint Mobility and Strength

	Right		Left	
	ROM	Strength[a]	ROM	Strength
Shoulder				
Flexion	0–160°	3/5	0–180°	5/5
Extension	0–60°	4/5	0–60°	5/5
Abduction	0–120°	3/5	0–180°	5/5
Adduction	0–60°	3/5	0–60°	5/5
Internal rotation	0–80°	4/5	0–80°	5/5
External rotation	0–25°	2/5	0–60°	5/5
Horizontal abduction		3/5		5/5

[a]Pain interfered with formal strength assessment. Grades represent observations of functional strength.

Assessment: Soft tissue injury to right shoulder and cervical spine resulting in pain and decreased mobility.

Treatment plan: Ultrasound and therapeutic exercise, 3× week for 3 weeks, to decrease pain and restore shoulder ROM.

Shirley Righteous, P.T.

Interim Note
Nancy Nice
May 30, 1997

Note: Client's course of treatment has been unavoidably interrupted due to a family emergency.

Physical Examination: After two weeks of treatment Nancy's pain had decreased to a level of 5 on a scale of 10. Tenderness to palpation has diminished significantly.

Joint Mobility and Strength

	Right (5/15)		Right (5/30)	
	ROM	Strength[a]	ROM	Strength
Shoulder				
Flexion	0–160°	3/5	0–165°	4/5[a]
Extension	0–60°	4/5	0–60°	5/5
Abduction	0–120°	3/5	0–140°	3/5
Adduction	0–60°	3/5	0–60°	4/5
Internal rotation	0–80°	4/5	0–80°	4/5
External rotation	0–25°	2/5	0–30°	3/5
Horizontal abduction		3/5		3/5

[a]Pain

Treatment Plan: Client provided with a home exercise program to help maintain status while away from treatment.

Shirley Righteous, P.T.

Interim Note
Nancy Nice
June 15, 1997

Subjective Data: Severity of right shoulder pain is reported at a level of 5 on a scale of 10. Pain no longer interferes with sleep. Pain does interfere with functional activities.

Physical Examination: Minimal tenderness to palpation noted.

Joint Mobility and Strength

	Right (5/15)		Right (5/30)		Right (6/15)	
	ROM	Strength[a]	ROM	Strength	ROM	Strength
Shoulder						
Flexion	0–160°	3/5	0–165°	4/5[a]	0–165°	3/5[a]
Extension	0–60°	4/5	0–60°	5/5	0–60°	5/5
Abduction	0–120°	3/5	0–140°	3/5	0–125°	3/5[a]
Adduction	0–60°	3/5	0–60°	4/5	0–60°	4/5
Internal rotation	0–80°	4/5	0–80°	4/5	0–80°	4/5[a]
External rotation	0–25°	2/5	0–30°	3/5	0–30°	3/5[a]
Horizontal abduction		3/5		3/5		3/5[a]

[a]Pain

Nancy has maintained progress made during first part of treatment with the exception of shoulder abduction. Pain in response to movement against resistance has also increased since 5/30. Overall pain level remains unchanged from 5/30. Client responded well to initial course of treatment.

Plan: Continue treatment program interrupted by family emergency. Goals remain to decrease pain, increase mobility, and restore function.

Shirley Righteous, P.T.

Interim Note
Nancy Nice
July 15, 1997

Subjective Data: Client reports pain severity has decreased to a level of 3 during the day and 5 at night on a scale of 10. Nancy reports consistent compliance with home exercise program. Limitations of function remain a problem. Personal hygiene, hair care, and moderately heavy housework remain difficult.

Physical Examination: Minimal tenderness to palpation at the apex of the shoulder. No other tenderness noted.

Joint Mobility and Strength

	Right (5/30)		Right (6/15)		Right (7/15)	
	ROM	Strength	ROM	Strength	ROM	Strength
Shoulder						
Flexion	0–165°	4/5[a]	0–165°	3/5[a]	0–175°	4/5
Extension	0–60°	5/5	0–60°	5/5	0–60°	5/5
Abduction	0–140°	3/5	0–125°	3/5[a]	0–140°	4/5[a]
Adduction	0–60°	4/5	0–60°	4/5	0–60°	5/5
Internal rotation	0–80°	4/5	0–80°	4/5[a]	0–80°	5/5
External rotation	0–30°	3/5	0–30°	3/5[a]	0–45°	3/5[a]
Horizontal abduction		3/5		3/5[a]		4/5

[a]Pain

Improvement noted in both ROM and strength.

Plan: Continue treating client in accordance with previous plan. Reduce frequency to weekly rechecks if progress continues at the present rate.

Shirley Righteous, P.T.

Discharge Note
Nancy Nice
August 15, 1997

Subjective Data: Client is now pain-free and has resumed all previous activity.

Physical Examination: Client is pain-free to palpation.

Joint Mobility and Strength

	Right (5/30)		Right (6/15)		Right (7/15)	
	ROM	Strength	ROM	Strength	ROM	Strength
Shoulder						
Flexion	0–165°	3/5[a]	0–175°	4/5	0–180°	5/5
Extension	0–60°	5/5	0–60°	5/5	0–60°	5/5
Abduction	0–125°	3/5[a]	0–140°	4/5[a]	0–180°	5/5
Adduction	0–60°	4/5	0–60°	5/5	0–60°	5/5
Internal rotation	0–80°	4/5[a]	0–80°	5/5	0–80°	5/5
External rotation	0–30°	3/5[a]	0–45°	3/5[a]	0–60°	5/5
Horizontal abduction		3/5[a]		4/5		5/5

[a]Pain

Plan: Client to continue on a home exercise program and notify this therapist of any change in condition. No further treatment required at this time. Client has been discontinued from therapy.

Shirley Righteous, P.T.

RESPONSE TO CASE STUDY 6.2

Subjective information provided by Farley Davidson:
Client expresses a desire to be able to animate his tattoo with his arm muscles as he did prior to his accident.

Objective information that would have been helpful:
Elbow flexor strength comparisons determined by a quantified device. Body position and degree of stabilization noted. If norms for the device were available, they could have been cited.

Girth measurements with a metal metric tapemeasure taken at 5-cm increments from olecranon to axillary fold.

Photographs of scar area might have been taken at various time intervals. A metric tape in the picture would have assisted in presenting comparative visual information.

Goniometric measurements might have been taken. An indication of the position and degree of stabilization would help reproduce the measurements. A known standard guide for range of motion might have been cited.

A standardized upper extremity functional test could have been used to add objectivity to the functional status comments. Time to complete activities could have been assessed.

RESPONSE TO CASE STUDY 7.1

Independent Physical Therapists, Inc. (IPT, Inc.) will find it advantageous to follow guidelines of the Joint Commission on the Accreditation of Healthcare Organizations (JCAHO) in developing a plan for monitoring quality assurance. The revision of IPT, Inc.'s existing quality assurance (QA) plan will follow the JCAHO model.

Steps One and Two: Responsibility Assignment and Identification of Activities (see Chapter 7, Example 7.4)

Step Three: Selection of Important Aspects of Organizational Activity

1. Client and family involvement in treatment planning
2. Quality of outside services

Steps Four and Five: Identification of Clinical Indicators and Establishment of Thresholds

Aspect: Client and family involvement in treatment planning.
Indicators: Documentation of client and/or family involvement in treatment planning in the initial treatment plan.
Threshold: 0% (All treatment plans shall contain documentation of client and/or family involvement in treatment planning or an acceptable rationale for the absence of client and/or family involvement shall be provided.)

Aspect: Quality of outside services

Indicators: Documentation of client and therapist satisfaction with the timeliness of services, timeliness of reports, and outcomes of outside services from equipment suppliers, prosthetists, and orthotists.

Threshold: 3% (In 97% of cases, both the client and therapist shall indicate satisfaction with the quality of outside services to which the clients of IPT, Inc. have been referred by IPT, Inc. therapists.)

Step Six: Implement the Monitoring Process

Client and/or family involvement in treatment planning:

The current chart review process will include the review of the initial treatment plan to determine if client and/or family involvement in treatment planning has been documented. If not, an acceptable rationale for its omission shall be provided. Results shall be reported quarterly.

Quality of outside services:

Client and therapist satisfaction with the quality of outside services shall be monitored through the use of a satisfaction survey. This survey will be given to both the therapist and the client each time a referral for an outside consult is made. Results of these surveys shall be complied on a quarterly basis. Specific complaints shall be acted upon whenever feasible. Results of the surveys shall be reported upon monthly along with the results from other client satisfaction monitors.

Steps Seven and Eight: Problem Identification and Resolution

When the monitoring process indicates that the established thresholds have been exceeded, problems will be identified and analyzed by appropriate parties. Once a problem has been identified, action will be taken to bring performance in line with established thresholds.

Steps Nine and Ten: Outcome Assessment and Reporting

All outcomes of actions shall be evaluated and the results documented. IPT, Inc. will report the outcomes of the QA process to the board and all staff on a bimonthly basis.

RESPONSE TO CASE STUDY 8.1

In appendix Figure 8.1 (which follows) four changes were made to deal with the problem of undesired client traffic patterns. These changes and the expected results are described below.

1. The employee parking lot was moved to the opposite side of the building near customer parking.
2. A third entrance to the facility was added near employee parking.
3. The secondary entrance was restricted to delivery personnel. Keeping this entrance locked on the outside and the installation of a buzzer system

facilitated this purpose. The parking area near this door now is reserved for delivery vehicles.

4. The new traffic flow pattern of arriving and departing employees brought them through less congested areas.

5. If customers did use the employee entrance, they would be nearer to the reception area than the staff offices. They would be less likely to drop in on therapists unannounced.

RESPONSE TO CASE STUDY 9.1

Before Independent Physical Therapists, Inc. (IPT, Inc.) adopts the suggested marketing strategy, there are several steps that should be taken. They are:

1. Completion of a strategic business plan. Before IPT, Inc. can even begin to talk about marketing techniques it should have completed the strategic business planning process. This is then used to make marketing decisions.

2. Analyze and define the target market. A practice the size of IPT, Inc. can least afford an expensive and ineffective marketing effort. To minimize the risk of failure, IPT, Inc. should obtain as much information as possible about its environment and the characteristics of its customers. Based on this information, IPT, Inc. should identify segments of the whole market toward which it will target its marketing efforts. Once a segment is selected, demand measurement and forecasting will help measure the potential volumes of business.

3. Selection of a marketing strategy. Once the target market is selected and understood, IPT, Inc. must determine how its services (do or will) meet market needs. Here is where IPT, Inc. should balance the importance of the product, the place it is available, the price of the product, and promotional activities such as advertising.

4. Once the marketing mix is determined, IPT, Inc. is ready to consider marketing communications. IPT, Inc. could use advertising, personal sales, or promotional events. The selection process should weigh effectiveness and cost considerations. The choice will be influenced by the goals to be achieved. A method should be established to evaluate the success of the selected method.

RESPONSE TO CASE STUDY 10.1

The therapist responsible for supervising the student is an agent of the employer. In this case, the employer was a hospital. Although each person is responsible for his or her own actions, in this case the liability passes to the employer under the vicarious liability doctrine called respondeat superior. This doctrine holds the master responsible for the acts of his servants. It is common practice to allow a student who has already been instructed, supervised, and evaluated to carry out the acts they have been judged competent to carry out. So the hospital would not be negligent for allowing the student to apply the pylon. Failure to provide adequate supervision as the treatment progressed was the ultimate basis for the negligence claim against the hospital.

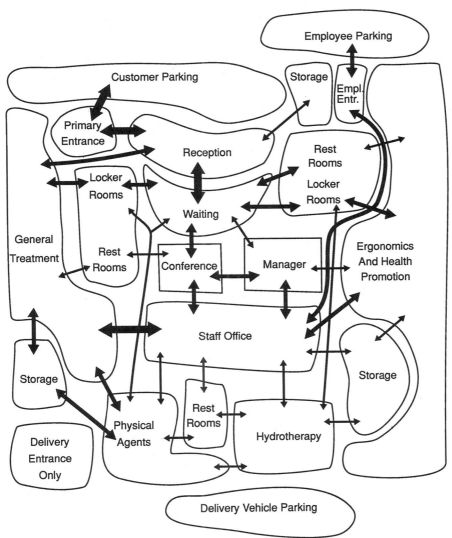

Figure 8.1.   Modification of facility plan presented in Case Study 8.1.

By the way, Stan Upnshout was too upset by this upheaval to attend his graduation ceremony at Upstate U.

RESPONSE TO CASE STUDY 10.2

In any lawsuit alleging negligence involving an employer, there may be an effort by the employer to show that they are not liable for the negligent act. As a defense, an employer may show that the employee was acting outside of the usual position description or that the incident did not take place at work.

The hospital had not yet taken any action on Anna Roll's proposal which clearly made her action outside of her position description. Second, no permission was granted from the nursing staff for the client to leave the hospital grounds. The policy requiring permission for clients to leave was something Anna should have been well aware of.

Anna rolled a gutter ball this time. She was found personally negligent. On top of this, her employer filed a claim for compensation for the legal costs involved in its own defense. Since Anna did not have personal liability insurance she was obligated to pay the legal costs of her own defense, reimburse her former employer, and pay the compensatory damages to the client's family herself.

Anna now works two jobs to pay off her debts. One job entails doing fill-in work through an agency which provides personal liability insurance for all its employees. Her other source of income is her winnings from bowling.

RESPONSE TO CASE STUDY 10.3

A manager has the responsibility to supervise an employee to ensure the safe fulfillment of duties. Delegation is appropriate only if the delegated action is within the capabilities of the employee. In this case, Patham failed to act prudently. She neither supervised nor delegated appropriately.

In a general partnership, both owners equally share the liability. In a limited partnership, the owner not present would share in the liability but to a lesser extent than her partner. This is not because she was not present or because she was not the cause of the problem but, rather, because she has less responsibility for the business than her partner.

In a professional corporation, liability for the acts of employees involved in providing services is assigned to the professional members of the corporation. In this case, both Patham and Bakeum were found liable for the negligent act.

As a result of this encounter with the legal system the two therapists sought advice from a risk management consultant to minimize the potential for future claims of liability. They also reformed their business into two solo proprietorships. While the two practices operate in the same location and share the same support services, one business is principally a general physical therapy practice and the other is limited to clients with back problems.

THREE RESPONSES TO CASE STUDY 11.1

Response I—Quick Ethics Check

Potential Answers	Legal?	Balanced?	Your Feeling
Only positives	Yes	No	Uncomfortable
Be truthful	Yes	Yes	Very comfortable
Avoid negatives	Yes	No	Comfortable

Response II—Decision Tree

Is there an ethical problem?
>   Yes →   Conflict between fidelity and
>   truthfulness

Can it be confirmed?
>   Yes →   Introspection, feelings

Do you have relevant
information that you can
assess?
>   Yes →   Workplace history, experience in
>   the position

Are there significant ethical
implications and consequences?
>   Yes →   Many, see Model III

Can you identify alternatives to
address the problem?
>   Yes →   At least three

Can you ethically weigh the
alternatives with confidence?
>   Yes →   Autonomy most important in this
>   situation

Can you confidently justify your
choice on ethical principles?
>   Yes →   By applying the four principles
>   Answer 2 is choice

Did you reassess all alternatives
before implementing your
choice?
>   Yes   No →   Reassess all alternatives
>   ↓

An ethical option may be evident

Response III—Formal Ethical Analysis

Problem: Fidelity to employer is in conflict with obligation to be truthful
to potential coworkers.

Alternatives	Some Likely Consequences
Answer 1: Only positives	They may hire on because of your incomplete information and be unhappy. Your employer will recognize your loyalty. With additional staff better care may be provided. Pressure on staff will be reduced. With additional staff there may be time to talk with manager about your observations and feelings which may increase the chance of you continuing to stay on.
Answer 2: Be truthful	Few if any potential employees will be interested in the positions. Your manager will be very concerned about the lack of applicants and your apparent disloyalty to her and the institution. Your future in the department will be in jeopardy. Care will not be improved. Continued pressure on staff will contribute to a continuation of the high turnover rate and may even increase the rate.
Answer 3: Avoid negatives	The pool of potential employees will diminish. You will feel good that you did not mislead anyone. And, most of the implications listed for answer 2 are applicable here also. Other considerations: Politics within the department and the institution, economic impact, philosophy of treatment, etc.

Applicable Ethical Criteria in Perceived Order of Importance

Rank	Principle
1	Autonomy
2	Beneficience
3	Nonmaleficence
4	Justice

Value Statements

Autonomy (A)	Truthfulness is very important at all times. I should respect my obligation to my manager and institution. I should keep my word.

Individuals seeking information should be
given the information they need to make
decisions that affect them.

Beneficence (B)   More staff members will benefit the clientele.
Forewarning potential coworkers of the
problems they will encounter will help the
institution recruit employees who fit well
and who will stay.
Insight into the realities of the position will
help keep those who do not fit "our" mold
from entering into a situation they would
find very uncomfortable.

Nonmaleficence (N)   A balanced answer will help protect the
welfare of the potential new employee.
Failure to increase the staff soon will result in
longer client waiting lists and additional
potential client discomfort.
The reputations of the institution and
department will be diminished.

Justice (J)   Be fair to potential employees by presenting a
balanced picture of the situation.
Be fair to employer by emphasizing positive
aspects of the job.

Rank order value statements (for this example, only the most important
in each category are listed here).

Rank	Statement
1	A. Respect obligations to the institution. (value = 4)
2	B. Do what benefits clients. (value = 3)
3	N. Increase staff to decrease client discomfort. (value = 2)
4	J. Be fair to employer. (value = 1)

Weight each alternative according to its perceived promotion of each of
the value statements.

Alternatives	Value Statements and Relative Ratings					Totals
	A (×4)	B (×3)	N (×2)	J (×1)		
Only positives	100%	100%	100%	100%	=	10
Be truthful	0%	10%	10%	0%	=	<1
Avoid negatives	50%	0%	5%	50%	=	<3

The ethical choice is alternative 1 based on the value hierarchy used in
this abbreviated example. Other conclusions could be reached using different value hierarchies.

APPENDIX B

Integrated Case Studies

INTEGRATED CASE STUDY 1
GENERAL HOSPITAL

Reorganizing an Acute Care Hospital's Physical Therapy Department

General Hospital (GH) is a 250-bed general acute care hospital. It has been in existence for 70 years serving the residents of its community. The GH mission is to provide medical services for community residents regardless of age, race, religion, or ability to pay. In the past, GH has been able to fulfill its mission due to a high daily census, good reimbursement, and a large number of community residents who have been willing and able to donate money to the hospital.

At present, GH's organizational structure is based on grouping staff by function. Under this structure each function has a department head regardless of size (i.e., number of employees) or type of staff (Fig. 1). Personnel, equipment, supplies, and space are dedicated exclusively to a department.

Over the past several years GH's financial position has shifted. Census now averages 125 patients per day. Staff size has decreased accordingly. Reimbursement is decreasing as Medicare and Medicaid pay less for services. The local community is less willing to support charity care. The hospital's president is looking for ways to decrease costs. She is considering a reorganization. Physical, Occupational, and Speech Therapy are presently independent departments (Fig. 1).

Please make recommendations regarding potential reorganization of the various therapy departments to enhance efficiency and decrease costs. List both positive and negative consequences of the changes you are recommending.

In Appendix C you will find one reasonable response to the problems encountered in this integrated case study.

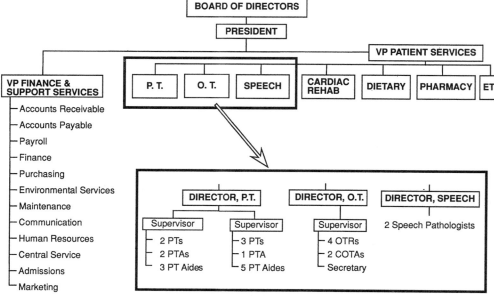

Figure 1. Current organizational structure of GH.

INTEGRATED CASE STUDY 2
GOOD HANDS PHYSICAL THERAPY CLINIC

Expanding a Small Private Practice

The Good Hands Physical Therapy Clinic (GHPTC) is owned and operated by two entrepreneurial physical therapists. Their private practice, GHPTC, celebrated its first year of operation this month. GHPTC defines its business as the provision of outpatient services on contract to the managed care market. This includes PPOs, HMOs, and IPAs. The goal of GHPTC is to grow as rapidly as possible. To achieve this goal, GHPTC's strategy has been to undercut the competition's prices while maintaining a high quality service. Consistent with these goals and objectives, the owners of GHPTC have set high quality standards and have cut their prices to the bone.

GHPTC currently employs its two owners, one full time physical therapist, an aide, and a receptionist. The clinic is operating at full capacity. Clients are able to begin therapy within three days of referral. No client waits longer than 15 minutes except in an emergency. Therapy is provided on an individualized basis. A physical therapist provides all of the direct care including the most routine modalities.

At present, GHPTC is operating at the breakeven point. Cash flow has been adequate to meet monthly accounts payable. Occasional shortfalls are handled with a line of credit from the local bank. To date, GHPTC has not had to incur any long-term debt. The owners have invested their savings to provide start-up costs. They have no more personal resources to invest. The owners' only income is a competitive salary from GHPTC. Between client care and the business office, the owners average 60-hour work weeks.

The owners of GHPTC are at a decision point in the life of their new enterprise. To meet their goals, they must aggressively seek additional business. To seek new business, they must be in a position to provide physical therapy services to additional clients. This is something they cannot do at their current staffing level while maintaining their current service delivery patterns.

The addition of a physical therapist to the GHPTC staff poses three problems. First, physical therapists are hard to hire. It takes about four months to recruit and orient an experienced therapist. Second, if past experience is valid, GHPTC will not have the luxury of four months time to recruit a physical therapist between the signing of a new managed care contract and the start of their service obligations. Third, GHPTC is operating at the breakeven point. The salary for an additional physical therapist would have to be financed by debt until an additional contract could be obtain and revenues generated. GHPTC's current line of credit would cover the salary of a physical therapist for one month.

The owners of GHPTC find themselves in a not uncommon "cart or the horse" dilemma. They need to add additional capacity to the GHPTC staff to market their services and grow. To hire an additional therapist before they have a known buyer is a substantial financial risk.

What options do these two entrepreneurs have? Of the available options which would you recommend?

Answers to this integrated case study are presented in Appendix C.

INTEGRATED CASE STUDY 3
EVERY BODY'S HEALTH MAINTENANCE ORGANIZATION

Providing Physical Therapy Services for an HMO

The owners of Good Hands Physical Therapy Clinic (GHPTC) have just received a request for proposal (RFP) from Every Body's Health Maintenance Organization (EHMO). EHMO is looking for a physical therapy clinic to provide for all of the physical therapy needs of its members. EHMO wishes to enter into a capitated arrangement for these services. Under a capitated arrangement, EHMO will pay the chosen physical therapy provider a preset amount per member per month. In return, the provider will meet the physical therapy needs of EHMO's members. According to the RFP, the successful bidder will demonstrate their ability to provide high quality services within the scope of EHMO's benefit plan. EHMO defines quality in terms of staff skill mix and member satisfaction. Other information contained in the RFP included:

Historical Utilization Data: Annual

Current Membership	45,000
Annual Member Months (AMM)	540,000
PT Visit/Member Month (MM)	0.03
PT Referrals	2,700
PT Visits	16,200
Average Length of PT Visit	45 minutes
PT Visits/Referral	6

EHMO predicts that membership will increase by an average of 15% per year over the next two years.

Scope of Physical Therapy Benefits

EHMO members are entitled to receive physical therapy services upon referral to an authorized provider by the member's primary physician. Members are entitled to receive a maximum of 80 outpatient physical therapy visits annually. EHMO covers only those services which are deemed medically reasonable and necessary based on the members diagnosis and prognosis for benefit. EHMO does not cover experimental treatments.

Utilization Control and Monitoring

EHMO medical staff determines which members are in need of physical therapy services. The physical therapy provider is encouraged to work actively with the EHMO medical staff to determine the amount of services required.

The owners of GHPTC would like the contract. They intend to prepare and submit a proposal. They believe the successful bidder will be selected on the basis of quality and cost per member per month. The owners of GHPTC must 1) determine the per member rate they will require from EHMO to provide the requested services and 2) assemble their business proposal. You are to outline the analysis that GHPTC management should perform to determine their per member per month price bid? What kinds of nonfinancial information might GHPTC include in its proposal to EHMO?

See Appendix C for suggested means of dealing with with this situation.

INTEGRATED CASE STUDY 4
WHAT'S A MANAGER TO DO?

Noncompetitive Physical Therapist Salaries in a Home Health Agency

Home Sweet Home (HSH) Home Health Agency is the second largest provider of home care services in its community. It provides nursing services, physical therapy, occupational therapy, speech and language pathology, social services, respiratory therapy, nurse aides, and personal care attendants. HSH will also provide homemaker services. The majority of HSH's referrals require the provision of nursing and physical therapy services. HSH has been unable to recruit enough physical therapists to meet its demand. Because of this, HSH has had to turn away 40 referrals in the past month. This has lead to an overall decline in services and revenues. The Executive Director of HHS has responded to this downturn with a freeze on salaries and a freeze on the hiring of new staff with the exception of physical therapists.

The Physical Therapy Manager of HHS has just been informed by his physical therapists that their salaries are $3 to $4 per hour lower than their peers at other home health agencies. They have obtained this information from professional associates, advertisements, and from interviewing with HSH's competitors. The manager is inclined to believe this information based on rumors he has heard elsewhere.

What, if anything, should the Physical Therapy Manager do in response to this new information? Does he need more information? If so, what and for what purpose?

Refer to Appendix C for some answers to this integrated case study.

INTEGRATED CASE STUDY 5
DIGNITY MANOR, INC.

Developing a Facility Plan for a Vertically Integrated Corporation Focusing on Older Adults

Dignity Manor, Inc. (DMI) is a vertically integrated health care organization which owns a skilled nursing home, an assisted care apartment building, a home health agency, and a retirement community of four-unit apartment buildings.

The Board of Directors of DMI has decided to enter into a new consumer market with a new product. The target group is healthy elderly individuals residing in the communities surrounding the DMI complex. The new product is a health promotion and fitness club for those over 50 years of age. Several reasons for this decision have been discussed. First, there is no fitness facility within a 75-mile radius. Second, there is a significant underserved market for these services. The DMI complex is a community of 7000 people. The surrounding townships have another 8000 residents. The general area has a long tradition of attracting new retirees. Third, in response to a survey conducted through the local newspaper over 3500 individuals in the target age group indicated interest in joining a fitness center for older adults. This was 72% of the respondents. Finally, a fitness center within the DMI complex that was open to the public would immediately increase local community members' familiarity with DMI.

In the future, this familiarity might be the basis for choosing the DMI complex for residential and/or health care service.

As the Director of Physical Therapy you have been asked to be a member of the fitness center planning committee. You were chosen because you provided the major input on the remodeling of DMI nursing home. You also had experience working in a sports physical therapy and fitness center before assuming your current position. You see this project as a potential future opportunity through which you could combine your interests in fitness and aging. You have been asked to prepare a schematic diagram for a 10,000 square foot facility which would support fitness activities appropriate for healthy older adults. You suggest to the Board that it would be wise to consider an injury treatment and rehabilitation space within the facility. When questioned about this, you explained to the Board that many of the fitness center members will have private insurance and could be billed for physical therapy services. You added that, since direct access legislation has been passed in the state, a client could consult with and be treated by a physical therapist without physician referral. These additional thoughts were well received by the Board who indicated that you should include a small physical therapy treatment area in the plan.

Your task is to make a schematic diagram of this 10,000 square foot facility. Follow the steps presented in Chapter 8. Produce an activity description list which you can group into related functional activities. Then make several alternative schematic drawings. Indicate the anticipated traffic flows in each of your optional drawings. Be sure to identify by name the types of rooms that will be required to meet your objectives.

Compare your thoughts with those of the authors by consulting Appendix C.

APPENDIX C

Suggested Responses to Integrated Case Studies

SUGGESTED RESPONSE TO INTEGRATED
CASE STUDY 1
GENERAL HOSPITAL

The restructuring of any organization will have both positive and negative consequences. The recommended structure for the rehabilitation services departments of General Hospital (GH) can be found in integrated case study Figure 2. The potential positive and negative consequences of adopting the recommended structure are as follows:

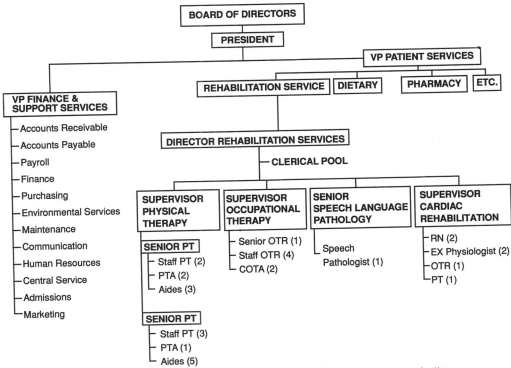

Figure 2. Suggested response to Integrated Case Study 1 question related to reorganization of GH.

Potential Positive Consequences

1. The total number of middle mangers has been reduced and replaced by senior clinical positions. This should result in a salary cost savings.

2. Combining similar departments will allow for more effective sharing of resources including equipment, space, support personnel, and management.

3. Larger clinical departments continue to offer employees a career ladder through the use of senior clinical positions.

Potential Negative Consequences

1. The employees who are in the position of Director at the time of the restructuring are likely to leave the organization. This is particularly true if salaries are frozen or reduced in the process.

2. Remaining employees who believe they have been negatively affected by the restructuring are more likely to become less effective and, possibly, disruptive to the operation of the restructured department.

3. Professional staff may feel that the importance of their profession has been diminished if the manager of the new combined structure is not a member of their profession.

4. Previously underutilized support personnel may be called upon to work harder without additional compensation as they provide services to more departments. This may be viewed as unfair.

The success of the recommended restructuring will depend on the sensitivity and response of the new manager to the negative as well as positive consequences.

SUGGESTED RESPONSE TO INTEGRATED CASE STUDY 2 GOOD HANDS PHYSICAL THERAPY CLINIC

The owners of Good Hands Physical Therapy Clinic (GHPTC) have several alternative actions which they can follow to alleviate their current situation. These include but are not limited to:

1. Continuing operations at the current level while hoping to find a customer who will give enough lead time to add capacity. It could be a long wait.

2. A review and modification of current practice patterns. Modifications could be made to increase capacity. Under this approach, GHPTC must balance its personal commitment to current standards, the impact of any changes on current customer satisfaction, and the impact on its marketing effectiveness. A review of community standards of practice may assist with this assessment.

3. Seek additional outside financing from the bank or other lender to cover the cost of additional staff while GHPTC markets its services.

Because the owners' assets are limited, and GHPTC has not been profitable, this option could be inadequate to meet the need. A solid business plan and financial projections would be essential.

4. Attempt to recruit a physical therapist who is already employed or unavailable until some future date. If the newly recruited physical therapist will agree to remain in another employment situation until needed, GHPTC's problem will be resolved. Similarly, GHPTC could employ an additional physical therapist and one of the owners could take temporary employment elsewhere. To work, there must be some incentive to make it worthwhile to potential candidates. The owners may have incentive, but desire is another matter.

5. Seek an additional partner. A partner willing to commit financial resources now and/or time when needed could also be the answer.

The owners could implement two or more of the possible alternatives. The first alternative is not an option if GHPTC is committed to its stated goal of growth. The choice of options should be based on the principal of risk minimization and the values of the owners.

SUGGESTED RESPONSE TO INTEGRATED CASE STUDY 3 EVERY BODY'S HEALTH MAINTENANCE ORGANIZATION

Good Hands Physical Therapy Clinic (GHPTC) must base its per member month bid on an estimate of the additional costs which will be incurred plus whatever profit margin they hope to achieve. To do this, they must develop projections of the following:

1. Salary, benefits, and FICA costs;
   To develop an accurate projection of salary costs GHPTC must develop estimates of:
   A. The amount of indirect time associated with the direct services utilized by EHMO members;
   B. The productivity expectations of direct care employees;
   C. The skill mix required to meet EHMO service needs;
   D. The time required by administrative and nonclinical support personnel for record management, billing, customer support, etc.;
   E. Required man-hours worked and paid.

2. Cost of supplies and other expenses for clinical and support services;
3. Small tools expenses;
4. Capital equipment expenses;
5. Facilities requirements and expenses;
6. Other operating expenses for things such as such as staff education and recruitment;
7. Indirect expenses associated with the additional volume.

The total of these direct and indirect expenses which will be incurred due to the additional service volume should then be inflated by the rate of profit GHPTC would like from operations. The total of expenses and profit would be divided by the annual projected member months used to estimated expenses. The result will be the rate per member month which would be submitted with the service proposal.

GHPTC may wish to include information about staffing practices, quality assurance activities and outcomes, utilization review practices, service evaluation practices and outcomes, current customer satisfaction activities and outcomes, and professional affiliations and certifications as part of their proposal. Price bids being equal, EHMO will likely chose the provider which demonstrates a history of quality service and self-monitoring.

SUGGESTED RESPONSE TO INTEGRATED CASE STUDY 4 WHAT'S A MANAGER TO DO?

First, the Physical Therapy Manager of Home Sweet Home (HSH) Home Health Agency needs more information. He needs to know the following:

1. What do HSH's current physical therapists hope will be the outcome of their efforts at sharing the salary information? Is this a informal demand for higher wages for themselves? Do they really plan to leave because they believe they can make more money elsewhere?

2. What are the salaries being offered by other home health agencies? If they are truly higher, are there conditions attached to them such as years of experience, irregular hours, fewer benefits, or less desirable working conditions? All conditions considered, how do the salaries at HSH compare?

3. How does the expense of higher salaries compare to the lost revenue which has resulted from HSH's inability to meet demands for service? Remember, the shortage of physical therapy services has affected revenue from the provision of other agency services as well.

The Physical Therapy Manager needs to act upon the information he has obtained. If the information shared by his staff proves to be inaccurate, he must share the results of his investigation with them. If this new salary information proves to be accurate, he should share it with the Executive Director of HSH. In doing so, he should present:

1. The results of his investigation;

2. His assessment of the impact on the organization including his financial analysis;

3. His recommendations for a response and a supporting rationale;

4. His assessment of the outcome, if any, which would result from a failure to follow his recommendations.

Having taken these steps, the Physical Therapy Manager has met his obligation as an advocate for both his staff and the organization. The employees' concerns and information will have been considered and utilized by the organization in the decision-making process.

SUGGESTED RESPONSE TO INTEGRATED
CASE STUDY 5
DIGNITY MANOR, INC.

Although the assignment was clear, make a schematic drawing for 10,000 square feet of space, there were several assumptions you, the reader, had to make. Among these assumptions were: How many staff? What kinds of equipment? How many members will the fitness center have to serve? How many hours a day and how many days a week will the facility be open? How many physical therapy (PT) clients will there be? The facility design depended to a large extent how you chose to answer these questions. Rather than use one schematic design, a discussion of suggested considerations that apply to any answer to this situation will be presented.

The examples of activities that might have designated areas in the proposed facility are:

Administrative Areas
>   Fitness office
>   PT office
>   Membership office
>   Director's office
>   First aid area
>   Storage

Activity Areas
>   Examination area
>   Consultation room
>   Gymnasium for ball sports, aerobic dance
>   Equipment room for loaning out equipment
>   Swimming pool
>   Recreational whirlpool
>   Sauna
>   Cardiorespiratory endurance testing and training equipment
>   Strength testing and training equipment
>   Flexibility exercise area
>   balance testing and training
>   Body composition measurement
>   Weight control programing
>   Posture measurement and training
>   Relaxation and stress reduction training
>   Massage
>   Nutrition instruction
>   Storage

Support Areas
>   Parking
>   Entrances and exits
>   Control point to check membership, security
>   Reception
>   Waiting

Locker rooms
Rest rooms
Showers
Lounge area with amenities (phone, TV, vending machines)
Beauty and barber shop
Refreshment bar
Health food sales
Athletic clothing and equipment sales
Injury prevention and rehabilitation equipment products
Injury care products
Storage

Comments

1. The charge was to formulate a facility plan for a fitness center for older adults which also has a basic PT space. This should have resulted in a small percentage of the overall space allocated to PT.

2. Check Table 8.1 to see if your rough space allocations would accommodate the equipment and activities you anticipate in each designated area.

3. Was storage approximately 1000 square feet (10%)?

4. Does traffic flow interfere with any activity(ies)?

5. Does everyone pass a point of control where membership can be checked and information can be given?

6. The majority of the fitness exercise equipment could be used by club members as well as PT clients. Therefore, there may not have been a need for special exercise equipment for PT.

7. Common usage could have been made for reception, waiting, locker, conference, storage, and rest rooms as well as entrances, parking, and secretarial staff. However, separate fitness and PT staff rooms are suggested.

8. If massages were offered to fitness center members, then cubicles would be needed which could be shared by PT and the masseurs. Otherwise, PT needed at least one cubicle.

9. Some thought would be given to defining which electrophysiological agents are therapeutic and should be administered by PT and which, if any, are for fitness purposes and could be administered by a technician. This is an example of a question that has legal, ethical, and fiscal implications for the physical therapist planner. It would be incongruous to have the same electrical stimulation treatments available in the same building where one was charged for at a high rate and the other was free or much less expensive.

10. Is cardiovascular fitness testing a PT or a fitness center activity or is it done by both services? Who would conduct the cardiovascular fitness testing? PT? ATC? Exercise Physiologist? On-the-job trained person? The division of labor becomes an ethical and economic concern. Who operates out of which office could also become an identification problem for club members.

11. Will the PT area double as the first aid station? Will ice, compres-

sion, and elevation be a billed PT treatment? Will these services be rendered by an athletic trainer working for the fitness center and be a benefit of membership at no charge?

12. Is there room for expansion? Is there some flexibility so that areas could be reconfigured?

13. Is the facility accessible to disabled individuals? While the intent was to attract healthy individuals, anyone who wishes to improve his/her physical status may seek membership. Residents of the existing DMI operations in particular would be likely to join the fitness club since it would be near their residences.

APPENDIX D

Glossary of Terms

Accountability refers to the requirement for objective information from the health care providers which demonstrates that they provide quality services, use resources wisely, and produce reasonable and predictable outcomes.

Accounts Payable are amounts owed by the company to creditors who sold them goods or services on credit. A liability.

Accounts Receivable are amounts owed to the company from customers who were sold goods or services on credit. An asset.

Accreditation is given after the provider demonstrates compliance with the performance or competence standards of the accrediting organization. (See **CARF** and **JCAHO**)

Affiliated Providers include hospitals, medical clinics, or practice partners.

Age Discrimination is defined as the unlawful employment practice of discriminating against any individual because of such individual's age.

American Hospital Association (AHA) is a national association of hospitals.

American Physical Therapy Association (APTA) is the major national professional organization representing physical therapists.

Assets are economic resources that are owned by an organization and are expected to benefit future operations.

Autonomy is the ethical principle which says that the wishes of competent individuals must be honored.

Balance Sheet is a financial statement that indicates what assets the firm owns and how those assets are financed in the form of liabilities or ownership interest. It summarizes this information as of a particular date.

Behavior Formalization is the work design parameter by which the work processes of the organization are standardized. It is used to increase efficiency and consistency.

Beneficence is the ethical principle which guides us to enhance the welfare of others.

Budgets are used to determine how much and what kind of resources should be used to reach a desired level of outcome. A budget is the development of financial plans relating to future operations. A budget is a projection at the beginning of the period of what the income statement will reflect at the end of the period.

Business Plan is the document used to represent the results of the strategic planning process.

Bylaws are rules adapted by an organization chiefly for the government of its members and the regulation of its affairs. They constrain policies and procedures. It usually requires an act of the organization's board of directors to change the bylaws.

Capital Costs are costs associated with the purchase of large items which are utilized to produce goods or services over an extended period of time. They are related to the purchase of equipment, buildings, and land. Costs associated with new business or service start-up can also be "capitalized."

Capitation Pricing is common to managed care. Here the service provider gets paid a set amount of payment per period per member. The amount paid is based on projections of utilization of goods and services.

Cash Flow Statement demonstrates how an organization's cash balances change over a specific period of time.

Chart of Accounts is a listing of the account titles and account numbers being used by a given business. It includes accounts for assets, liabilities, owner's equity, revenue, and expenses. It helps the business track money spent and money earned.

Coaching is a popular method of helping employees improve performance. It is a face to face process used to analyze and improve performance.

Common Law is the result of court decisions taken when there is no statutory law related to a case.

Comparative Financial Statements are used to compare financial information of different types and from different periods. A common-size statement is used for vertical analysis by scanning columns of entries. The comparison of financial information from different periods allows for the identification of trends that might affect the future of the organization. This is referred to as horizontal analysis.

Comparison Method is a performance appraisal method in which the rater ranks members of a work group according to some standard such as efficiency. This method is of little value for jobs that require multiple skills. Use of this method can create bad feelings and negative peer pressure within the work group.

Competitive Strategy reflects an organization's plan for defending and taking a market share from its current and future competitors.

Contingency Theories of Management postulate that management style is contingent on characteristics of the manager, the group, and the situation.

Cost Centers are segments of the organization which incur costs. Each cost center uses appropriate accounts from the total chart of accounts.

Cost Characteristics are used as a way to define how costs will respond or behave in response to changes in the level of business activity. They are variable, semi-variable, or fixed costs and direct or indirect.

Cost Plus Pricing takes the total expenses (costs) plus the desired net income and divides by the projected volume of units sold to arrive at the selling price per unit. It ignores competitors prices and the perceived value of the services and could result in under- or overpricing.

Cost-Volume-Profit Analysis relates cost with revenue.

Critical Incident Method is a performance appraisal method in which the manager keeps an ongoing record of incidents of positive and negative performance. This record is used at the end of the evaluation period to judge overall performance.

Current Ratio compares current assets to current liabilities. The current ratio is calculated by dividing current assets by current liabilities.

Debt Ratio compares total liabilities to total assets. Debt ratio is calculated by dividing total liabilities by total assets. This ratio gives the percentage of the organization's assets that is financed through borrowing.

Demand Measurement and Forecasting is performed to quantify current and potential market demand and to link specific demand forecasts to analysis of environmental factors, market characteristics, and market segments.

Demographics refers to the set of personal characteristics which can be used to describe groups of people, such as age, sex, family structure, education, and income.

Depreciation Cost is the amount of capital cost which can be allocated to a specific operating period as an offset against revenue for that time period.

Diagnostic-Related Groups (DRGs) are a set of mutually exclusive categories that are used by Medicare to describe a client's medical condition and purportedly his or her medical needs. Hospitals are paid a predetermined amount per admission for each client, dependent on the client's DRG category, regardless of the costs of the services provided.

Direct Costs are directly associated with the production of a unit of goods or service.

Direct Health Care Provider would be one that deals directly with the person receiving the health care services. A hospital, health department, physician, orthotist, pharmacist, and physical therapist are all direct care providers.

Documentation is a process involving systematic gathering of information, recording information in a synthesized form, organizing the synthesized information, and producing a document.

Earnings Statement (See **Income Statement**)

Environment of an organization is everything that is outside of its structure including its technology, markets, competitors, geographical location, outside regulation, the economy, political climate, and even the weather.

Environmental Analysis looks at external factors which may impact on the future success of the organization and determines what are the trends, opportunities, and threats that face the organization now and in the future.

Environmental Complexity refers to the amount of sophisticated knowledge needed about an organization's products, customers, etc. For example, a simple environment is one where the knowledge needed is easily understood.

Environmental Diversity ranges from integrated to diversified. It refers to the diversity of products or services, clients, and geographical distribution of markets.

Environmental Hostility refers to the predictability of an organization's environment. An unpredictable environment causes the organization to face an unpredictable demand.

Environmental Stability has to do with both the rate of change as well as the predictability of change. The more unstable or dynamic an organization's environment, the more difficult it is to predict future needs and activities.

Equipment Planning is the process of identifying and justifying requests for capital equipment.

Essay Appraisal Method is a performance appraisal method in which the rater writes an essay describing the strengths and weaknesses of the employee. This method has questionable reliability and validity. It is time consuming and relevant information may be missed and/or irrelevant information may be included.

Ethics is the branch of philosophy which focuses on morality.

Expenses represent the amount of money spent by a business to produce goods and services during a specific period of time. Usually a business has more expense categories than it does revenue and capital categories. There are different types of expenses, operating costs and capital costs, and different characteristics of expenses, variable, semi-variable, and fixed, and they can be directly or indirectly related to the production of goods or services.

External Funding is funds that come from sources other than operations. Examples of external funding sources are banks, shareholders, the government, philanthropists, and private investors.

Facilities Planning refers to the process of planning for the physical structure which will house an organization. This includes the building, building layout, and the building grounds.

Fee Schedule is the schedule which sets forth the prices for goods and services. It lists all the goods and services available and prices for each by unit of measure.

Financial Cost-Benefit Analysis is written in the form of a projected income statement. It compares the potential of projected financial benefit (revenue) with the projected costs (expenses).

Financial Management refers broadly to the use of financial information to evaluate and direct the activities of an organization. Financial information can be used to evaluate an organization's ability to generate revenue through the sale of goods and services. It can be used to determine when and how an organization spends its financial resources.

Financial Statements are reports which describe the financial position and operating results of an organization. The two major financial statements are the balance sheet and the income statement. These statements summarize financial information collected over a specific period of time.

Financial Strategy answers three basic but critical questions: How will the organization be managed so that it will remain financially viable? How will profits be spent or losses covered? How will the organization pay for planned investments?

Fiscal Year refers to any 12-month cycle which an organization considers its operating year. Fiscal year cycles do not have to match the calendar year.

Fixed Costs remain unchanged despite changes in business volume. The fixed cost per unit of measure will decrease with increased volume while the total fixed cost remains unchanged.

Full Time Equivalency (FTE) is a standard measure which organizations use to describe labor resources. It represents 2080 man-hours paid.

Fundamental Principles are an adopted set of values by which executive management evaluates the performance of the organization and its members.

Going Rate Pricing keeps the prices at the average levels charged by the industry and/or competitors. This is a common strategy among health care providers.

Graphic Rating Scale is a performance appraisal system in which the rater evaluates an employee against a preestablished standard using a five- or seven-point scale. The points on the ordinal scale are assigned labels from outstanding to unsatisfactory. This method is thought to have poor reliability between raters and provides no feedback to the "average" performer.

Health Care Financing Administration (HCFA) is the governmental agency overseeing the Medicare program.

Health Care Industry encompasses all of the products and services offered by a multitude of individuals and organizations which contribute to health maintenance or improvement.

Health Care Provider is any individual or organization that makes available services or products which contribute to health maintenance or health improvement.

Health Maintenance Organization (HMO) can be both a payer for and a provider of health care services. HMO members receive health care services in return for a fixed payment which covers a specific period. (See **PGP** and **IPA**)

High Performance Theory by Schermerhorn proposes that to achieve high levels of performance people must have the right abilities and support and be motivated to exert the necessary level of effort.

Horizontal Specialization deals with the breadth or scope of the job (i.e., how many different tasks are contained on the job, how broad or narrow are each of these tasks). The less tasks and the more narrow the tasks, the more specialized they are.

Human Relations Model of Management is an extension of the traditional model of management with the addition of management's efforts to provide each individual worker with a sense of belonging and importance. Management can accomplish this by keeping workers informed, listening to their feedback, and allowing some self-control and self-direction in routine matters. Given an individual sense of belonging and importance, workers will accept authority and provide a reasonable level of cooperation and performance.

Human Resource Model of Management goes beyond the human relations model in recognizing that workers also want the opportunity to develop and apply all of their skills in the performance of their work. The human resource model argues that the organization can benefit if it supports and encourages full participation of all workers.

Hybrid Law is an interpretation of the applicability of a statutory law.

Income Statement is a report used to evaluate the performance of an organization by comparing money spent (expenses) to money earned (revenues) for a specific period. It demonstrates the net income or loss for the period. It is also referred to as the **Earnings Statement**, **Statement of Operations**, and **Profit and Loss Statement**.

Indirect Costs are necessary for the production of the organization's goods and/or services but are indirectly associated with a unit of goods or service. Indirect costs are allocated to the cost of producing a unit and generally decrease as volume or output increases. Examples might be administration, financial services, building, or utilities.

Indirect Health Care Provider makes available products and services that allow the direct care providers to meet the needs of the clients they serve.

Individual Practice Association (IPA) is a type of HMO. The IPA functions like the group practice HMO except that the physicians contract independently with the HMO. Enrollees receive services at the physician practice location instead of one central location.

Job Design (See **Work Design**)

Joint Commission on Accreditation of Hospitals (JCAHO) develops and monitors standards to analyze, review, evaluate, and, where necessary, improve the quality of clinical practice. It establishes specific guidelines for health care providers to follow.

Justice is the ethical principle which dictates fairness.

Labor Productivity is a measure of the productivity of human resources.

Law reflects the ethics of society through democratic processes which result in the election of legislators by the majority of the voters.

Liabilities are debts.

Liability is defined as a duty that must be performed. Liability can be shared between parties or vicariously because of relationships between parties.

Licensure Laws refer to state statutes which define the type, scope, and requirements to practice certain regulated professions such as physical therapy.

Life Cycle Theory by Hersey and Blanchard focuses on the "maturity" of those managed as the key indicator for leadership style.

Malpractice is the term used to define a situation of professional negligence.

Managed Care Organizations function as a link between providers and consumers. As an intermediary, managed care organizations seek to control the utilization and/or cost of health care services. They also assume responsibility for the quality of health care services.

Management is the part of an organization that provides direction and supervision.

Management by Objective is a performance appraisal method in which the rater ranks employees based on their success at achieving specific performance goals. This approach focuses on outcome, but not method. It may penalize employees who fail to achieve goals due to factors outside their control.

Management Theory is a body of knowledge which attempts to provide models that can help organizations manage human resources. These models find their basis in assumptions and research related to human behavior.

Market Analysis looks at the consumer side of the product and service exchange process.

Market Segmentation serves to focus an organization's marketing efforts. To be effective, an organization must concentrate its marketing efforts on those markets it can serve well. Markets may be segmented on the basis of size, location, wants and needs of a specific group, buying habits, or other differentiating characteristics.

Market Share Pricing is often used by new businesses. The price is set low to attract volume but results in minimal income. The hope is that, long-term, increased volume will provide increased income.

Marketing is a process which brings together the activities of sales, advertising, market research, new product development, customer service, and distribution.

Marketing Communications encompasses all of the methods used to communicate with a target market including media advertising, promotions, and direct personal sales.

Marketing Mix refers to the interrelationship of product, place, price, and promotion on the organization's ability to market its output.

Marketing Strategy refers to the methods chosen to meet the needs and wants of the targeted market segments. It serves to define the organization's customers and the products/services that will be sold. It also defines organizational policy related to pricing, advertising, and promotion.

Marketing Tasks define what must be accomplished by the marketing strategy to influence the market demand for the organization's output.

Mass Production systems produce large quantities of like products. This results in standardized production, formalized behavior, and structure reflective of the classic bureaucracy.

Medicaid (Title XIX of the Social Security Act) is a complex program that is jointly funded by the state and federal government and administered by the individual states. It provides health care benefits for the poor, elderly, and disabled; federal legislation mandates minimal coverage and a state may choose to provide services at or above this minimum.

Medical Record refers to all of the documentation which a health care provider collects and retains pertaining to individual clients. The medical record is owned by the provider. The provider has a legal obligation to maintain and protect the medical records of its clients. The client has a legal right to access his or her medical record.

Medical Staff Bylaws guide and regulate the actions of the medical staff that provides services within the facility. Bylaws set guidelines regarding medical staff credentials, organizational membership classes, membership rights and responsibilities, member responsibilities, and medical staff committees and their functions.

Medicare (Title XVIII of the Social Security Act) is designed to cover certain health care costs of individuals over age 65 and certain disabled people under age 65.

Mission (See **Fundamental Principles**)

Motivation Theory (See **Management Theory**)

Negligence is the term used to describe a situation in which harm has been inflicted on another.

Net Cash Flow refers to the income after annual operating expenses have been covered.

Nonmaleficence is the ethical principle which directs a moral person to do no harm to another.

Notes Payable are amounts owed by the company which are evidenced by formal promissory agreements for specific amounts of money plus interest due at a future date (loans). A liability.

Operating Core is the part of an organization that actually does the work of the organization.

Operating Costs are costs which can be related to the day to day activities of a business. This includes costs for salary, supplies, merchandise for resale, linens, etc.

Operations refers to all of the day to day activities of an organization. Each organizational activity can be associated with money spent, money earned, or both.

Organization and Management Strategy will address issues related to what must be done, assignment of management accountability, organizational structure to support the strategic plan, and human resource needs.

Organizational Chart is the pictorial representation of the organizational structure.

Organizational Design is the process of arranging the activity of an organization into a whole.

Organizational Structure is the outcome of the process of organizational design. It refers to the relationship between organizational segments.

Owner's Equity represents that portion of the organization's assets which is owned by the owners. Owners are the shareholders of the organization.

Payback Period is the length of time necessary to recover the entire cost of an investment from the resulting annual net cash flow. It is a tool used by businesses to evaluate potential capital expenditures.

Performance Appraisal is done to accurately assess an employee's performance in relation to performance expectations.

Performance Criteria Based Method is a performance appraisal method that is based on specific objective performance criteria. The Performance Criteria Based Method comes from the employee's position description. The major functions of the position are defined in terms of performance indicators.

Performance Discrepancies can be defined as anything that an employee is doing, not doing, or doing incorrectly that is different from the expected performance.

Performance Expectations define the tasks of an employee. They are communicated to the employees through a variety of channels including job descriptions, policies and procedures, or job orders specific to individual tasks.

Policies and Procedures answer the question of what, who, where, and how an activity shall take place.

Policy is a statement of what an organization or part of an organization will do in a given situation and who will be responsible for the action.

Position Descriptions are used by organizations to formalize basic performance expectations.

Preferred Provider Organization (PPO) is a network of providers who have agreed to provide services at a discounted rate and to comply with preadmission and ongoing utilization review in anticipation of a guaranteed volume of business.

Prepaid Group Plan (PGP) is a type of HMO. There are two types of PGPs, the staff model and the group model. The staff model employs its own physicians who practice out of the HMO facility. Group model HMOs contract with an independent group of physicians who provide services exclusively to enrollees of the HMO at the group practice location.

Primary Care Provider is the initial point of contact between the health care delivery system and the client. It is the entry point into the health care system.

Private Law deals with the rights and obligations in activities involving other people. Private law is also called civil law.

Problem-Oriented Medical Record (POMR) is a medical record documentation system. Part of the system requires notes to be written in a specific format (Subjective information, Objective information, Assessment, and Plan).

Procedure is a detailed statement of when, where, and how an activity should be accomplished.

Process Production refers to the continuous flow of production. Process production organizations tend to be highly automated, with a highly skilled work force that spends time maintaining equipment.

Production/Service Strategy addresses planning issues related to how, where, and in what volume the necessary work will be accomplished.

Productivity is the relationship between the input of resources and the output of a product.

Professional Socialization, sometimes referred to as organizational socialization, can be described as the process whereby a member of an organization acquires an understanding of the organization's value system and behavioral norms.

Profit and Loss Statement (See **Income Statement**)

Program Evaluation is a process whereby the outcomes of human services can be evaluated.

Prospective Payment established a new way to pay hospitals for the care provided to Medicare clients. All admitted clients are assigned to one of 467 diagnostic-related groups (DRGs).

Public Law defines a person's rights and obligations in relationship to society and the various levels of government.

Quality Assurance is defined by the JCAHO as a process designed to objectively and systematically monitor and evaluate the quality and appropriateness of client care, pursue opportunities to improve client care, and resolve identified problems.

Quality Circles are worker groups used by Japanese management to maximize worker involvement and input in the work setting.

Quick Ratio compares liquid assets to current liabilities. Liquid assets include cash and those assets that can be quickly converted to cash.

Ratio Analysis allows comparisons to be made between pieces of financial information.

Receivable Turnover Ratio gives the average number of days it takes to convert accounts receivable (credit sales) into cash. It is calculated by dividing the annual credit sales by the current receivables.

Recruitment can be looked upon as the search for talent.

Rehabilitation Act of 1973 prohibits employment discrimination against the handicapped.

Research and Development Strategy is used by an organization whose activity is dependent on product/service innovation or differentiation.

Return on Assets is used to evaluate an organization's ability to earn a return on funds supplied from all sources. It is calculated by dividing net income plus interest expenses by total assets.

Return on Investment is the annual net income from an investment expressed as a percentage of the average amount invested. It is a tool used by businesses to evaluate potential capital expenditures.

Revenue is the income received by a business for goods or services sold during a specific period of time.

Revenue Forecasting is a process of predicting how many units of goods or services a business will sell during a specific period.

Revenue Productivity Ratio indicates the amount of revenue generated for each dollar of salary expense. It is calculated by dividing total revenue from services by related salary expenses.

Robinson-Patman Act prohibits the seller from charging different prices to comparable customers unless the price differences are based on real cost differences.

Secondary Care Providers make available equipment, skill, or expertise not provided at the primary care level.

Semi-Variable Costs are in part based on total volume and in part based on some other factor such as time. These can be looked at as the cost of availability and the cost of usage.

Sexual Harassment is defined as unwelcome sexual advances, request for sexual favors, and other verbal or physical conduct of a sexual nature which are the basis for employment decisions or have the effect of interfering with an individual's work performance.

SOAP Documentation Format is a medical record documentation format which gained popularity as an entity separate from the POMR system.

Statement of Operations (See **Income Statement**)

Statute of Limitations refers to a time period within which a claimant may file a legal claim of medical malpractice.

Step Variable Costs is when a particular resource is only available in set quantities. With step variable costs, the goal is to maximize utilization of each step.

Strategic Business Plan is a document used to represent the results of the strategic planning process.

Strategic Goal is a statement of what is to be accomplished.

Strategic Objective is a statement that compliments the goal by stating how a strategic goal is to be achieved.

Strategic Planning is the term used to describe an organizational planning process. It represents a collection of decisions an organization had made about its goals and the strategies (course of action) it will follow to achieve those goals.

Support Services is the part of the organization that provides technical or other types of support services to management and the operating core.

Tax Equity and Fiscal Responsibility Act (TEFRA) was enacted in 1982 by federal legislation. This act altered the method of reimbursement for inpatient hospital care from a retrospective cost basis to a prospective diagnosis-based system, i.e., DRGs. The prospective method paid hospitals for the cost of patient care. The diagnostic-based system pays a predetermined amount based on diagnosis. This amount is paid regardless of the actual cost of service.

Technology refers to the body of knowledge required to complete the special task of the organization.

Tertiary Provider provides specialized care. A university medical center which acts as a regional diagnostic and treatment center for community hospitals would be an example.

Theory X and Theory Y are theoretical models about human behavior in the work set-ting developed by McGregor to help managers increase worker productivity.

Theory Z is Ouchi's management model based on the Japanese style of management and worker motivation.

Third Party Payer is someone other than the client receiving health care services who pays for the services.

Title VII of the Civil Rights Act prohibits discrimination on the basis of race, color, religion, sex, or national origin in any term, condition, or privilege of employment.

Title XVIII of the Social Security Act (See **Medicare**)

Title XIX of the Social Security Act (See **Medicaid**)

Traditional Model of Management solves the problem of managing workers by providing them with a limited number of rules and techniques which can be learned and repeated. Consistency of the performance is maintained by close supervision. The organization provides reasonable working conditions, equitable treatment, and fair pay. In return, the worker provides a reasonable level of performance.

Training is the process by which job-related skills are taught. The more complex and nonroutine the skills needed, the more training required.

Unit of Measure refers to the way items are packaged for sale. Units of measure for services can be time or activity based.

Unit Production is a distinct organizational system associated with technical systems. Outputs, dependent on a customer's requirements, were ad hoc or nonstandard.

Universal Coverage refers to a health care reimbursement system which would provide health care insurance to all Americans.

Utilization Review is defined as a written program that endeavors to ensure appropriate allocation of the organization's resources by striving to provide quality patient care in the most cost-efficient manner.

Variable Costs increase or decrease in direct proportion to volume of business activity.

Variance is a deviation from what has been planned. When money earned or spent deviates from the budgeted or projected level it is referred to as a variance. Variances can be positive or negative and generally indicate a need for management attention.

Vertical Integration describes the relationship which would exist if all components of a process, product, or service were controlled by one organization. A health care provider who provides all types of primary, secondary, and tertiary care would be a vertically integrated provider.

Vertical Specialization deals with the depth of the job. It separates the performance of tasks from the management of the task. The more specialized the job, the less control the employee will have over the work.

Work Design refers to the way in which an organization structures and regulates the activities of its employees. It is a process, and the outcome of this process is the creation of a set of employee performance expectations that is unique to the organization and the specific job performed. The intended outcome of the work design process is regulation of employee behavior.

INDEX

Page numbers in *italics* denote figures and examples; those followed by "t" denote tables.